MODERN JAPAN: A CONCISE SURVEY

Modern Japan

A Concise Survey

Sir Hugh Cortazzi

St. Martin's Press   New York

First published in the United States of America in 1993

Printed in Great Britain

ISBN 0–312–10630–0

Library of Congress Cataloging-in-Publication Data
Cortazzi, Hugh.
Modern Japan : a concise survey / Hugh Cortazzi.
p.   cm.
Includes index.
ISBN 0–312–10630–0
1. Japan.   I. Title.
DS806.C78   1993
952.04—dc20   93–27056
                                    CIP

Contents

List of Tables and Figures

Maps

Table

Figures

Preface

This short book is an attempt to give the basic facts about modern Japan which an intelligent person visiting the country or going to live there is likely to want to have at his fingertips or at least readily available. It does not pretend to be comprehensive. Nor can it hope to provide a substitute for the detailed study of particular aspects which may interest readers with specific needs. For instance, anyone going to Japan to live will need the advice of a good tax accountant when dealing with his taxes. He or she is also likely to require the advice of a specialist on questions of contract or of employment. But it is hoped that this book will at least provide a starting point.

This is not another book trying to analyse Japanese ways and attitudes. It is primarily a factual survey.

Statistics which have been included where necessary are as up to date as possible. But although there is no lack of statistics these are not always consistent, and fully up-to-date statistics are not immediately available. The statistics should, accordingly, be regarded as primarily an indication of magnitudes and trends rather than as a source of accurate and current figures.

In general the facts and information have been selected on the basis that the author would have liked to have had such a brief survey available to him when he was British Ambassador to Japan to provide briefing for visiting ministers and officials, and to give to new members of his staff to study before coming out to Japan or to use on arrival.

Chapter 1 provides general background, including basic information about geography, the people, language, history and culture. Chapters 2 to 10 contain a survey of modern Japan and its institutions. Chapter 2 describes the political framework including the Constitution and the Diet. Chapter 3 reviews the organization and functions of central and local government. Chapter 4 gives an overview of the Japanese legal system and of law enforcement. Chapter 5 looks at Japanese foreign and defence policy. Chapters 6, 7 and 8 attempt to cover the Japanese economy. Chapter 6 deals with finance, including banking and securities, Chapter 7 with industry and trade, Chapter 8 with Japanese agriculture, construction and transport. Chapter 9 reviews the position of labour in the economy and the provisions for health and welfare.

Chapter 10 looks at education, cultural and religious organizations, and the media.

June 1993   Sir Hugh Cortazzi

Note: Japanese names are reproduced in the Japanese order, that is, surname first followed by given name. Long vowels have been marked except for well-known place names such as Tokyo and Osaka.

Acknowledgement: The author and publishers are grateful to Dodwell Marketing Consultants, Tokyo, for permission to reproduce the two charts from their *Industrial Groupings in Japan* (10th edn, 1992–3).

Sketch Map of Japan

Map of Japanese Prefectures

1 The Setting

1.1 GEOGRAPHY

Japan consists of four main islands and some 3900 smaller ones. The main islands are: Hokkaidō in the north; Honshū, which is the largest of the four and is the central island; Shikoku, which lies on the southern flank of Honshū; and Kyūshū, the southern island. The most important of the lesser islands are the Ryūkyū (Loo-Choo) group to the north of Taiwan (formerly Formosa), which include the island of Okinawa; and the Amami–Oshima islands which lie to the South of Kyūshū. Other significant islands are Tsushima in the straits between Japan and Korea, the Oki islands and Sado in the Japan Sea, and a series of islands to the south of central Honshū including the Bonin or Ogasawara islands, of which Iwojima is one. Japan also claims the islands of Etorofu, Kunashiri, the Habomai group and Shikotan which are the southernmost islands in the Kurile chain but which were occupied by Soviet forces in 1945 and which have not yet been returned to Japan by Russia.

The territory of Japan stretches from 45° 33' north at the northern tip of Cape Soya in Hokkaidō to about latitude 25°. Tokyo, the capital, lies at 35° north and is roughly on the same latitude as Algiers. The Japanese islands form an arc from the cool and temperate north of Hokkaidō to the semi-tropical southern Ryūkyū islands.

The Japanese islands come under the influence of the Asian continental system, but this is tempered by a warm current (the *kuroshio*, literally 'black tide') which splits and flows up the west and east coasts of Japan. Japan is also affected by cold currents from the area of the Kuriles. Winters in Hokkaidō are severe and heavy snow tends to fall in winter along the western side of the mountain ranges in Honshū. On the eastern side of the mountains winters are generally cool but dry and there is a good deal of sunshine. Summers are hot and humid, especially in central and southern Japan, with a distinct rainy season (*tsuyu*) lasting for about 40 days from late June through July. Japan has a high annual rainfall averaging some 1700–1800 mm. The Japanese islands, especially Kyūshū, Shikoku and Honshū, lie in the path of many typhoons spawned in areas to the south or west of Japan.

1

Some 75–80 per cent of the land area is mountainous and is not available for general cultivation or habitation. The mountains are steep and precipitous. The highest is Mount Fuji, a dormant volcano, whose summit is 3776 metres above sea level. The Japan Alps which lie to the north of Mt Fuji also include mountains in the 3000 metre range. These mountains resulted from volcanic eruptions and there are still many active volcanoes in the Japanese islands.

Off the eastern seaboard there is a deep submarine trench. The huge and sudden differences of height and depth cause great stresses and strains which result in numerous earthquakes. These have often caused severe damage and loss of life.

There are few natural plains. The largest is the Kantō plain in the area round Tokyo. Another relatively flat area is the Kansai in the neighbourhood of Japan's second city, Osaka.

Rivers are generally short and fast running. Flooding has been a serious problem, especially in the rainy season or when the winter snows melt.

The climate is suitable for wet rice cultivation and rice is grown from the southern part of Hokkaidō to Kyūshū. In a few southern areas two crops of rice are possible but more often wet rice in the summer is combined with a winter wheat crop. However as a result of over-production some areas are now being left fallow or only provide a single crop. The mountainous nature of the land has meant that terracing has been essential for rice cultivation and allocation of water supplies has been a key factor in the development of Japanese agriculture.

In the Pleistocene era (perhaps some 150 000 years ago) the Japanese islands were connected to the mainland of Asia by land bridges and what is now the Japan Sea was once a huge lake. As a result the flora and fauna of Japan and the Asian continent are similar.

The Japanese islands have only limited mineral resources, most of which are no longer economic to mine. Coal which was found in workable quantities in Hokkaidō and Kyūshū was of low calorific value. Copper, gold (for example, on the island of Sado) as well as iron ore were also mined, and small quantities of oil have been found especially in the Niigata area on the Japan Sea Coast.

1.2 PEOPLE

Prehistoric man came to the Japanese islands perhaps some 200 000 years ago. The Japanese race is considered to be of Ural-Altaic stock. They are Mongoloid, but with some admixture from south China,

South East Asia and Polynesia. The Japanese were not, however, the only indigenous inhabitants of the Japanese islands. The **Ainu**, who now represent a tiny minority of the inhabitants of Hokkaidō and have almost disappeared as a separate race, are ethnically entirely different from the Japanese, being more hairy and less yellow-skinned. They are probably of the same racial origin as some of the Uralic peoples of Siberia. The Ainu were dominant in Hokkaidō (whose old name was Ezo) until the nineteenth century and in northern Honshū until about 1000 years ago. The **Kumaso**, who may have been of similar racial origin as the Ainu and lived in areas further south, were defeated and exterminated or absorbed by people of Japanese race some 1500 years ago.

1.3 LANGUAGE

The genetic origins of the Japanese language have not been clearly established. It is quite different from that of the Ainu, but has syntactical resemblances to Korean. It also has some similarities to Altaic languages. There seem in addition to have been some Malayo-Polynesian influence on Japanese vocabulary. However, the only really kindred language is that spoken in the Ryūkyū islands. This can be regarded as a derivative of Japanese with an admixture of Chinese.

Japanese is polysyllabic and agglutinative, almost without stress and tones, and is thus totally different from Chinese, which is monosyllabic, tonal and without inflexions. Japanese consists of forty-eight basic sounds which may be defined as being the five vowels and the consonants k, s, t, n, h, m, y, r and w followed by a vowel (although there is no yi, ye or wu). The single consonant 'n' was added later because the final 'n' in Chinese words as imported into Japanese did not exist in ancient Japanese. The consonant 't' is subject to inflexion, becoming 'd' or 'z'; 's' can also become 'z'; 'k' can become 'g', and 'h' become 'b' or 'p' (*hu* came to be pronounced *fu*) thus adding considerably to the number of different syllables available.

In vocabulary and structure Japanese was enriched and changed when writing was introduced from China in the fifth century AD. The language has been transformed again in recent years by the adoption of innumerable foreign words, primarily of English origin.

Chinese was the first written language with which the Japanese came in contact in the sixth century AD. It was adopted as the language of administration and scholarship in much the same way as Latin was the language of scholarship and government in Europe.

Chinese characters were modified for the writing of syllables to represent Japanese particles and endings. These adapted characters came to be called **syllabaries**. The main syllabaries are *hiragana* and *katakana*. *Hiragana*, the more rounded of the two, is more generally used. *Katakana*, which is squarer, is, however, used for words of foreign origin and was used in telegrams.

Chinese ideograms (characters), called *kanji* in Japanese, were also adopted to represent Japanese words with similar meanings. The language was complicated, however, by the adoption at the same time of Chinese vocabulary using two or more characters together to cover things or ideas for which there was no appropriate Japanese word. Thus the Japanese word *kaze* meaning wind was represented by the Chinese character for wind (風), but a typhoon was a *taifū* (大風) or 'big wind', where *tai* and *fū* are pronunciations of the two characters as they sounded to Japanese ears many centuries ago. This oversimplifies the process of adaptation, as some Chinese characters came to be adopted at different times and with different sounds. The Japanese reading of a Chinese character is said to be the *kun* reading whereas the 'Chinese' reading is the *on*. But there are a number of different *on* readings; there are *kanon* (said to be the pronunciation of the people of Shensi or Kansu), *go-on* (said to be the pronunciation of the people of the Wu province), and *tō-in* (said to be the pronunciation of the T'ang dynasty). As a result, a Chinese character may be read in various ways in Japanese and only knowledge and practice can ensure that the correct reading is given for a Chinese character in modern Japanese. The character with the largest number of readings in Japanese is said to be the relatively simple character (生), which means to live, to give birth to, to be fresh and so on. There are two *on* readings: *sei* and *shō*, and some seventeen *kun* readings.

At elementary school a Japanese child is expected to master the 881 basic 'education *kanji*' or *kyōiku kanji*. At middle school the Japanese child is expected to learn a further 1000 characters or so in the list of those in current use (the *tōyō kanji*). If the characters approved for use in names are added the list amounts to about 2000 in all. Knowledge of these characters will enable a Japanese to read a newspaper, but to read Japanese literature a larger number of characters and a wider vocabulary are required.

While a literate Japanese can understand many notices in Chinese some characters used in modern Japanese are not the same as the characters used in modern China for the same things. For instance, the characters used in China and Japan for a railway station and a motor car are different. The Japanese and the Chinese, in simplifying characters in recent years, have often used different simplifications.

1.4 HISTORY AND CULTURE

1.4.1 The Prehistoric Era

A Stone Age culture began to develop in Japan after about 10 000 BC. Early inhabitants of the Japanese islands lived by fishing and hunting. They lived in small communities in pit houses of simple construction. They learnt to make pots for storage and for cooking. They also made figurines. Their pots were decorated with a rope pattern (*Jōmon*) and the age is called by historians the **Jōmon** period. It lasted until about 300 BC. In the final part of the period after about 2000 BC rice cultivation seems to have been introduced from the continent and to have spread from Kyūshū northwards.

The Jōmon or Stone Age was succeeded by the Bronze Age called in Japan the **Yayoi** period. In this period bronze and later iron tools and weapons were developed. Metal mirrors were imported from China and were copied by the Japanese who also made large bronze pieces shaped like bells and called *dōtaku*. In the Yayoi period pottery was made on the wheel. Some information about this period of Japanese history can be gleaned from early Chinese chronicles.

The Bronze Age was succeeded by the Iron Age and the **Kofun** or burial mound era in Japan. This began about 250–300 AD and lasted until about the seventh century. Over ten thousand tombs dating from this period have been found, the greatest concentrations being in the Kansai area and in northern Kyūshū. The classical shape of a tomb was the so-called 'keyhole' type (*zempōkōen*). One of the largest, near Osaka, is said to be that of the leader known today as the Emperor Nintoku. Around the tombs were a number of clay figures called *haniwa* of animals, human beings and buildings. These may have been intended as substitutes for sacrificial victims.

The earliest records purporting to give the history of Japan are contained in the *Kojiki* ('Records of ancient matters') written down in 712 AD in Japanese in an adaption of Chinese characters and the *Nihongi* or *Nihonshoki* ('Chronicles of Japan') written in classical Chinese. These bring together the various legends about the origin of Japan. According to these myths the gods Izanagi and Izanami together produced the Japanese islands and various other deities. The most important of these deities were Amaterasu-omikami-no-mikoto, the sun goddess, and her brother Susanoo-no-mikoto, who was given dominion over the sea. The two gods quarrelled violently and Amaterasu who was shocked by her brother's behaviour, retired to a cave, causing the world to become dark. She was eventually enticed out by an entertainment including a lewd dance. Susanoo was banished from heaven and went off to the Izumo district of Japan (now part of Shimane prefecture) where he killed an eight-forked serpent. Amaterasu wanted to bestow the sovereignty of Japan on one of her children but first needed Susanoo's agreement. This was eventually obtained after he had been promised a new palace (now the great shrine of Izumo, that is, Taisha). Another 'palace' was built on Mount Takachiho in Kyūshū and in due course the sons of the gods of the place moved against chiefs opposed to them in the Yamato district of Honshū (in the Kansai). One of these was given the name Jimmu, who according to legend was the first Emperor of Japan and ancestor of the present Emperor. He is alleged to have reigned from the year 660 BC. This is clearly incorrect and all dates before about 400 AD are probably spurious. One legendary hero was Prince Yamato-Takeru-no-Mikoto who defeated the Kumaso in Kyūshū but died after being deceived by a deity.

The earliest Japanese state seems to have been established after a struggle between various groups in Kyūshū and Honshū. The conflict was apparently won by the Kyūshū people who eventually conquered the Kansai but their dominion was challenged by various groups and was not easily achieved. The chieftains of the victorious group came to be called *Tenshi* or *Tennō*, a word now translated as Emperor. They rarely seem to have exercised real power but depended for their status on their priestly role resulting from their alleged descent from the sun goddess.

There were three main elements in the society of this early period. These were the *uji* which were groups of families bound together by loyalty to a leader. They depended on certain occupational groups or *be/tomo* who performed prescribed functions and the *yakko* or slaves, who carried out the menial tasks.

The indigenous Japanese religion, to which the name **Shintō** (literally 'the way of the gods') has been given, dates back to this early period. The Japanese pantheon of Shintō gods is shadowy and confused and most Japanese Shintō shrines are dedicated to later gods such as the warrior Hachiman. The imperial shrines of Ise are, however, devoted to the worship of Amaterasu. Images of Japanese gods were never made and the *shintai* (literally 'god body') in a shrine is often just a mirror.

Shintō in its early manifestations was, as was natural and inevitable in a primitive agricultural society, largely a form of nature worship and cult of fertility. Nature was both bountiful and beautiful. Natural disasters, which are frequent in Japan, were ascribed to the misbehaviour of man or of the gods who had to be propitiated by offerings of food and drink. Pollution was thought to be abhorrent to the gods and ritual purification was an essential part of Shintō rites. Some of the earliest Japanese writings consist of *norito*, which are a form of Shintō prayers.

1.4.2 Confucianism and Buddhism

First recorded contacts with China date back to the early years of the fifth century when a Chinese sage called Wani is said to have arrived in Japan with a number of Chinese texts. This marked the beginning of Confucian teaching in Japan which was to have a profound impact on Japanese life and thought. Confucianism is essentially a philosophy of life said to have been taught by Kong Qiu (c.551–478 BC) known to us as Confucius and to the Japanese as Kōshi. The most important Confucian text was the *Analects*, a collection of sayings of the master.

Confucius claimed that he was primarily concerned with practical and moral questions. His main wish was to restore the society which had, he thought, existed in earlier times, and which was based on a harmonious and hierarchical system. He was a conservative and fundamentally opposed to change. He placed great emphasis on the family and hence on filial piety. He asserted that the supreme virtue was benevolence but believed that ritual and hierarchy must be maintained.

The Japanese in due course developed Confucian concepts to suit their own purposes. The emphasis on family led to the development of the *ie* or house system. The hierarchical element in Confucian thought was combined with ideas of service to make loyalty (*chū*) and obligation (*giri*) paramount virtues in Japan. Confucian concepts of ritual behaviour were the origin of Japanese forms of politeness. In Confucianism women had a lowly status and this attitude was adopted in Japan.

The official date given for the introduction of Buddhism into Japan is 552 AD, but it is probable that Buddhist scriptures and concepts reached Japan through Korea some years before this.

Buddhism originated from the life and teaching of Siddhartha Gautama who was born in India in about 446 BC. Gautama was the son of a prince who at the age of twnty-nine renounced his life of luxury and spent six years in ascetic practices and meditation. Seated under a *bo* tree he achieved enlightenment and become a Buddha, meaning one who has awakened to the truth. He was given the honorary name of Sakyamuni (in Japanese, Shaka) meaning the silent sage. Gautama did not claim to be God. He stressed *dharma* (the true eternal law). Life was suffering. Nothing was constant; everything was transient. A man's life or *karma* was both a sequel to what occurred earlier and a prelude to what was to follow. Hence came the Buddhist belief in reincarnation. The 'self' did not exist. The objective and subjective worlds were one and the same. To achieve an end to suffering the causes had to be extinguished. Lust and desire could be eradicated by spiritual discipline and meditation as well as by the pursuit of the middle way which involved neither suffering nor pleasure. This led ultimately to *nirvana* or the absence of all causes of suffering. Running through all the teachings of Gautama is a spirit of compassion and kindness as well as a strong wish to help others to find enlightenment.

The 'three treasures' of Buddhism are the Buddha, the law and the order of monks. The 'five precepts' are not to kill, not to steal, not to act immorally (that is, not to fornicate), not to lie and not to drink intoxicating liquor. The 'four noble truths' are: all existence is suffering; the cause of suffering is desire; the cause can be prevented; the way to prevent suffering is through the eightfold path. This consists of right views, right aims, right words (or speech), right action, right living, right efforts, right mind (that is, right understanding of the non-existence of self), right rapture (that is, the ecstasy of perfect knowledge or enlightenment, leading to *nirvana*).

In Japan Buddhism was adapted and mixed with Confucian and indigenous ideas to produce a peculiarly Japanese amalgam. It permeated Japanese life, thought and culture up to the nineteenth century. It is a dominant feature in much of Japan's art and literature.

The Buddhist sects which came to Japan were essentially of the **Mahayana** (greater vehicle) form from China. The Mahayana sects recognized that the ideals of Gautama were unattainable by the majority of people and substituted the ideal of the compassionate **Bodhisattva** or aspirant to Buddhahood who worked for the salvation of all human beings so that they too could become Buddhas. The emphasis was placed on the discovery of the Buddha nature in every human being. Gautama was transformed from a human teacher into a transcendant being or god. A large Buddhist pantheon was developed including *Shaka, Dainichi Nyorai* (*Roshana* or *Vairocana*), *Yakushi Nyorai*, the healing Buddha, and *Amida* (Amitabha) the Buddha of the western paradise. Among the most popular of the other Buddhist 'deities' in Japan were *Miroku* (Maitreya), the Buddha of the future; *Kannon* (Kuanyin or Avalokitesvara), the personification of mercy; and *Jizō* (Kshitigarbha) who vowed to deliver all creatures from hell and who in Japan is the special protector of children.

1.4.3 The Beginnings of Japanese Civilization

Buddhism was welcomed by some of the leading Japanese in the sixth century AD. But the priests of the indigenous cults and the soldiers were opposed to Buddhism, which threatened their position in the primitive Japanese state. In 587 Soga no Umako defeated the leading opponents of Buddhism and arranged for his niece to become Empress in her own right under the name Suiko. He also had another nephew, Prince Umayado, appointed Crown Prince. The Prince is known today as Shōtoku-Taishi and is generally regarded as the patron saint of Japanese Buddhism.

In 604 the so-called 'constitution' of Shōtoku-Taishi was promulgated. This was in essence a set of seventeen principles and moral exhortations which were as much Confucian as Buddhist in origin. In 607 Shōtoku-Taishi founded the great temple of Hōryūji near what is now the city of Nara in the Kansai. In the same year an official emissary was sent to China to study Buddhism.

In 646 the **Taika** (great change) era was inaugurated by a new reform leader Fujiwara no Kamatari, the founder of the Fujiwara line which dominated the court for the next 400 years. The *Taihō* code of law promulgated in 701 was based on Chinese models and abolished the private title to land. The first land surveys were instituted and the first maps of Japanese estates (*shōen*) were produced. Land was supposed to be allocated on the basis of the number of people to be fed from the land. This system was known as *ku-bun-den* (literally mouth-division-rice field). A land tax was also established. But although superficially Japan had become a Chinese-style state the Chinese system of tenure and taxation never took root in Japan and the provinces tended to remain under traditional control.

Japan was changing and the arts inspired by Buddhism began to flourish. Numerous palaces were built, which sadly no longer exist.

Buddhist temples were built on Chinese models and Buddhist sculpture developed under Korean influence. The oldest surviving Buddhist sculpture in Japan is that of the Asuka *daibutsu* cast in bronze, apparently in the year 609. Alhough damaged and repaired, the image, which is in the Asukadera at Asuka, south of Nara, still shows the skill of the early casters in bronze. The name given in art history to this era is **Asuka**. Other fine examples of Asuka-period sculpture include the wonderful *Kannon* in the Chūguji which is part of the Hōryūji and the incomparable *Miroku bosatsu* in the Kōryūji in Kyoto. Early paintings of this period owed much to T'ang influence; very few have survived. Some richly coloured murals dating back over 1300 years were found in the Takamatsuzuka tumulus near Asuka. Reproductions are displayed in the museum. Sadly the frescos of a similar date in the main hall (*hondō*) of the Hōryūji near Nara were damaged in a fire in 1949 but have been carefully restored.

1.4.4 Relations with Korea

Korea was the main gateway to Japan in the sixth century AD and Korea played an important part in the development of the Japanese state in the fifth and sixth centuries, during which Japanese groups exercised control of parts of southern Korea. The headquarters in Japan for relations with Korea at this period was Dazaifu in Kyūshū (south of the modern city of Fukuoka).

1.4.5 The Nara Period (710–784)

Until the beginning of the eighth century AD Japan had no fixed capital but the chieftains or 'Emperors' generally had their headquarters in the Kansai area near Nara and Osaka. In 710, during the reign of the Empress Gemmei the city of Heijōkyō (Nara) was chosen as the capital. It was built on the model of Ch'ang An (Sian), the capital of T'ang China, on a rectangular grid pattern. The city was not fortified.

The political history of the Nara period is the story of relations, between on the one hand, the titular sovereign and his or her advisers largely from the Fujiwara family, and on the other the increasingly powerful Buddhist hierarchy. Few titular sovereigns made any real impact on history even in these early times, but the Emperor Shōmu is remembered for the promotion of Buddhism in Japan, ordering the building of temples in all the provinces. Attempts were made to expand the power of the court over the provinces (*kuni*) of which by the beginning of the ninth century there were 66, but central control was in practice limited. The land allocation system was soon largely evaded and cultivators sought the protection of powerful local chiefs or monasteries. The gradual process which led to the development of Japanese-style feudalism in the twelfth century had already begun. But the court became the centre for an increasingly cultivated aristocracy and Japan's relative prosperity was shown by the building of the great temples of Nara which required huge quanitities of labour, great trees and large quantities of copper.

Buddhism, which brought Chinese civilization to Japan, was the religion of the court rather than of the people at this time. The six Buddhist sects introduced to Japan in the Nara period were intellectual in nature and had little popular appeal. But as Buddhism began to spread a typically Japanese compromise resulted in an amalgam of Shintō and Buddhism. Shintō gods were thus often treated as if they were manifestations of the Buddha and Buddhist deities as if they were Shintō gods.

The Nara period in art is often referred to as **Tempyō**, an epoch in which Buddhist sculpture and architecture reached their highest point. Few buildings have survived the ravages of earthquake, fire and war, but those that have survived, such as the the three-storey pagoda of the Yakushiji, the Sangatsudō of the Tōdaiji, the *kondō* and the *kōdō* of the Tōshōdaiji demonstrate the greatness of Nara architecture.

The Shōsōin, however, has come to symbolize Nara architecture. This was built in 756 to house the personal treasures of the Emperor Shōmu. The treasures, which were collected from as far away as Persia, form a unique collection. (Each autumn selected items are exhibited in the National Museum in Nara.) Some of the finest Buddhist sculptures of the period are in the Kōfukuji, the Sangatsudō of Tōdaiji and Shinyakushiji in Nara.

The great literary work of the Nara period is the *Manyōshū*, a collection of poems by various authors.

1.4.6 The Heian Period (784–1185)

In 784 the Emperor Kammu decided to move the court away from Nara to escape from the strong priestly influences there. In 794 a new capital, Heiankyō, was established at what is the modern city of Kyoto, north of Nara. Heiankyō was also laid out on the lines of the T'ang capital of Ch'ang-an, in a rectangular shape in the basin between the Kamo and Katsura rivers. An imperial palace of unprecedented splendour was built in the northern part of the city. In and around the city there were a large number of shrines and temples, some of which pre-date the founding of the city.

During the ninth century Chinese learning was dominant and official documents were all written in Chinese. Japanese monks went to China to study Buddhism and there were a number of official and unofficial missions from Japan to China. In 894 the famous Japanese scholar Sugawara no Michizane was chosen to lead a mission to China. He argued strongly against the mission on the grounds that conditions in China were unstable. The mission was called off but in 901 Michizane was accused of plotting against the throne and was banished to Kyūshū. He was rehabilitated after his death and is revered in Japan as the god of scholarship. He is known as Tenjin.

Throughout the Heian period until the eleventh century the Fujiwara family dominated the court by a series of carefully engineered marriages. The administrative offices introduced from China became largely titular and power tended to be in the hands of the palace chamberlains. Emperors abdicated fairly quickly and as many Emperors were minors, regents (*sesshō*) had to be appointed. Real power, however, tended to be in the hands of the *kampaku*, who was nominally an assistant to the Emperor. This office was filled by members of the Fujiwara family. The apogee of Fujiwara power was reached in the time of Fujiwara no Michizane (966–1028). In the eleventh and twelfth centuries the Emperors attempted after their nominal reigns to maintain control from their position as 'cloistered Emperors' (that is, they took the tonsure). This procedure was known as *inkyo*.

During the four centuries of intrigues and power broking which marked the Heian period the central government's hold on the provinces and on land revenues continued to decline. Even in the capital security from marauding monks and robbers could not be guaranteed. But the *emishi* ('barbarians') in northern Japan were gradually subdued and a northern headquarters was established at Hiraizumi in what is now Iwate prefecture.

During this period more popular forms of Buddhism spread to Japan. The two great sects of **Tendai** and **Shingon** were established by Saichō (Dengyō Daishi) and Kūkai (Kōbō Daishi) respectively. Tendai emphasised the impermanence of all things and asserted that the absolute is inherent in all phenomena. Meditation was an essential means to enlightenment. Shingon, a form of Tantric Buddhism, stressed mysticism, incantations, ritual and magic spells. The general feeling of the age was one of pessimism. This provided the basis for the development of 'Pure Land' Buddhism (**Jōdoshū**) or Amidism. The Amidist sects of which **Shinshū** was the most popular, emphasised the saving power of Amida, whose help was invoked by the *nembutsu* or calling on the name of Amida. Religion for most people in those days was more a matter of magic and ritual than of ethics and philosophy.

Heian civilization centred round the court. It was created and sustained by a few thousand nobles. In the tenth and eleventh centuries a unique and original culture of exquisite refinement, great aesthetic sensibility and discriminating taste was created in Japan. It was not philosophically profound and was more sentimental than rational. While the court had splendid costumes and rituals the lives of the aristocrats were far from luxurious. Simplicity and frugality marked their existence. They pursued with intensity the cult of beauty and the art of making love.

The prevailing sense of melancholy and pathos (*mono no aware*) was expressed in their poems which they exchanged on every possible occasion. Some of the best have been preserved in imperial collections of poetry of which the outstanding collection was the *Kokinshū* which was produced in 705. Ki no Tsurayuki, who wrote the preface to the collection, emphasised that 'The poetry of Japan has its roots in the human heart.'

Some of the greatest works in Japanese literature were produced by women in the Heian period. One of the world's finest novels, *The Tale of Genji*, was written in the early years of the eleventh century by the Lady Murasaki (Murasaki shikibu). A fascinating picture of the life of the Heian court is also contained in the *Makura-no-sōshi* ('The Pillow Book', or diary) of Sei Shōnagon, a contemporary of Murasaki Shikibu. Other novels and diaries of the period throw much light on the life and attitudes of the nobles at the Heian court.

Architecture and sculpture continued to flourish. Perhaps the most sublime of all the Heian buildings which have survived is the Byōdōin at Uji, south of Kyoto, which also contains a magnificent image of Amida by the sculptor Jōchō. Among other fine Heian period temples is Murōji, in the mountains to the east of Nara. One of Japan's great shrines, the Itsukushima shrine at Miyajima, dates from the end of the Heian period.

Japanese monks became masters of illumination and calligraphy. The great Heian period novels also inspired artists to produce scrolls (*emaki*) which told the story in pictures. Painting in the Chinese style was also developed. Fine lacquer wares were produced for the court and pottery was developed for popular use. Music (*gagaku*) which developed from Chinese models was an important part of court ritual.

1.4.7   The Kamakura Period (1185–1333)

A series of disturbances in the middle of the eleventh century led to
sharp rivalry between the leaders of two of the largest military clans
which had developed with the decline of the power of the court. These
were the Minamoto and the Taira.

In 1160, in the **Heiji** uprising, Taira no Kiyomori managed to defeat
Minamoto no Yoshitomo and for the next twenty years dominated the
court in Kyoto. But his arrogance and pride were overweening and
various plots were hatched against him. A large scale civil war (known
as the **Gempei** war) began in 1180. Kiyomori died in 1181 and the Taira
forces were finally defeated in 1185 at the sea battle of Dannoura
during which the boy Emperor Antoku was drowned. The Minamoto
were triumphant but there was jealousy between the two Minamoto
brothers. Yoritomo, the elder brother, was the better politician, while
the younger brother, Yoshitsune, was the better general. Yoshitsune,
with his faithful follower Benkei, was forced to flee to the north. In
1188 Yoshitsune, who became one of Japan's tragic heroes, was
obliged to commit suicide.

Yoritomo established his military headquarters (known as the
bakufu or tent government) at Kamakura not far from modern
Tokyo. In 1192 he had himself appointed *Seii – taishōgun* (literally
barbarian quelling general or shōgun). The court remained at Kyoto
but had no effective power. Yoritomo died in 1199 and was followed by
two other Minamoto shōguns, but the real power passed into the hands
of the Hōjō family who ruled as the shōgun's regents (*shikken*).
Constables were appointed to uphold the authority of the shōgunate
in the provinces and stewards were nominated to collect taxes. The
system of land tenure became still more complicated and inefficient.

Gradually the code of the warrior, which came eventually to be
called *bushidō*, was developed. This had three main sources, Confucian,
Buddhist and Shintō. Great emphasis was placed on absolute and
unconditional loyalty to his lord (*daimyō*). The samurai or warrior was
supposed to abhor underhand dealings and to despise money and
luxury. He must not display his emotions and should adhere to the
correct rules of etiquette and politeness. The preservation of his honour
was of paramount importance and he had to be prepared to commit
ritual suicide in defence of his honour.

During the early part of the Kamakura period some desultory trade
was maintained with China, but in 1259 Kublai Khan was proclaimed
Emperor of China. He soon demanded the submission of Japan. This

demand was rejected and the Mongols launched attempts in 1274 and 1281 to invade and conquer Japan. Their attacks in the neighbourhood of Hakata (Fukuoka) in Kyūshū were repelled with help from storms which came to be called divine winds (*kamikaze*). Although the invasion attempts were defeated the cost of the defence was considerable and undermined the power of the Kamakura *bakufu*.

While Amidism became ever more popular, an indigenous Buddhist sect was promoted by the priest Nichiren (1222–82) who stressed the importance for salvation of the Lotus Sutra. Nichiren, who was a fiery preacher and extremely intolerant, was one of Japan's earliest overt nationalists. **Nichirenshū** later split into a number of sub-sects.

The samurai were more attracted to **Zen** Buddhism which was introduced into Japan from China during the Kamakura period. Zen which puts great emphasis on meditation, denies the validity of logic in relation to religious beliefs. Enlightenment (*satori*) could be achieved by sudden inspiration. Zen has had a profound effect on Japanese culture. Its austerity inspired the Japanese preference for restraint and understatement, and its contempt of logic for pragmatism over theory. Zen identification with nature also underlies much of the Japanese aesthetic sense.

The most famous imperial collection of poetry in this period was the *Shinkokinshū* in which the prevailing mood was that of *yūgen* which implies 'mystery and depth'. One of the greatest poets of the period was the priest Saigyō.

Tales or *monogatari* took the form primarily of chronicles of war. The most famous of these is the *Heike monogatari* which tells the story of the Gempei wars in poetic prose.

Sculpture continued to flourish and was reinvigorated by a new realism. The greatest sculptor of the period is reputed to have been Unkei. Portrait sculpture was developed and many fine figures of Japanese patriarchs have been preserved. Examples of Kamakura period sculpture can be seen in many temples throughout Japan. An impressive group of statues from this time is in the Sanjūsangendō in Kyoto. Portrait paintings were also produced. The **Tosa** and **Kasuga** schools of painting which had concentrated on depicting court scenes coalesced and the style known as **Yamato-e** was developed.

An important craft of the period was the making of swords; Japan's greatest swordsmith is said to have been Masamune (1264–1343).

Lacquer wares continued to be produced in Kyoto and in Kamakura a special type of carved wooden lacquer wares *Kamakura-bori* was developed.

In architecture Chinese and Indian influences were strong. Some fine examples of Kamakura period temples are in Kamakura, for example, Engakuji, Kenchōji, and others.

1.4.3   The Ashikaga or Muromachi Period (1333–1573)

During almost two and a half centuries Japan was racked by almost constant civil wars. Lands were won and lost. Families prospered and were then cast down. It was a time of changing fortunes, of loyalty and of treachery, of heroism and of cruelty. But life went on. Towns grew up and the arts flourished under the patronage of the Ashikaga shōguns.

The first part of the period, from 1337 to 1392 was dominated by a split which led to the establishment of two lines of Emperors and two courts, the northern and the southern. This was the so-called *nambokuchō* period. Ashikaga Takauji who overthrew the weakened regime of the Hōjō regents in Kamakura in 1333 restored Emperor Godaigo who had been in exile in the Oki islands. But Godaigo, who wanted to return to the old system of land tenure and did not realise the weakness of his position, plotted to overthrow Takauji. This led to the schism and establishment of the two courts resulting in over five decades of civil strife. Finally the courts were reunited in Kyoto in 1392.

The two most famous Ashikaga shōguns were Yoshimitsu (1358–1408) and Yoshimasa (1436–90). Yoshimitsu built a fine palace for himself at Kitayama in Kyoto which included the famous Golden Pavilion (Kinkakuji). Yoshimasa was a weak leader who watched while Kyoto was largely destroyed during the destructive civil war which is called the Ōnin war (1467–77). However, after his retirement he built for himself the villa and temple known as the Silver Pavilion (Ginkakuji) where he patronised the arts, especially painting, the tea ceremony and the Nō drama.

This period of Japanese history is often called *sengoku* or the country at war. Apart from the plots and quarrels of the feudal leaders there were various risings termed *ikki*. These included uprisings by peasants and militant monks. Fortunately for the ordinary people medieval warfare in Japan, if almost constant, was on a small scale and did not involve firearms. These only reached Japan in 1542 when the first Portuguese arrived on the island of Tanegashima south of Kyūshū (see below).

Despite wars and natural disasters agricultural production increased as new land was brought under cultivation. Better tools and different types of crops also led to increases in productivity. Tea began to be grown in quantity. Crafts were developed to supply the needs of the samurai and silk weaving techniques were introduced from China. Coins were also imported from China and money was increasingly used instead of the old methods of barter. New towns developed and traders banded together to protect their interests. Trade with China and Korea was resumed.

In literature the most significant development was the beginning of the *Nō* theatre. *Nō* plays are not strictly dramas. They consist primarily of song, recitative and dance, and the dramatic elements are of relatively minor importance. *Nō* plays eschew realism and achieve much of their effect by symbolic actions. The texts are partly in prose and partly in verse. The themes were largely taken from traditional stories. They were generally staged at temples and shrines while some *Nō* performances were arranged by the shōgun or noblemen. *Kyōgen*, which were comic interludes, were performed between plays. The actors, who were all men, belonged to troupes which developed their own traditions. The outstanding figures in the development of the *Nō* in this period were Kanami (1333–84) and his son Zeami (1363–1443).

One of the greatest works of literature of the era was the *Taiheiki*, which described the first years of the schism between the two courts. Another work representative of the period was the *Tsurezuregusa*, a series of miscellaneous jottings by Yoshida Kenkō (c.1283–c.1352). This encapsulates many typical Japanese aesthetic ideas.

The arts flourished. Ink paintings were imported from China and a Zen style of painting, which was simple and direct in its appeal to the imagination was developed. One of the greatest Japanese artists of this style was Sesshū (1420–1506). Another school of painting which was established during this period was the **Kanō** school. This was essentially a development of the Tosa school with an admixture of Chinese elements. The first exponent of this style was Kanō Masanobu (1434–1530).

In architecture an important development was the building of a number of feudal castles with their watch towers and keeps. Another was the introduction into domestic architecture of the *tokonoma* (alcove) used to display a hanging scroll or a vase and of shelves nearby called *chigaidana*.

The Japanese had had gardens from early times and they were an important feature of Kyoto palaces. But no complete garden built before the Muromachi period has survived. In this period Japanese gardens were much influenced by Zen. Two broad types of garden were developed. These were the so-called stroll gardens (*kaiyūshiki*) in which a garden and its pond can be viewed from different angles and the 'dry mountain water' garden (*karesansui*) in which sand, rocks and moss play the main part. Perhaps the most famous *karesansui* garden in all Japan is that of Ryōanji temple in Kyoto. Another very famous *karesansui* garden is that of the Daisenin of Daitokuji temple in Kyoto. Apart from the gardens of Kinkakuji and Ginkakji famous and fine *kaiyūshiki* gardens of this period in Kyoto include those belonging to Saihōji (better known as Kokedera or the Moss temple) and Tenryūji.

The tea ceremony (*cha-no-yu*) became a popluar cult in the fifteenth century. Simplicity and austerity were essential features of the ceremony. The tea used in the ceremony was green powdered tea and the tea bowls were characterised by restrained glazes and irregularity. Seto, Shino, Shigaraki and Bizen wares were popular with the tea masters. With the tea ceremony, flower arrangement was developed into an art. The headquarters of the main tea ceremony schools, including the Urasenke and Omotesenke, are in Kyoto.

1.4.9 The Momoyama Period (1573–1616)

By the middle of the sixteenth century the Ashikaga shōguns were largely irrelevant. Feudal lords vied with one another to extend their domains and the country was in a state of anarchy.

One daring minor chieftain, Oda Nobunaga (1534–82) from Owari (now part of Aichi prefecture) siezed power in central Japan and in 1567 marched on Kyoto. He destroyed the monasteries of Hieizan with their militant monks in 1571 and after the last of the Ashikaga shōguns had plotted against him in 1573 he deposed the shōgun. From 1576 to 1579 he built a magnificent castle at Azuchi overlooking Lake Biwa near Kyoto. Oda Nobunaga continued to try to assert his authority throughout Japan but he was assassinated in 1582 in Kyoto by one of his generals, Akechi Mitsuhide.

Nobunaga was primarily a warrior. Tough, brave and ruthless, he was exceptionally cruel even in an age when cruelty was commonplace, but he was an outstanding figure in Japan's history, preparing the way for the re-establishment of law and order.

After Oda Nobunaga's death one of his former vassals, Toyotomi Hideyoshi (1537–98) took the lead. In 1590 he finally defeated his last enemies. In 1592 he became *Taikō* (retired regent), a name by which he is still known in Japan. But he retained the real power and in 1592 he ordered the invasion of Korea. At first the Japanese expedition was successful and a brief incursion was made across the Yalu river into China. The Chinese, to whom the Koreans had appealed, gradually pushed the Japanese back. Japanese forces were finally withdrawn after Hideyoshi's death in 1598.

Hideyoshi was a remarkable man. He was shrewd, passionate and frank, but he was ostentatious and his castle at Momoyama, south of Kyoto, had particularly gorgeous and splendid decorations. In the eyes of Japanese aesthetes his taste seemed vulgar. In his early years he was relatively humane but in his later years his affections and jealousies, combined with bouts of wild rage, led to horrifying excesses. The attack on Korea may have been intended as a way of occupying Japan's fighting men in other than internecine strife, but it has also been seen by some as an example of Hideyoshi's growing megalomania.

When Hideyoshi died the strongest of the *daimyō* was Tokugawa Ieyasu (1543–1616). He had been granted lands in the Kantō plain and had established his headquarters in Edo (the modern Tokyo). Hideyoshi had made Ieyasu one of five elders with responsibility for protecting the succession for his young son Hideyori. Ieyasu determined to assert his position and at the great battle of Sekigahara in 1600 he defeated his enemies among the *daimyō* and achieved control of the country. In 1603 he had himself proclaimed shōgun, but he could not feel totally secure while Hideyori remained in the stronghold of Osaka castle. On the pretext that Hideyori was plotting against him Ieyasu launched an attack on Osaka castle in 1614. The castle fell in 1615 after Hideyori had committed suicide. Ieyasu was supreme. The country was now a unified feudal state and at peace. The **Tokugawa** or **Edo** era had begun.

Ieyasu was primarily a military and practical ruler, cunning and unscrupulous. But his achievement in completing the unification of the country under his sway was considerable.

Various metaphors have been coined to describe the achievement of these three men. According to one, Oda Nobunaga quarried the stones for New Japan, Toyotomi Hideysohi rough-hewed them and Tokugawa Ieyasu finally set them in place.

In the Momoyama period Japanese art, especially painting, flourished. Some of the finest painters of the Kanō school, such as Eitoku and Sanraku were employed in painting colourful screens and sliding panels. Some magnificent sliding screens by Hasegawa Tōhaku (1539– 1610) can be seen in the little museum attached to the Chishakuin temple in Kyoto.

Japanese craftsmen were used to build elaborate gateways and pavilions. Some of those built for Momoyama castle, which was destroyed were removed to the Nishi-Honganji temple including the marvellous Hiunkaku pavilion and a fine Chinese-style gateway (*karamon*).

Industrial arts such as metalwork and lacquerware were also encouraged and tea bowls by outstanding Kyoto potters were in great demand by the devotees of the tea ceremony which reached its apogee under the great tea master Sen no Rikyū. Hideyoshi, who had a golden tea room made for his palace, patronised Sen no Rikyū but in a sudden fit of rage and jealousy the tea master was commanded by Hideyoshi to commit suicide.

Many fine castles were built during this period, including that at Himeji which is designated as a national treasure.

1.4.10   Traders and Missionaries: Japan's 'Christian Century' (1543– 1640)

The first Portuguese traders reached Japan in 1542 or 1543. They landed at the island of Tanegashima off southern Kyūshū where their firearms impressed the Japanese who soon managed to reproduce guns in increasing quantities. Trade was opened via Macao, but the journey by sea from Europe in those days was a hazardous one and took two to three years.

In 1549 Francis Xavier, a Jesuit priest later canonised, arrived in Japan to preach the gospel. He stayed for two years and established the first Jesuit mission to Japan. The missionaries faced immense difficulties in communicating with the Japanese. Even a suitable word for God had to be found. Their condemnation of Buddhism as idolatry inevitably aroused the fierce opposition of the Buddhist priests, while their denunciations of sodomy angered many of the samurai who had homosexual as well as heterosexual relationships. But they gradually made converts, especially in the southern island of Kyūshū.

In 1569 the Jesuit priest Luis Frois managed to have an interview with Oda Nobunaga in Kyoto. Nobunaga thought that the Christians could be useful to him in his conflict with the militant Buddhist monks on Hieizan and appeared to favour the missionaries, but his interest was purely tactical.

In 1582 the Jesuit visitor Valignano, as a means of gaining support in Japan, decided to take a group of four young Japanese of noble birth to Rome, which they eventually reached in 1585. They returned to Japan in 1590, but by then the position of the Christian community in Japan had deteriorated and the persecution of the Christians had begun, if at this stage in only a desultory way. Hideyoshi turned against the Christians in 1587 perhaps because the church, claiming to represent God on earth, was in the long run a threat to his rule and he issued a decree expelling the missionaries. The decree was not effectively implemented at this time and the missionaries were able to continue their work so long as they behaved with circumspection. Hideyoshi received Valignano and the four young *daimyō* in 1591 and the missionaries felt relatively optimistic about their future.

By about 1595 the Jesuits estimated that there were some 300 000 Christians in Japan. But in 1596 a Spanish galleon foundered off Shikoku. It is possible that the Spanish captain threatened that if his ship and cargo were not released 'the long arm of the King of Spain would reach Japan, where the Christians would rise in his favour'. At the same time Spanish Dominican friars who had arrived in Japan were behaving indiscreetly in their attempts to make converts. This led in 1597 to the crucifixion in Nagasaki of twenty-six Christian martyrs, and the Jesuit priests were forced to go into hiding.

The arrival from 1600 of Dutch and English traders complicated the position, as did an incident in Macao in 1608 in which Japanese seamen were killed. This led to the sinking of a Portuguese ship off Nagasaki in 1610. In 1614 an edict was promulgated proscribing Christianity in Japan. By this time the Japanese realised that they could do without the Portuguese traders.

In the next two decades persecution of the Christians increased in intensity and many were tortured as well as martyred. The final tragedy occurred in 1637–8. The peasants in the Shimabara peninsula in Kyūshū and the Amakusa islands, many of whom were Christians, revolted but were massacred. The Japanese authorities then cut off all contact with the outside world except for a small window at Nagasaki. The persecution of anyone suspected of being a Christian was further intensified. Despite the persecution some Japanese, however, managed to retain their faith in secret up to the reopening of Japan in the middle of the nineteenth century.

The English established a trading post in 1613 at Hirado in Kyūshū but they failed to make a profit and withdrew after ten years. The Dutch were more successful and after the expulsion of the Portuguese moved to Nagasaki where, throughout the years of Japan's seclusion from the rest of the world (1640–1853), they were allowed to maintain a small trading post on the artificial island of Dejima in Nagasaki bay.

The Jesuits brought a number of benefits to Japan. They taught Western-style painting, and **Namban** (southern barbarian) art, as the screens and other works of art depicting foreigners were called, had a vogue in Japan. The Jesuits also brought knowledge of Western map making and other scientific techniques. They introduced many new words to the Japanese language and learnt to speak Japanese

1.4.11   The Tokugawa (Edo) Period (1616–1853)

Tokugawa Ieyasu and his followers had two main objectives: They wanted to ensure their rule, and reward themselves handsomely. They did this by confiscating estates and moving any *daimyō* who seemed a potential threat.

The *daimyō* were divided into *fudai* (*daimyō* with a history of loyalty to the Tokugawa) and *tozama* (the 'outer' lords) whose fiefs were carefully segregated and watched. Under the so-called *sankinkōtai* system the *daimyō* had to spend part of their life in Edo, the Tokugawa capital, and when they returned to their fiefs they had to leave their families behind in Edo.

There were three Tokugawa houses – Owari (Nagoya), Kii (Wakayama) and Mito (Ibaragi) from whose ranks the shōguns were selected.

Society was rigidly divided into four classes (*shi-nō-kō-shō*), that is, samurai, farmers, artisans and merchants. There was very little mobility between the classes and the samurai regarded the merchants with contempt although they frequently had to turn to the merchants for funds. The farmers were nominally second in rank but were generally oppressed and exploited.

The samurai class, who numbered about 2 million in a total population during the period of around 25 million, were parasites on society. There were no wars and therefore they had no job to do. Their main function was to provide unswerving loyalty to their masters. This led to vendettas (*kataki-uchi*) of which the most notorious occurred in 1701. This was the subject of a famous play *Chūshingura* ('The treasury of the loyal retainers') known as the story of the 47 *Rōnin* (*rōnin* were masterless samurai).

The Tokugawa system of government was rigid. At the apex was the shōgun but his authority was for much of the period largely nominal and the administration was largely in the hands of the shōgun's advisers and chamberlains. The court in Kyoto was given no powers and had very limited resources. It was regarded as of no real importance. Criminal 'justice' was arbitrary and cruel. Menial and unclean tasks were left to the *hinin* and the *eta* who were little more than slaves and who were regarded as beyond the pale of society.

Agriculture was the mainstay of the economy as well as the main source of revenue for the shōgunate. But an increase in trade which followed the pacification of the country and the oppressive regime in agricultural districts led to a migration to the towns. Much effort had to be put into increasing agricultural production, but Japanese crops were liable to many natural disasters and periods of famine were frequent.

The rigidity of the regime and Japan's isolation led to other economic problems. There were various attempts at reform, but the land as farmed in Tokugawa days could hardly support such a large number of unproductive samurai. They were supposed to maintain an austere way of life but many wanted to enjoy a life of luxury.

The cities of Edo and Osaka grew and generally prospered. They had their pleasure quarters (the *Yoshiwara*) and the merchant class generally flourished. But there were frequent fires, and violence and disorder were rife in the cities.

Communications gradually improved and there was a good deal of traffic on the main 'highways' although none of these were usable by wheeled traffic. The most important highway was the Tōkaidō from Edo to Kyoto. The forty-seven stations on the road were made famous by the masterly series of prints by Hiroshige.

The comparative absence of civil strife and increased prosperity meant that more resources could be spent on education. But the Tokugawa were inimical to freedom of thought and demanded orthodoxy. In this climate Confucian studies flourished but many scholars concentrated on the revival of indigenous Japanese studies (termed *kokugaku*). Others attempted to learn from the West, especially in the fields of science and medicine, through Dutch studies (*rangaku*). Many *daimyō* established their own schools and there was a significant growth in literacy. But the emphasis in these schools was on Chinese and Confucian studies and such subjects as mathematics were frowned on as they were regarded as only appropriate for the despised merchant class.

Comparative prosperity and peace also provided a fertile base for the development of the arts and of literature. The theatre flourished and new dramatic forms were developed. The puppet theatre (*Bunraku* or *Jōruri*) became popular, especially in Osaka. One of the greatest writers of puppet dramas was Chikamatsu Monzaemon (1653–1724). Many of his plays were tragedies involving love themes and double suicides. They were written in a form of poetic prose much of which was chanted by a commentator or chorus.

Many of the puppet dramas were later adapted for use in the *Kabuki* theatre. This was a form of drama which became popular in both Edo and Osaka. It involved elaborate scenery and stylised acting. The actors were all men but some of the actors specialised in women's parts (*onna-gata*). There were three main types of *Kabuki* plays: period pieces, contemporary pieces and dance plays.

The novel became popular, especially with the merchant class. One of the greatest novelists of the seventeenth century was Ihara (or Ibara) Saikaku (1642–93) who wrote about erotic life, samurai behaviour and merchant attitudes. In the eighteenth century one of the most famous writers was Ueda Akinari (1734–1809) whose collection of stories the *Ugetsu monogatari* deals mainly with ghosts and supernatural phenomena. In the nineteenth century a number of *kokkeibon* or humorous books were produced. The *Hizakurige* ('Shank's mare') by Jippensha Ikku (1765–1831) tells the picaresque story of two wags travelling along the Tōkaidō.

While the aristocrats continued to write *tanka* (short poems of 5, 7, 5, 7 and 7 syllables), a new form of verse derived from the linked verse which had become a popular game in the Ashikaga period was the *haiku*. *Haiku* are short verses of 5, 7 and 5 syllables. They are the briefest of vignettes, designed to appeal to the reader's imagination. They should include some reference to the season and their words which are chosen for their beauty and rhythm are allusive. The greatest haiku poet is generally considered to be Matsuo Bashō (1644–94), but Taniguchi Buson (1716–84) and Kobayashi Issa (1763–1827) are also famous *haiku* poets of the period.

Painting flourished. Both the Kanō and Tosa schools produced many famous artists. The **Rimpa** school of decorative painting symbolizes one important element of the art of the Tokugawa period. Among the greatest artists of this school were Tawaraya Sōtatsu (? –1643), Ōgata Kōrin (1658–1716) and Maruyama Ōkyō (1733–1795). Kōrin's brother was the famous potter Kenzan the First. Painting in the Chinese style also flourished.

One of the most significant artistic development in the Tokugawa period was the Japanese print (*hanga*) normally referred to under the name *Ukiyo*-e (literally, 'pictures of the floating world') (the term *Nishiki-e* is also used). The earliest prints were in black and white and derived from genre painting. Colour printing was only developed in the middle of the eighteenth century. The print required the co-operation of the artist, the maker of the blocks and the printer. In some complicated prints there were as many as ten different blocks. Iwasa Matabei (1578–1650) is traditionlly regarded as the first Japanese print artist. Many of the names of the greatest print artists are well known in the west. They include Kiyonobu, Harunobu, Utamaro, Toyokuni, Sharaku, Hokusai and Hiroshige. Subjects ranged from courtesans and actors to scenery, flowers and birds.

The art of making ceramics was boosted by the arrival of a number of able Korean potters as well as by the increasing demand in a time of peace for tea bowls, tableware and ornaments. Kyoto became a major ceramic centre, as did Seto and Mino near Nagoya. Kutani ware was developed in Kaga (now Ishikawa prefecture). Kilns at Hagi (Yamaguchi prefecture) produced fine tea bowls with a pinkish glaze. But it was in Kyūshū that the ceramic art particularly flourished. Korean potters were active at Karatsu (Saga prefecture) and Satsuma (Kagoshima prefecture). At Arita, porcelain ware was produced in large quantities, both for export to South East Asia and to Europe via Holland and for use by the nobility and the merchant class. Arita ware is generally called Imari which includes the famous Kakiemon-style ware which became deservedly popular in Europe where it was widely copied. Nabeshima ware, also made in the Arita area, was primarily intended for the Nabeshima clan and their friends.

Lacquer, cloisonné (*shippō*) and metalwork were in demand, and Japanese craftsmen perfected their techniques.

Some of the finest gardens especially of the *kaiyūshiki* type, were built in Kyoto and elsewhere. In Kyoto the imperial gardens of the Sento palace and the Katsura and Shūgakuin detached palaces are outstanding. The three great gardens of Japan outside Kyoto dating from this period are the Kairakuen at Mito, the Kōrakuen at Okayama and Kenrokuen at Kanazawa.

Japanese houses became more refined and marginally more comfortable. Numerous temples and shrines were built or rebuilt. The most striking Tokugawa building was the mausoleum erected at Nikkō for Tokugawa Ieyasu. The Tōshōgu shrine is either magnificent or gaudy depending on one's taste; it can be regarded as a form of Japanese rococo. Its setting among huge cryptomeria trees is particularly fine.

1.4.12   The Reopening of Japan and the Meiji Restoration (1853–68)

By the middle of the nineteenth century Japan's international isolation was an anachronism which could not continue. The rigidity and corruption of the Tokugawa regime was holding back Japan's economic and intellectual development. There was widespread discontent, particularly among the *tozama daimyō* who chafed under the Tokugawa hegemony.

The catalyst for change was provided by the foreign powers, in particular the United States of America. American whalers in the north Pacific needed to be able to shelter from storms and take on water and supplies. The denial of access to Japanese ports was seen by the American government as unacceptable and an expedition to Japan to try to persuade, or rather force, the Japanese to open some ports was sent under the command of Commodore Perry in 1853. In 1854 he managed to conclude a treaty with the Japanese regime which opened the ports of Nagasaki, Hakodate and Shimoda to US vessels. The British, Russians, French and Dutch soon concluded similar agreements. An American Consul, Townsend Harris, was appointed to Shimoda and after protracted and difficult negotiations managed in 1858 to persuade the Japanese authorities to conclude a new treaty which ensured the opening in 1859 of Kanagawa (in fact, Yokohama) as a further treaty port near Edo. The treaty also provided for extra-territorial rights for foreign residents in the treaty ports (that is, they were subject to their *home*, not Japanese, jurisdiction). Lord Elgin for Britain concluded a similar treaty and the other powers quickly followed suit.

The conclusion of the treaties demonstrated the weakness of the shōgunate (*bakufu*). Their opponents, taking advantage of popular feelings against foreigners, stepped up their attacks on the regime.

Following the opening of Yokohama in 1859 foreign traders, particularly British and to a lesser extent French, took up residence in the treaty ports. They were a fairly unscrupulous lot and Yokohama in these early years had similarities to a Wild West town. The presence of the foreigners was resented and attacks on foreign residents and diplomats were frequent.

In 1862 a British merchant from Shanghai was murdered at Namamugi on the Tōkaidō near Yokohama by retainers of the *daimyō* of Satsuma (now Kagoshima prefecture) in southern Kyūshū. The British demanded the punishment of the assassins and an indemnity. The *bakufu* were unable to force the Satsuma fief (one of the main *tozama daimyō*) to comply and in 1863 a British fleet bombarded Kagoshima, setting the town on fire. This was not a clear-cut victory for the British but enmity quickly turned to friendship as the Satsuma leaders saw in Britain a source of support against the Tokugawa. In 1864 the straits of Shimonoseki were closed to foreign shipping by the anti-foreign Chōshū clan (another leading *tozama daimyō*). The British took the lead in forcing the reopening of the straits and bombarded Shimonoseki. In due course Chōshū leaders looked to Britain for support.

Gradually the position and remaining power of the shōgunate was undermined. The opposition concentrated on trying to get the support of the Emperor and his enfeebled court in Kyoto. In 1867, following the appointment of the last of the Tokugawa shōguns (Keiki) and of the boy Emperor Mutsuhito (known in history as the Emperor Meiji) the conflict came to a head and the shōgun was induced to resign. But his followers did not give in without a fight and were only finally defeated in early 1869. The Tokugawa era, however, ended in 1868 with the assumption of nominal power by the Emperor.

One of the first acts of the new government, made up largely of court nobles and samurai from the *tozama* fiefs, was to move the capital from Kyoto to Edo, which was renamed Tokyo.

The British, who gave at least tacit support to the forces opposing the *bakufu*, and the French who supported the Tokugawa with a military mission, played a marginal if important role in the revolution. But the real leaders were the young samurai, especially from the *tozama* fiefs of Satsuma and Chōshū who were later known as the Satchō oligarchy. Some of these new leaders had been smuggled out to study briefly in Britain. A number, including Saigo Takamori, the Satsuma general, and Itō Hirobumi of Chōshū had friendly contacts with a young British scholar–diplomat, Ernest Satow. The British Minister, Sir Harry Parkes, was an irascible and arrogant man but he was influential and ensured that Britain played an important role in the modernization of Japan.

1.4.13 The Meiji Era (1868–1912)

There was at first little consensus on the objectives to be pursued after the fall of the Tokugawa. Some of the conservative *daimyō* wanted to maintain the old feudal system. They all agreed, however, that Japan must become strong so that the treaties which were regarded as unequal with their extra-territorial provisions could be amended. The younger samurai saw that this could only be achieved if Japan was modernised and the old regime destroyed. Japan had to be unified and they decided that the Emperor with his heriditary priestly status should be turned into the symbol which would unify the Japanese people in all walks of life. His status was accordingly exalted and state Shintō developed to ensure that his 'divine' position was recognised. Shintō shrines were divorced from Buddhist temples and in parts of Japan Buddhist temples were damaged.

The new leaders launched what was to be a major revolution. The fiefs and the old class structure were abolished. The samurai were pensioned off (their pensions were soon eroded) and conscription was introduced. The fiefs were abolished and a new land tax system introduced.

The Japanese assiduously studied the reasons for Western success and in 1871 a major mission was sent abroad under the leadership of a court noble, Iwakura Tomomi, but including such young leaders as Itō Hirobumi, to make a detailed study of Western economies. They also tried unsuccessfully to have the unequal treaties renegotiated. They were forced to recognise that to achieve acceptable amendments to the treaties Japan had to introduce a Western-type legal system and start to catch up with Western countries. Efforts at modernisation were redoubled. New legal systems were devised and the administrative system modernised. Teachers and engineers were recruited from Western countries, particularly Britain. The telegraph and lighthouses were introduced with British help. In 1872 the first railway, from Yokohama to Tokyo, which had been built by British engineers, was opened. A banking system based on Western models was developed and industrial enterprises were started under government auspices. Western habits and costume were also promoted and the court was remodelled on European lines.

Inevitably these revolutionary changes aroused the opposition of conservative elements among the former samurai. The opposition culminated in a rebellion (known as the Satsuma rebellion or the **Seinan** war) in 1877 led by Saigo Takamori of Satsuma. The rebels were defeated and Saigo had himself beheaded by one of his followers rather than be captured by the imperial forces. The conscripts had managed to defeat the former samurai.

The speed of change also led to economic problems while the import of Western ideas induced demands for a less autocratic regime and a parliamentary sytem. The government responded to the latter by the encouragement of nationalist sentiments and by indoctrinating the people through the education system. They also promised in due course to introduce a constitution.

Itō Hirobumi was given the task of studying Western constitutions and drawing up one suitable for Japan. His draft was an amalgam but owed much to the German (Prussian) model. The so-called Meiji Constitution was unveiled in 1889 and was declared to be a grant from the Emperor, whose supremacy was confirmed. The Emperor, who was described as 'sacred and inviolable', retained the power to declare war, to conclude treaties and to prorogue or adjourn the Diet. He was also supreme commander of the armed forces. The cabinet was responsible to the Emperor, not to the Diet. The Diet was made up of two houses: the upper house was a house of peers while the lower house was elected on a limited suffrage.

The first Prime Minister under the new constitutition was General Yamagata Aritomo from Chōshū. Elections for the Diet were held in 1890. The government encountered immediate difficulties and the first few years of parliamentary institutions in Japan were troubled by squabbles, electoral malpractice and corruption. But by the middle of the decade Itō Hirobumi had managed to work out a *modus vivendi* between the government and the political parties in the Diet.

An important slogan of the Meiji government was 'a rich country and a strong army' (*fukoku-kyōhei*). This slogan underlined the government's efforts to amend the treaties, and their determination not to be left out in the Western scramble in the nineteenth century to divide up China. An excuse for a Japanese attack on China was found in 1894. Much to the surprise of many Western observers, the Japanese forces easily defeated the Chinese and in 1895 the Japanese, in the Treaty of Shimonoseki, exacted the spoils which they considered appropriate including the cession to Japan of Formosa (now Taiwan) and the Liaotung (Liaodong) Peninsula. The treaty was, however, considered by the Russian, German and French governments as a threat to their interests in China and they launched what was termed the Triple Intervention to force the Japanese to disgorge some of their gains. This aroused extreme Japanese resentment but the Japanese government had to give in as Japan was not strong enough to take on all three powers. Britain, which had finally agreed in 1894 to a revision of the treaties (the revision came into effect in 1899), carefully refrained from supporting the Triple Intervention and this stood the British in good stead with the Japanese government.

The main Japanese interest at this time was in Korea and Manchuria, but their interests conflicted with those of Russia. The Japanese were suspicious of Russian intentions in the Far East, as were the British in India. These mutual suspicions and Japanese fears of a further triple intervention were major factors in the conclusion of the Anglo-Japanese Alliance of 1902. In 1904 Japanese efforts to reach an acceptable arrangement with Russia foundered and war was declared. The Anglo-Japanese Alliance ensured that the other European powers did not intervene, but Japanese forces encountered stubborn Russian defences and the seige of Port Arthur was long and bloody. The Russian fleet which was sent from Europe was annihilated in the battle of Tsushima (the battle of the Japan Sea) by the Japanese naval forces commanded by Admiral Tōgō Heihachiro. In 1905 a peace treaty between Japan and Russia was signed at Portsmouth, New Hampshire. The Japanese gained most of their objectives but were forced by outside pressure to accept compromises that were highly unpopular in Japan. Japan was exhausted by the war and needed a period of peace.

The Anglo-Japanese Alliance was revised in 1905 and again in 1911, but it had largely served its purpose and was of declining importance. Korea became a Japanese protectorate in 1905 and was annexed by Japan in 1910. Japan now had a firm foothold on the mainland of Asia.

The origins of Japanese imperialism are complicated, but a major factor was undoubtedly the desire to achieve equality with the Western imperial powers and to demonstrate that Japan was a great power not only in Asia but also in the world.

To be a great power Japan needed her own heavy industry and the ability to build warships and manufacture armaments. At first Japanese naval ships were built in Britain, but by the end of the Russo-Japanese war Japan had built up her basic industry and was able to supply most of her own needs. She also developed her textile industry and became an increasingly important trading power. But the Japanese standard of living was low and much still needed to be done to develop the country's infrastructure.

The Meiji period saw the early development of the large Japanese conglomerates known as the *zaibatsu*, including the Mitsui, Mitsubishi, Sumitomo and Yasuda groups. Japanese banks, trading companies and industrial firms were becoming an increasing force in the Japanese economy.

Society changed vastly during the Meiji period, but by the 1890s there was a sharp reaction to Westernisation and a determination to maintain and revive traditional values. The hierarchy had changed radically. The main power rested with the bureaucracy and increasingly with the armed services and the leaders of industry. The farmers remained poor and the workforce was exploited.

Ways of thought and language were also altered drastically by contacts with the West. Indeed a whole new vocabulary had to be invented to cover such Western concepts as freedom, democracy and competition. The written language became more accessible and had to be adapted to newspapers, which despite rigid censorship developed a wide readership throughout Japan during the Meiji period.

Great emphasis was placed on education and by the end of the century most Japanese were literate despite the complexity of the language. Japanese high schools and universities (both public and private) were developed and a hierarchy of prestigious educational institutions emerged, with the Imperial University of Tokyo at the apex.

In literature the novel received a particular boost as translations from foreign languages became popular. Naturalism, realism and romanticism all found their exponents. One of the great naturalist Japanese novelists of the period was Tayama Katai (1872–1930). Among the greatest novelists of the Meiji period, many of whose works have been translated into English, were Natsume Sōseki (1867–1916) and Mori Ōgai (1862–1922).

Tanka and *haiku* continued to be written. The outstanding producer of *haiku* in this period was probably Masaoka Shiki (1867–1902). Free verse forms were also tried, notably by Ishikawa Takuboku (1886–1912).

The *Kabuki* retained its popularity but there were also some relatively successful attempts at producing Western-style dramas.

In the arts, Western influence at first seemed to crush the spirit of traditional forms and in lacquer, cloisonné, pottery and porcelain as well as in metalwork, Western demand led to a deterioration in design and taste.

Painting in Western style (*yōga*) became popular, but there was a counter-reaction from painters in the traditional styles. They took some elements from Western painting and developed a new style of Japanese painting which is termed **Nihonga**.

Western-style architecture, which was more suited to public buildings than traditional Japanese forms, became popular. One British architect, Josiah Conder (1852–1920), is remembered in Japan for his designs of a number of important Meiji buildings.

1.4.14   The Taishō (1912–1926) and Shōwa (1926–1945) Eras

The death of the Emperor Meiji in 1912 marked the end of an era in which Japan had emerged from seclusion and achieved the status of a world power. But imperialist pressures were growing, especially in the Japanese army.

With the outbreak of war in 1914 the Japanese government, seeing the chance to improve Japan's position in the Far East, entered the war against Germany. Japanese forces seized the German base in the Shantung (Shandong) Peninsula and occupied the Pacific islands which had been German colonies.

With the other powers fully involved in Europe the Japanese decided to expand their influence in China. A list of twenty-one demands was drawn up and presented to the Chinese government in 1915. Under pressure from America and Britain the demands were somewhat modified but they still amounted to forcing the Chinese to concede a special role to Japan in China.

In 1917 the Japanese agreed to provide naval assistance to the allies in the Mediterranean. Japanese forces also took part in joint operations in Siberia after the Russian Revolution had occurred.

At the Versailles Peace Conference in 1919 the Japanese clashed with the Americans over China and were forced to agree that the former German Pacific islands which they had occupied and hoped to annex were placed under a League of Nations mandate. The Japanese deeply resented the discrimination practised in California against people of Japanese origin and tried to get a clause inserted in the charter of the League of Nations banning racial discrimination. This failed, largely owing to American opposition.

The British, concerned by growing American–Japanese hostility, arranged for a conference to be held in Washington in 1921 to consider the problems of the Far East and the Pacific. The resulting four-power pact between the USA, Britain, France and Japan which replaced the Anglo-Japanese Alliance had little substance and the main attention was focused on the agreement between Britain, the USA and Japan under which the ratio of capital ships in the navies of the three countries was to be 5:5:3. Japan had wanted parity.

In Japan the retirement of the old guard of Meiji leaders, the so-called *genrō* (elder statesman), gave the Diet a chance to assert its authority, but there was no consensus on how to proceed. For a time in the 1920s it seemed just possible that Japan might move towards a more democratic system. But the political parties consisted largely of venal politicians divided more by personal loyalties and jealousies than by policy differences. Japan could not escape the world slump and there was much discontent, both among industrial workers and farmers as the Japanese standard of living remained low. Socialist movements were banned and oppressive policies were reinforced by the first 'Peace Preservation' law of 1925. This led in 1928 to the arrest of some 1600 suspected Communists.

The naval conference in Washington in 1930 gave the Japanese a marginal improvement in their permitted ratio of naval vessels but the result was greeted with disappointment in Japan. The Prime Minister, Hamaguchi Osachi (1870–1931), forced the Privy Council to accept the agreement, but he was assassinated soon afterwards. Japan's period of what one commentator has called 'government by assassination' had begun.

The army now took the initiative. On the night of 18–19 September 1931 the Kwantung (Guandong) army launched a sudden attack on the Chinese garrison in Mukden in retribution for alleged attacks on the tracks of the South Manchurian railway by the Chinese army. In fact these incidents had been fabricated by the Japanese army. Vain attempts were made from Tokyo to control subsequent events, but by December 1931 the Japanese army controlled most of southern Manchuria. By January 1933 Manchuria had been subjugated.

The League of Nations was unable and unwilling to take effective steps to deal with Japanese aggression. A League of Nations commission of inquiry under Lord Lytton concluded that the Japanese actions were unjustified. The Japanese responded by walking out of the League.

Right-wing extremism and chauvinism were encouraged by Japanese success in Manchuria. In February 1932 Prime Minister Inukai Tsuyoshi (1855–1932) was murdered by a group of young officers. Other incidents followed, culminating in the *ni-ni-roku jiken*, an incident which began on 26 February 1936. A group of some 1400 officers and men under the leadership of young army officers seized control of the central part of Tokyo and assassinated the Finance Minister, the Lord Keeper of the Privy Seal and the Inspector General of Military Education. The Shōwa Emperor (Hirohito), in whose name the rebels pretended to be acting, was furious and demanded firm action. Martial law was proclaimed and the rebels were surrounded by loyal troops. Nineteen of the rebels, who had expected leniency, were executed, but the army used the incident as an excuse to strengthen its hold on power and bolster its imperialist ambitions.

Japanese fascism differed from German Nazism and Italian Fascism. Its base was among agricultural rather than industrial workers. It was nourished by a Japanese sense of racial superiority and belief in their divine mission. Loyalty to the Emperor was considered to override all other moral principles. Central to Japanese fascism was the concept of *kokutai* which may be translated as 'the national polity' or 'the national essence'. Japanese fascism was backed up by a special police force (the *tokkō*) and by the military police (*kempeitai*). Their task was to apprehend those who had committed 'thought crimes' and 'convert' them to orthodox views. Between 1928 and 1941 some 74 000 people had been arrested for such crimes although only some 5000 were prosecuted. At the end of the war some 2500 political prisoners were released.

Japanese fascism was reinforced by further developments in China. On 7 July 1937 a clash between Japanese and Chinese troops at the Marco Polo bridge on the outskirts of Peking (Beijing) provided the excuse for a Japanese attack on China. Tientsin (Tianjian) and Peking (Beijing) were soon occupied. Japanese forces moved up the Yangtse (Yangzi) river and on 13 Decemeber 1937 Nanking (Nanjing) was occupied in an orgy of murder, rape and looting. Japanese atrocities were now known to the whole world. The Japanese soon controlled most of the Chinese coast and large inland areas but they did not succeed in subjugating China.

In 1936 the Japanese had signed an anti-Comintern pact with Germany. In September 1940 a tripartite pact was concluded with Germany and Italy.

The Americans, increasingly concerned by the rise in Japanese power in Asia, were intent on reducing Japanese access to raw materials. So the Japanese army turned towards the south. After the fall of France in 1940 they managed to obtain bases in Indo-China, but their main interest was in the oil and other resources of the Netherlands East Indies (now Indonesia).

Negotiations for an understanding with the USA in 1941 foundered on American insistence that Japan should guarantee the integrity of its Asian neighbours. The military and naval authorities, with the backing of General Tōjō Hideki (1884–1948), who became Prime Minister in October 1941, decided to launch pre-emptive strikes against the Americans and the British. The American fleet was attacked with devastating results in Pearl Harbor on 7 December 1941 before the Japanese declaration of war had reached the Americans. At the same time an attack was launched against British possessions in the Far East.

At first Japanese forces achieved overwhelming victories. They soon had control of the Philippines, Malaya, Singapore and the Netherlands East Indies as well as the bulk of Burma. Their forces moved rapidly south and West and seemed ready to strike at India and Australia.

In the territories which they occupied, Japanese treatment of the civilian populations did nothing to endear them to the people they claimed to be liberating. Their treatment of allied prisoners of war was at best inhumane and at worst savagely cruel.

However, the tide began to turn against Japan. In 1943, after a bloody battle, the Japanese were forced out of the Pacific island of Guadalcanal. In 1944 American naval forces inflicted a decisive defeat on the Japanese off Leyte. In early 1945 the Americans regained most of the Philippines and US Marines landed first on Iwojima and then on the Japanese island of Okinawa. Colossal bombing raids were launched against Japanese cities and much of Japanese industry, infrastructure and housing was destroyed. Only the cities of Kyoto and Nara were spared by the bombers.

Following the fall of Germany in May 1945 it should have been obvious to the Japanese leadership that Japan was defeated and that further resistance could only end in the destruction of Japan. But it took until mid-August 1945, following the dropping of the atomic bombs on Hiroshima and Nagasaki, before a decision to surrender was made. The military did all they could to hide the real facts from the Japanese people and urged suicide rather than surrender. It was only after the unprecedented intervention of the Emperor in person that the Japanese at last agreed to the unconditional surrender which the allied powers had demanded. In the final days the Japanese government had wriggled hard to try to find a formula which protected the position of the Emperor. He for his part was willing to accept the Allied terms, which made it clear that the authority of the Emperor must be subject to the Supreme Commander of the Allied Powers (SCAP). Despite an abortive attempt by military hard liners to stop him by seizing the tape of the broadcast the Emperor broadcast the decison to surrender on 15 August 1945. The actual surrender ceremony took place on board the USS Missouri in Tokyo Bay on 2 September 1945. The war was at last over.

These were not good years for literature and the arts, which were expected to conform to the requirements of Japanese fascism. But some great novels were produced and a number of fine painters in the *Nihonga* tradition were able to develop their art. One of the most remarkable novelists of the early part of this period was Akutagawa

Ryūnosuke (1892–1927). The prize for literature established in his name is now perhaps the most prestigious in Japan. Among the many outstanding figures in this period of twentieth-century Japanese literature who went on writing in the post-war period were Tanizaki Junichiro (1886–1965) and Kawabata Yasunari (1899–1972), who won the Nobel prize for literature in 1968.

One significant artistic movement which managed to survive and develop was the *mingei* (literally, 'folk craft movement'). This was a movement whose leading philosopher was Yanagi Sōetsu and whose leaders included the British potter Bernard Leach and his Japanese potter friends such as Hamada Shōji. It aimed to revitalise the Japanese craft tradition, especially in the making of pots for everyday use.

1.4.15   Post-war Japan (1945–)

In August 1945 Japan was defeated, impoverished and almost starving. Sixty-six Japanese cities had been largely destroyed by air raids and Japan's industry and infrastructure were in ruins.

The country was occupied by allied forces, mainly American, between September 1945 and April 1952. The Supreme Commander Allied Powers (SCAP) was General Douglas MacArthur of the US Army.

SCAP decided to operate through the Japanese administration. The first task was demilitarization. Nearly seven million Japanese, including civilians, had to be brought back to Japan from overseas and the armed forces disbanded. The main proponents of Japanese imperialism and fascism were purged from public life and some 6000 Japanese accused of war crimes in occupied territories and against Allied prisoners of war were tried by Allied courts. An international military tribunal tried twenty-eight Japanese leaders.

Political prisoners were released and human rights guaranteed. The education system was reformed on American lines. State Shintō was abolished.

A major land reform was instituted. The old industrial combines which formed the *zaibatsu* were broken up. Labour Unions were permitted and encouraged.

Perhaps the most significant of all reforms was the drafting and enactment of a new constitution (see Chapter 2 and Appendix 1).

The Japanese economy was in chaos and the Americans had to provide food and other aid. Inflation was rampant and was only brought under control by drastic measures proposed by Joseph Dodge, an American banker. The Americans also provided expert advice on management and quality control which contributed greatly to subsequent Japanese industrial success.

The Korean War which broke out in June 1950 provided a major stimulus to the Japanese economy through special procurements for the American forces.

The new democratic constitution provided the basis for a new political order. The conservative forces were revamped into what eventually became the Liberal Democratic Party (LDP). The Socialists provided the main opposition, but they were divided between right wing social democrats and left-wing Marxists. This split eventually led to the division of the party into two groups – the Japan Socialist Party (JSP) on the left and the Democratic Socialist Party (DSP) on the right. A relatively strong Japan Communist Party (JCP) which advocated violent revolution also emerged. In 1950 General MacArthur denounced the JCP and action was taken against its leaders under the Subversive Activities Law which was enacted in 1952.

In 1947 the JSP leader Katayama Tetsu (1887–1978) formed a coalition government, but it lasted less than a year. This was the only occasion in which since the end of the Second World War the Japanese government has not been headed by a conservative-inclined politician. The outstanding Japanese politician of the immediate post-war years was Yoshida Shigeru (1878–1967).

A peace treaty (text in Appendix 2), largely drafted by the Americans, was signed at San Francisco in September 1951. It came into force after ratification on 28 April 1952. The terms of the peace treaty were moderate, but Japan had to cede the territories which it had gained in its imperialist era. There were only limited provisions for reparations. Neither the Soviet Union nor the People's Republic of China was a party to the Treaty, but under American pressure the Japanese subsequently concluded a peace treaty with the Nationalist Chinese regime in Taiwan.

The Japanese also concluded a security treaty with the United States which permitted United States forces to remain in Japan and at the request of the Japanese authorities to give assistance in the event of internal disturbances. This latter clause was bitterly criticised by the Japanese opposition. It was eventually dropped in the revised treaty concluded in 1960, but the revised treaty itself aroused fierce opposition in Japan and was only ratified after disturbances which forced the resignation of Kishi Nobusuke (1896–1987) as Prime Minister and the cancellation of the proposed visit to Japan by the US President General Dwight Eisenhower.

Japanese life has changed dramatically in the post-war years, but the political scene has remained much the same. The LDP has remained in power throughout but has responded to public pressure by adapting its economic and social policies. It has also regularly shuffled the political pack to balance the factions and appease political and public opinion. The electoral system of multi-member constituencies has remained largely unaltered, allowing money to play an important role in Japanese political life. There has been much talk about the need for radical political reform but little or no effective action has been taken so far. The bureaucracy, whose senior officials are some of the cream of educated Japanese, have provided continuity and competence and ensured that the game of politics has not been too damaging to Japan's position and development. A list of Japanese Prime Ministers since the end of the second World War in 1945 is given in Appendix 4.

Economic recovery was at first relatively slow but during the term of office of Prime Minister Ikeda Hayato (1899–1965) who proclaimed a policy of doubling Japanese income, a major leap forward occurred. This was partly spurred on by the need to build Japan's infrastructure to meet the requirements of the Olymic Games which were held in Tokyo in 1964. Between 1955 and 1970 Japanese GNP grew at an average annual rate of 10.3 per cent. Japanese living standards, which had been low in the immediate post-war years, improved dramatically.

Japanese industry after the end of the Occupation was enabled to regroup. The pre-war *zaibatsu* gave way to the looser groupings of the *keiretsu* (see Chapter 7). Manufacturing industry was helped by favourable financial arrangements and by protectionist measures administered by the Ministry of International Trade and Industry (MITI). Japanese success was also spurred on by the competition which was encouraged by the authorities and by the traditional attitudes and loyalties of Japanese management and workforce. An important factor in minimising labour troubles was the fact that most unions were company unions who co-operated with managements to improve the competitive positions of their firms.

Japanese defence and foreign policies in post-war years have been modified to meet the changing circumstances of the times. These are discussed in Chapter 5.

Post-war Japanese educational reforms were amended to suit Japanese economic requirements and to reinforce Japanese traditional values (see Chapter 10). Literature and the arts were revitalised and the Japanese language was modified to meet the changing needs of the age.

The Japanese novel achieved world renown. Among the many Japanese novelists whose works have been translated into English Mishima Yukio (1925–70) became particularly famous following his dramatic ritual suicide in the Tokyo headquarters of the Ground Self-Defence Forces.

In the performing arts there have been significant developments in drama and music. Japanese orchestras, conductors, soloists, dancers and singers are now among the best in the world.

In the visual arts both *yōga* and *Nihonga* have been popular and produced a number of great artists to follow in the footsteps of Umehara Ryuzaburo (1888–1986) in *yōga* and Yokoyama Taikan (1868–1958) in *Nihonga*.

The essential rebuilding of modern Japan and increasing prosperity enabled Japanese architects not only to design some very striking new buildings but also to achieve world fame. Tange Kenzō and Isozaki Arata among others have achieved such fame and have made outstanding contributions to Japan's new public buildings.

2 The Political Framework

2.1 THE CONSTITUTION

The present Japanese Constitution was promulgated on 3 November 1946 and came into force on 3 May 1947. It was officially an amended version of the so-called Meiji Constitution of 1889 but was in substance a new constitution.

The Potsdam Declaration of August 1945 had called for the removal of 'all obstacles to the revival and strengthening of democratic tendencies among the Japanese people. Freedom of speech, of religion, and of thought, as well as respect for the fundamental human rights, shall be established'. The declaration also called for the establishment 'in accordance with the will of the Japanese people' of 'a peacefully inclined and responsible government'.

Various efforts were made by Japanese politicians in the final months of 1945 to produce proposals for revision of the Meiji Constitution. These proposals, however, proved totally unacceptable to the Supreme Commander Allied Powers (SCAP). A draft for a new constitution was prepared in the government section of SCAP and delivered to the Japanese cabinet on 13 February 1946. The cabinet, warned that if it did not accept the draft, at least in principle, the Emperor might be tried as a war criminal capitulated and produced a draft based on the SCAP model. The only basic change made by the Japanese cabinet was that there should be a bicameral legislature rather than an unicameral one proposed by the Americans. The Emperor, having indicated his acceptance of the formula suggested to cover the imperial status, the amended constitution was approved unanimously by the House of Representatives and the House of Peers.

Chapter I of the new Constitution deals with the position of the Emperor. Under Article 1 he is declared to be 'the symbol of the State and of the unity of the people, deriving his position from the will of the people with whom resides the sovereign power'. He is empowered to act in matters of state only 'on the advice and approval of the Cabinet' and as 'provided for in this Constitution and he shall not have powers related to government'. The Emperor's ten functions, as defined in Article 7, include convoking the Diet, dissolving the House of Representatives, awarding honours, and receiving foreign ambassadors. However, in each case he can only act 'with the advice and approval of the Cabinet'.

Under the Meiji Constitution the Emperor had been 'sacred and inviolable'. He was 'the head of the Empire, combining in Himself the rights of sovereignty'. He exercised 'the legislative power with the consent of the Imperial Diet' which he convoked, opened, prorogued and dissolved. He could issue decrees when the Diet was not in session. He was the supreme commander of the forces and declared war, made peace and concluded treaties. The Meiji Constitution was granted by the Emperor. The provisions of the new constitution thus totally changed the Emperor's status and powers. He is not even described as Head of State but only as 'the symbol of the State'.

Chapter II of the new Constitution consists of only one article, the famous Article 9, confirming Japan's commitment to peace. The interpretation of this article, which is of major significance for modern Japan has been the subject of much controversy. It reads:

> Aspiring sincerely to an international peace based on justice and order, the Japanese people forever renounce war as a sovereign right of the nation and the threat or use of force as a means of settling international disputes.
>
> In order to accomplish the aim of the preceding paragraph, land, sea, and air forces, as well as other war potential, will never be maintained. The right of belligerency of the state will not be recognised.

This article has been interpreted as permitting the establishment of Self-Defence Forces.

Chapter III (Articles 10–40) covers the rights and duties of the people. It is a great advance on the old constitution, which emphasised duties rather than rights. Some of the more important articles are:

(i) Article 13 provides that 'All of the people shall be respected as individuals. Their right to life, liberty, and the pursuit of happiness shall, to the extent that it does not interfere with public welfare, be the supreme consideration in legislation and in other government affairs.'

(ii) Article 14 provides for equality under the law and declares that 'there shall be no discrimination in political, economic or social relations because of race, creed, sex, social status or family origin'. It also abolished the peerage and declared that 'No privilege shall accompany any honour, decoration or any distinction.'

(iii) Article 15 includes provisions for universal adult suffrage and the secret ballot.

(iv) Article 19 declares that 'Freedom of thought and conscience shall not be violated.'

(v) Article 20 asserts that 'freedom of religion is guaranteed to all'. It also provides that the State must not grant privileges to any religious organization and 'shall refrain from religious education or any other religious activity'.

Chapter IV (Articles 41–64) covers the Diet. Under Article 41 the Diet is declared to be 'the highest organ of state power' and 'the sole law-making organ'. The term of office of Members of the House of Representatives is limited by the Constitution to a maximum of four years, whereas that of Members of the House of Councillors is stipulated as being six years, with half the members being elected every three years. Members generally cannot be arrested while the Diet is in session and their speeches in the Diet are regarded as privileged. An ordinary session of the Diet must be held once a year but extraordinary sessions may be convoked. Other Articles cover general rules of procedure. An important provision is in Article 59. This provides that:

> A bill which is passed by the House of Representatives, and upon which the House of Councillors makes a decision different from that of the House of Representatives, becomes a law when passed a second time by the House of Representatives by a majority of two-thirds or more of the members present.

In the case of the budget and of treaties requiring Diet approval, the Constitution provides that if the House of Councillors makes amendments which are not acceptable to the House of Representatives, the budget and the treaties approved by the lower house become law after thirty days.

Chapter V (Articles 65–75) deals with the Cabinet in whom executive power is vested. They are collectively responsible to the Diet and must be civilians. (Under the Meiji Constitution the Prime Minister and other members of the Cabinet were frequently from the Army or the Navy, and the Army and Navy Ministers were generally serving members of the Forces). The Prime Minister has to be designated by the Diet from among its members. If the two houses disagree on the designation of the Prime Minister, the decision of the House of

Representatives stands. Cabinet Ministers, called Ministers of State, are appointed by the Prime Minister, who may remove them as he chooses. The Cabinet's functions include (Article 73) the administration of the law, the conduct of foreign affairs, concluding treaties, and administering the civil service.

Chapter VI (Articles 76–82) makes provisions for the judiciary. Article 76 declares that 'The whole judiciary power is vested in a Supreme Court and in such inferior courts as are established by law' and that 'All judges shall be independent in the exercise of their conscience and shall be bound only by this Constitution and the laws.' Supreme Court judges have to be confirmed in their appointments by the electorate at the first election after their appointment (Article 79). Article 81 makes it clear that 'The Supreme Court is the court of last resort with power to determine the constitutionality of any law, order, regulation or official act.' However, the Japanese Supreme Court is not a constitutional court and any member of the public bringing a case to the Supreme Court challenging the constitutional validity of public actions must show a direct and personal injury. A declaration that an act is unconstitutional requires the assent of at least eight of the fifteen judges of the Supreme Court.

Chapter VII (Articles 83–91) covers finance and provides that expenditure by the state and new taxes must be approved by the Diet.

Chapter VIII (Articles 92–95) deals very superficially with local self-government. The most important provision is that the chief executive officers (that is, governors of prefectures and mayors) are to be elected. Before the war they were appointed by the central government.

Chapter IX (Article 96) provides that amendments to the constitution have to be initiated in the Diet and approved by two-thirds or more of all the members of each House. Amendments have then to be submitted to a referendum and approved by a majority of the votes cast.

There have been discusssions from time to time of amendments to the Constitution on the grounds that it was imposed by the Americans during the Occupation and is not in various respects 'appropriate' to Japan's needs today. When the LDP was formed from conservative groupings in 1955 it placed strong emphasis on constitutional revision and in 1956 a law was passed establishing a commission on the constitution. During its seven-year existence many proposals for revision were made to the commission. However, the commission concluded that although some of the provisions of the constitution could be criticised, there were no serious defects in the constitution, it was functioning well and enjoyed popular support. Although a majority of the commission favoured revision it made no formal recommendations. One reason for this was that it would clearly be extremely difficult to obtain the necessary majorities for the approval of amendments.

Chapter X (Articles (97–99) is entitled 'Supreme Law'. Article 97 proclaims, rather unconvincingly in the light of the history of modern Japan, that 'The fundamental human rights by this Constitution guaranteed to the people of Japan are the fruits of the age-old struggle of man to be free' and 'are conferred upon this and future generations in trust, to be held for all times inviolate'. Article 98 confirms that the constitution is 'the supreme law of the nation'.

The full text of the Constitution is given in Appendix 1.

2.2 THE EMPEROR

Under the new constitution the role of the Emperor is largely symbolic and ceremonial. He thus has some of the functions of a Western-style constitutional monarch, but he is not described as Head of State and because of the traditional Japanese concept of a ruler descended from the gods who created Japan and who consequently had a semi-priestly role, he does not play the same popular role as does, for instance, the Queen of England. He and the other members of the imperial family tend to be kept secluded from too many contacts with the Japanese people if only because of the paranoiac fear by the police of possible terrorist attacks.

The English title Emperor has only been used since the latter half of the nineteenth century. It was adopted to give the Japanese sovereign a title equivalent to that of the Emperors of China, Russia and Germany and that of Queen Victoria who became Empress of India. The Japanese title of the sovereign is *Tennō* (or formerly *Tenshi*) which may be regarded as 'son of heaven'. The full title is *Tennō Heika*, that is, His Majesty the Emperor, and he is usually referred to briefly as *Heika*, that is, His Majesty or Your Majesty.

The term *Mikado* (literally, 'noble gate'), which was much used by foreigners in the latter part of the nineteenth century (cf. Gilbert and Sullivan's *The Mikado*) is no longer used.

The present Emperor of Japan is, according to Japanese traditions, the 125th Emperor since the mythological founding of Japan in 660 BC by the first Emperor, Jimmu. The present Emperor was proclaimed on 7 January 1989 on the death of his father. His given name is Akihito, but this name is never used when referring to him, that is, he should not be termed the Emperor Akihito, but simply the Emperor. He was born in Tokyo on 23 December 1933 and is the elder son of the late Emperor Hirohito (now termed after his era name *Shōwa*) and the Empress Nagako (now the Empress Dowager or *Kōtaigō*),. The Emperor studied at the Gakushūin schools and University (the Gakushūin was before the war the Peers' college). He has made a special taxonomic study of gobiid fish and is a member of the Ichthyological Society of Japan whose journal has carried a number of papers by him. He came of age in 1952, when he was officially invested as Crown Prince of Japan. In 1953 he attended the Coronation of Queen Elizabeth II of England. In 1959 he married Miss Shōda Michiko, now the Japanese Empress Michiko. His enthronement ceremonies, including the traditional rites of dedication in the *Dajōsai* took place in November 1990.

The Empress (*KōgōHeika*) Michiko, born in Tokyo on 20 October 1934, is the eldest daughter of Mr and Mrs Shōda Hidesaburo. Mr Shōda Hidesaburo was the former president of a flour manufacturing company. The Empress attended the Sacred Heart middle and high schools and the Sacred Heart University where she specialised in English literature. She plays the piano and the harp while the Emperor plays the cello.

The Emperor and Empress have three children. Their eldest son, the Crown Prince (*Kōtaishi*), has the given name of Naruhito and the title of *Hiro-no-miya*, or Prince Hiro. He was born on 23 February 1960 and graduated from the Department of History at Gakushūin University in March 1982, where he did a special study of maritime transport in the Seto Inland Sea in the medieval period. In July 1983 he went to England to study at Merton College, Oxford, where he studied transport on the River Thames in the latter half of the eighteenth century. He returned to Japan in October 1985 and resumed his postgraduate studies at the Gakushūin University. He plays the viola and the violin. An announcement was made in January 1993 of the Crown Prince's engagement to Miss Owada Masako (aged 29), the daughter of the Administrative Vice-Minister in the Ministry of Foreign Affairs and a member of the Diplomatic Service who had studied at Harvard and Oxford (Balliol College). The wedding took place on 9 June 1993.

A note on the other members of the imperial family and the imperial household is given in Appendix 3.

2.3 THE DIET (PARLIAMENT)

Under Article 41 of the new constitution the Diet is 'the highest organ of state power' and 'the sole law-making body'.

The Diet consists of two houses. The upper house, or House of Councillors, and the lower house, or House of Representatives.

The upper house has 252 members with a fixed term of office of six years. Half are elected every three years at an election normally held in July.

The House of Representatives currently has a total membership of 512. An election to the House of Representatives must be held at least once every four years, but the Cabinet (in practice the Prime Minister of the day) has the right to ask for a dissolution of the lower house before the prescribed four years has expired.

The Diet is convoked by an imperial rescript on the decision of the Cabinet. An ordinary session of the Diet must be held once a year for a term of 150 days to consider the budget and related fiscal measures. In addition, extraordinary sessions may be convoked on the decision of the Cabinet to consider other bills or if demanded by a quarter or more of the total members of either house of the Diet. An extraordinary session must be convoked after a general election has been held following the expiration of the term of office of members of the House of Representatives or after a regular election for members of the House of Councillors. A special session of the Diet must be called after a general election following dissolution of the House of Representatives when an election takes place in less than the statutory four years. The length of an extraordinary or a special session is decided by the two houses. An ordinary session may be extended once. A special or extraordinary session may be extended twice.

When the Diet is convoked, the Cabinet resigns and a Prime Minister is designated and elected by members of the two houses. The Prime Minister must be a member of either the lower or the upper house.

At the beginning of each session an opening ceremony in the presence of the Emperor is held in the chamber of the House of Councillors. After the opening ceremony for an ordinary session policy speeches are delivered by the Prime Minister, the Foreign Minister, the Finance Minister and the Minister for the Economic Planning Agency. In the case of an extraordinary session the Prime Minister gives a policy speech which may be followed by speeches by other ministers. These policy speeches are followed by interpellations from selected representatives of the parties. Interpellations take the form of questions but these may be protracted and are designed to enable the questioner to criticise the policies of the government. The Japanese Diet does not conduct general debates in the Westminster style and although many questions are asked of ministers and, in committees, of senior officials there is no equivalent of Westminster's daily question time and the regular sessions of Prime Minister's questions.

Each House has both plenary and committee meetings. As a rule plenary sessions are open to the public. Business cannot be transacted unless a quorum of one-third of total membership is present. All decisions are taken by a majority of those present (unless otherwise provided, for example, by amendments to the constitution). Votes can be oral, standing or by open ballot. In the case of oral votes the speaker asks if any member objects, and if there are none the measure is approved. A standing vote is called if there is an objection. If the Speaker decides that the number of members standing exceeds those sitting down he declares that the standing members are in a majority and the measure is approved. An open ballot vote is taken if the Speaker deems this necessary or it is demanded by one fifth of the members present. In open ballot votes those in favour cast white ballot tablets with their names in black on the tablet whilst those against cast green (blue) ballot tablets with their names in red. Oral voting is generally used to decide such matters as resignation of officers, leave of absence, protocol issues and petitions.

During sessions the House of Councillors normally meets at 10 a.m. on Mondays, Wednesdays and Fridays while the House of Representatives normally meets at 2 p.m. on Tuesdays, Thursdays and Fridays.

Committees are either standing or special. The House of Councillors and the House of Representatives each have standing Committees covering the Cabinet, local administration, judicial affairs, foreign affairs, finance, education, social and labour questions, agriculture (with forestry and fisheries), commerce and industry, transport, communications, construction, budget, audit, and rules and administration. In addition to these sixteen committees the House of Representatives has two other committees, for science and technology, and environment. Every Diet member has to serve on at least one committee. Membership of committees is allocated to political parties in proportion to their numerical strength in the respective houses. Half of the members must be present for a quorum. The budget committee has fifty members. The size of the other committees varies between twenty and forty.

Committees are not open to the public but media representatives may attend as observers and report the proceedings. Other observers may be admitted if space permits and the chairman's prior approval has been obtained. As committee meetings are not held in public, records are not published, but minutes are made, printed and distributed to all members of the house and copies are deposited in the National Diet Library, from where copies are sent to local libraries. A committee may decide to hold a closed meeting and to keep the minutes confidential.

Committees are presided over by a chairman who is responsible for keeping order and arranging business. Committees make decisions by a majority of those present, subject to there being a quorum of over half the members of the committee. The committee chairman has a casting vote in the case of a tie but does not normally vote.

Most of the normal work of the Diet is done in committee. Committees may undertake investigations and call government officials and other witnesses. Committees may propose bills and pass resolutions.

The standing committee on the budget covers the whole spectrum of government business. It is therefore of particular importance. The audit committee also has extensive responsibilities covering all organs of government. The rules and administration committee has a wide remit, deciding such matters as composition of committees, protocol and all questions related to the smooth operation of the Diet.

Special committees, which are of two types, may be established on the decision of the respective houses. One type of special committee is investigative and is empowered to look into specific matters referred to it. The other type is for consideration of particular measures. Some special committees may be re-established in each session, for example, on disasters, on election laws, on prices and on traffic safety.

Petitions may be presented to either house, which may remit the petition to a committee if it considers this appropriate.

If proceedings are proposed to remove a judge the two Houses have to set up a 'judges' indictment committee' and a 'judges' impeachment court'.

Laws and Diet decisions normally require the concurrence of both houses. If the House of Councillors amends a bill received from the House of Representatives or vice versa the bill must be remitted to the other house for further consideration. If the amended bill is not approved by the other house a conference committee of both houses is called to try to thrash out an agreement.

In the case of budget bills and treaties, as well as resolutions on the appointment of the Prime Minister, the House of Representatives is supreme and can overrule the upper house. Similarly, if a bill is passed by the lower house with a majority of two-thirds or more or if the upper house fails to take action within the specified time the will of the House of Representatives prevails. The budget must be submitted first to the lower house. Resolutions of no confidence in the government can only be introduced and passed in the House of Representatives. If such a resolution is passed or a vote of confidence is defeated the Cabinet must either resign or the house must be dissolved within ten days of the passage of the resolution. A resolution of no confidence requires the assent of at least fifty members.

Most bills which become law are introduced by the Cabinet, but bills can be (and are from time to time) introduced by ordinary members of the Diet. Such bills require the support of at least twenty members of the House of Representatives, or if introduced in the House of Councillors, of at least ten members of that house. Bills with budgetary implications require the support of at least fifty members of the House of Representatives or twenty members of the House of Councillors.

In an emergency, if the lower house has been dissolved and no elected House of Representatives exists pending an election, an emergency session of the upper house may be called and take provisional measures.

Each house has its own secretariat and legislative bureau. The National Diet Library, which is open to the public, is Japan's central library.

Members of the two houses are allocated offices in three seven-storey buildings behind the Diet building. Every Diet member is provided with a generous salary, exemption from arrest while the Diet is in session and freedom from liability for his actions and speeches within the house. He also receives free housing, a free pass on the railways or a generous monthly allowance for air fares, plus two secretaries and various office allowances.

The House of Councillors is presided over by the President of the House while the House of Representatives is presided over by the Speaker. The President and the Speaker sit on a dais with the members' seats arranged in a semi-circle facing them. Cabinet ministers sit in seats arranged on either side of the dais. Just behind the President's seat in the House of Councillors is the throne used by the Emperor during opening ceremonies.

The Speaker and the Vice-Speaker are each elected separately by secret ballot, whereas the Prime Minister is elected by open ballot. If the elections are held after a general election for members of the House of Representatives the Secretary General takes the chair during the elections. The Speaker and the Vice-Speaker are expected to act in a neutral fashion and generally resign from their parties while in office. Traditionally the Speaker has been chosen from the government party and the Vice-Speaker from the main opposition party.

The first Diet building was made of wood. It was completed for the first Diet session in 1890, but was burnt down in January 1891. The present building was completed in 1936. The House of Councillors occupies the left wing and the House of Representatives the right wing on the two sides of the central tower. The central porch is used exclusively by the Emperor and visiting heads of state.

2.3.1 Elections

Under the current electoral laws all Japanese citizens over the age of twenty have the right to vote. Candidates for the lower house must be at least twenty-five years old. There are 130 electoral districts for the House of Representatives, which send 512 members to the house. Each electoral district sends between two and six members, except for the Amami–Oshima islands to the South of Kyūshū which only send one member to the house.

In elections to the upper house, where candidates must be at least thirty years of age, one hundred members are elected from the nation as a whole on the basis of proportional representation. The remaining 152 are elected by prefectures. The forty-seven Japanese prefectures send two to eight members to the upper house depending on the size of their population.

A general election must be held within forty days of the dissolution of the House of Representatives or if the term of office of members has expired within thirty days. The election campaign proper is limited to fifteen days for lower-house elections and eighteen days for those of the upper-house. Before the election campaign proper begins various political activities, which in practice amount to campaigning, are permitted. Members and candidates have their own groups of supporters in the various parts of their constituency and much of their time has to be spent cultivating these groups, called *kōenkai*.

Candidates file their notification of candidacy on the prescribed day with the local election administration commission and receive the necessary certification enabling them to campaign officially. The rules governing campaign activities and expenditure are strict. Door-to-door canvassing is not permitted and there are limits on speeches, rallies and the use of posters and leaflets. But many of these rules are dead letters and during election campaigns noise pollution is all-pervasive as candidates go round with loudspeaker vans canvassing support.

Voting is secret and each voter has only one vote, although constituencies return more than one member. This means that in a medium-sized constituency of, say, four members, where the electorate is fairly evenly divided between supporters of the government and of the opposition the parties could lose if they put up more candidates than they could expect to have returned and candidates may find themselves competing for votes from their own party supporters. This has been a major factor in the growth of factions within the Liberal Democratic party (LPD). It has also encouraged local co-operation between opposition parties. An advantage of the medium-sized constituency system is that it makes landslides unlikely and thus helps to maintain stability. There is also less chance of a government being elected on a minority of the votes cast. But it makes electioneering and maintaining support in a largish constituency extremely expensive and time-consuming. In the past candidates were expected to make cash donations to their supporters on the occasions of, for instance, weddings and funerals. Such donations have now been ruled out, or at least limited to occasions where the candidate or member is present in person.

Various attempts have been made at wider political reform to reduce the role of money in politics in Japan but so far with limited success. Some have advocated the adoption of the single-member constituency system on the Westminster model. But no progress has so far (June 1993) been made with this proposal because there would almost certainly be more losers than winners and there would be great problems in dividing the constituencies and drawing up boundary lines. It has also been suggested that the single-member constituency system should be combined as in Germany, with a proportional representation system, but proportional representation is not thought to have worked particularly well in the upper house where 100 of the 252 members are elected by a proportional representation system.

A major problem about the present constituency system is that it is very much weighted in favour of agricultural districts, where the government have had much of their support, at the expense of the cities and industrial areas, where the opposition has had the bulk of its support. In some cases the value of a vote in a country constituency has been more than three times the value of a vote in a metropolitan area. This has led to appeals to the Supreme Court to declare such arrangements unconstitutional. The court has called for reallocation to ensure that the weight of rural votes does not exceed three times that of metropolitan votes. Some changes have been made but they have made little difference to the imbalance.

Because of the problem of cultivating a constituency there has been a tendency for sons to succeed their fathers as members. These so-called second generation politicians amount to almost one-third of members in the lower house. The LDP has tended to draw recruits not only from business but also from the civil service, while the socialists have concentrated on recruits from labour unions.

Doubt is sometimes expressed about the reality of parliamentary democracy in Japan. One reason for such doubt is the imbalance between rural and city constituencies. Another is the role of money in political campaigning. A third is the way in which the Diet operates. In Japan, confrontation in the Westminster style is eschewed. Compromises are sought and the opposition placated by occasional sops. It is also argued that (as at Westminster) party loyalty is fiercely maintained and free votes are practically unknown. Finally, it is suggested that a country cannot be a true democracy if a single party has had, as in Japan, a virtual monopoly of power for over forty years. All these criticisms have some validity, but public opinion does affect the attitudes of members and the LDP could not have held on to power for so long if it had not responded to the wishes of its supporters (for example, for improvements in living standards and social welfare). The failure of the opposition parties to produce coherent alternative policies and unify has also been a major factor. Perhaps Japanese parliamentary democracy might best be described as 'Japanese style' democracy.

2.4 POLITICAL PARTIES (as of 14 June 1993)

*The Liberal Democratic Party (*LDP – *Jimintō)* was formed in 1955 as a result of the amalgamation of the Liberal Party and the Japan Democratic Party. Both were conservative parties. The conservatives have formed all Japanese governments since 1948 and the LDP has been the party of government since its formation.

The LDP on its formation declared that in home affairs its aim was 'to stabilize the people's livelihood and to promote public welfare'. In international affairs its objective was said to be 'to adjust and establish various conditions for peace'. The party was to be a party for the people, pacifism, democracy, and 'parliamentarism'. It was to have 'progressive ideas' and to seek 'the realization of a welfare state'. It upholds the principles of a free market economy. These objectives have been varied over the years. In particular the LDP has modified its pacifism and supported increases in the defence budget. It has also tried to limit welfare expenditure. In November 1985 the party adopted a new party platform which called for a place of honour for Japan in the international community, educational reform, greater social participation by young people and women, a sound home environment, small government, renewed economic growth, and the enhancement of living conditions.

The LDP's hold on power has been due partly to the way in which it has reflected the wishes of the electorate for economic progress and partly because of the failure of the opposition parties to unite and produce convincing alternative policies.

The party's main supporters have been farmers and businessmen including medium- and small-scale enterprises, for example, retailing. This has led the party to resist liberalization of imports of agricultural products and changes in the laws limiting competition from department stores affecting small retailers. They have also opposed alterations in consituency boundaries and representation to reflect the movement of the rural population to metropolitan areas. The support of the main business organisations has been reflected in the emphasis placed on economic policy and the concentration on the development of industry at the expense of public welfare. The financial backing given to the party by, for example, the Securities' companies has slowed the progress of financial reform and liberalization.

In foreign affairs the party has accepted the need for close relations with the United States and this has been the cornerstone of Japanese foreign policy for decades. The party has thus supported, if sometimes reluctantly, the concessions needed from Japan to keep the relationship on a relatively even keel.

The LDP tried in the 1950s and early 1960s to work for a modification of the constitution and in particular of Article 9, but in recent years this isssue has not been pressed. The party's emphasis on economic policy has also been reflected in its handling of relations with foreign countries. Economic advantage rather than principle has been a dominant feature of Japanese foreign policy under successive LDP governments.

The party's main weakness is its division into factions (see Appendix 8) which coalesce around individual leaders with access to substantial electoral funds. In the early post-war years the relationship was essentially one of a party boss (known as *oyabun* in Japanese) and his clients or followers (known as *kobun*). In the 1980s relationships within factions became more collegial and factions thought of themselves as belonging to a village *(mura)*. Factions tended in the past to have not more than fifty members but in the 1970s and 1980s some factions grew to more than 100 members. One factor which has, however, prevented the total domination of the party by one or two large factions has been the fact that members of the same faction do not want to have to compete with other members of the same faction in a constituency. An aspirant for membership of the Diet, in shopping around the various factions for support, thus tends to look for a faction which may not already be represented in his favoured constituency. Strong factions offer not only access to funds but also to government posts and to membership of Diet committees to suit the interests of Diet members. These are paralleled by party committees which maintain close relations with relevant industries and bureaucrats. These relationships enable members to win favours for their own constituencies in the allocation of government funding. 'Pork barrel' politics is generally more valuable in the Japanese electoral scene than attitudes towards policy issues. Indeed, policy differences between factions are rarely discernible. Factional strength thus owes practically nothing to the pressure of public opinion. This has led observers to declare that the LDP is neither liberal, nor democratic nor a party in the normal sense of that word.

The Japan Socialist Party (JSP – Nihonshakaitō)   which has been the largest opposition party since the coming to power in 1948 of the conservatives in Japan, has recently decided to call itself, in English the Social Democratic Party of Japan (SDJP). In 1955 the party adopted a platform based on Marxism–Leninism. In January 1986, at its fiftieth party convention, the JSP agreed a new declaration based on the social democratic model of West European social democratic parties. In practice the JSP has seemed to remain dominated by out-dated Marxist–Leninist dogma. It has failed to produce convincing economic policies and its adamant opposition to the United States and the Self-Defence Forces, while somewhat modified in recent years has meant that party policies are seen to be based more on ideology than on realities.

The JSP's main support has come from the left-wing unions, especially those in the public sector which belonged to the federation of unions called *Sōhyō* now merged into a new federation called *Rengō*. The JSP has had some backing among disaffected farmers and small businessmen as well as among blue- and white-collar workers, but its inability to produce coherent economic policies has eroded much of this support. It has done relatively well in elections when it has attracted protest votes from people disillusioned by the venality and corruption perceived among LDP members and by scandals involving government ministers. Such boosts in the JSP's popularity have, however, generally been short-lived, not least because of the party's failure to organize itself effectively and to produce leaders of stature with popular appeal. The JSP has also had its share of factionalism, although JSP factionalism has been based more on ideological than personal grounds. The apparently permanent failure to gain power has been a factor which has led to irresponsibility in making policy proposals. Party members recognize that they will never be in a position to implement their proposals.

The Kōmeitō (Clean Government Party)   was established in November 1964 as the political arm of Sōka Gakkai, a lay organisation affiliated with the Nichiren Shoshū sect of Buddhism. (See Chapter 1 for a brief explanation of Nichirenshū (1222–82).) At its formation, Kōmeitō was a religious party dominated by Sōka Gakkai. This led to difficulties for the party and the formal connection with Sōka Gakkai was severed in 1970, although the party still looks to Sōka Gakkai members as its main source of support. In 1970 the party declared that it was 'a national political party committed to a centrist ideology based on respect for humanity'. The platform also stressed 'humanitarian socialism', an independent foreign policy based on peace, the upholding of the Constitution, basic human rights, and parliamentary democracy. Following a setback in the elections in December 1972 the party expressed its readiness to co-operate with the Communists in the Diet, but the arrangements proved difficult and in 1975 the party reverted to a more moderate position. In recent years it has tended to co-operate with the moderate Democratic Socialist Party

(DSP) (see below). It has denounced the scandals involving the LDP but it has not itself been immune from scandals. It has been willing to support the LDP on limited issues.

The Democratic Socialist Party (DSP – Minshatō) was established in January 1960 by dissident members of the right wing of the JSP. Its policies, based on those of Western European social democratic parties, have been pragmatic. Its guiding principle is to 'reject dictatorship of either the left or the right and achieve socialism by stages while preserving parliamentary democracy'. The DSP sought initially to work with the JSP and the Kōmeitō to form a coalition government opposed to both the LDP and the Communists. These efforts failed and the party has tended in recent years to co-operate with Kōmeitō and occasionally with the LDP. Its current policies call for the maintenance of Japan–US security arrangements, retention of a minimal self-defence capability and opposition to nuclear weapons. Its main support has come from moderate trade unions but its organization is weak and it has only limited popular backing.

The Japan Communist Party (JCP – Nihon Kyōsantō) remains a Marxist–Leninist party. But its policies have been relatively flexible and in recent years it has followed a line independent of those of the Chinese Communist Party and the former Soviet Communist Party. It has also endorsed the parliamentary system and thus rejects the need for violent revolution in Japan. It is well organized and has a relatively stable income (largely due to the sales of its newspaper *Akahata* (Red Flag)). Its support comes mainly from committed Marxists and left-wing trade unionists but it also attracts support from those disaffected with the established order. It has consistently refused to align itself with the other opposition parties in the Diet and is thus isolated on the left.

The United Social Democratic Party (Shakai Minshū Rengō or Shaminren) formed in 1978 by dissidents from the JSP in 1978 has only minimal representation in the Diet and is of limited significance. *Rengō*, the recently formed group of moderate unions had some success in winning seats in the upper house election in 1989 but failed to win any seats in the upper house election in 1992. On this occasion *The New Japan Party (Nihon Shintō)* led by the former governor of Kumamoto prefecture, Hosokawa Morihiro, who had previously belonged to the

LDP, won four seats on a platform calling for political and administrative reform.

While the LDP had a comfortable majority in the lower house it has had (until June 1993) to rely on support from Kōmeitō and the DSP in the upper house. This meant that the LDP had to be pragmatic and cautious. It also meant that political reform, which is urgently needed and which would require the parties and politicians to make sacrifices, has been difficult to achieve. Pressures for reform mounted in the spring of 1993 in the wake of political scandals. On 18 June 1993 a vote of no confidence in the government of Prime Minister Miyazawa was passed in the House of Representatives following the defection of members of the Hata faction of the LDP. This forced a general election, and opened up the prospect of possibly far-reaching changes in the political scene in Japan.

POSTSCRIPT

The Hata faction decided to call itself for the campaign the Japan Renewal Party (Nihon Shinseitō). Another small breakaway group from the LDP set up the Japan Harbinger party (Nihon Sakigaketō). Nine parties accordingly took part in the election on 18 July. The rump of the LDP won 223 seats. This was one more than they had had when the election was called and the party could count on the support of at least five independents. The Socialists calling themselves SDJP lost heavily, gaining only 70 seats against 134 before the election. Mr Hata's Shinseitō won 55 seats, Mr Hosokawa's Nihon Shintō won 35 seats, and Sakigake 13. The remaining seats were divided between Kōmeitō with 51, the DSP 15, the JCP 15, Shaminren 4, Independents 30. The results mean that unless a minority government were formed a coalition commanding at least 247 seats would be required. The opposition groups together could form a majority if they were able to agree on joint policies but their views on, for example, foreign-policy issues were so different that a stable and lasting coalition could hardly be formed. The attitudes of the conservative groups in Shinseitō, Nihon Shintō and the Sakigake party were crucial to the outcome. Reflecting the rainy weather and disillusionment with politicians, only 67.2 per cent of the electorate voted.

3 Government

3.1 CENTRAL GOVERNMENT

3.1.1 The Cabinet

The Cabinet consists of the Prime Minister and not more than twenty Ministers of State. A majority of these must also be Diet members. In practice, although there have been occasional exceptions, all members of the Cabinet are members of the Diet, with a large majority being members of the House of Representatives. Cabinet ministers are appointed and dismissed at the discretion of the Prime Minister.

The Prime Minister of Japan is elected by the Diet from among its members. He and the members of the Cabinet are jointly accountable to the Diet and if the Prime Minister resigns or dies the Cabinet resigns *en masse*. An acting Prime Minister may, however, be appointed on a temporary basis from among serving cabinet ministers in the case of illness or absence abroad of the duly elected Prime Minister.

The Prime Minister normally attempts to achieve through appointments to Cabinet posts a balance between the various factions in the LDP. To become a minister, Diet members usually have to have been re-elected a minimum of five times. Reshuffles take place on an average of once a year and most ministries change hands in the reshuffles with a majority of ministers being new to Cabinet posts. This gives the appearance of a Cabinet appointed on the 'Buggin's turn' principle. The main exceptions are appointments to key posts such as Minister of Finance and Chief Cabinet Secretary. Other key posts which do not always change are the Minister of Foreign Affairs and the Minister of International Trade and Industry. Experience in such key posts is normally sought by faction leaders aspiring to be selected as Prime Minister. Ex-cabinet ministers may move back into the Cabinet in another post (or even the same post) at a subsequent reshuffle or under a different Prime Minister and no stigma attaches to resignation from the Cabinet as the result of a reshuffle.

The Japanese Cabinet is defined under the constitution as 'the highest executive authority of government'. It is jointly responsible for formulating government policies and directing the various Japanese ministries. It has to approve the draft budget before submission to the Diet and draft legislation for submission to the Diet on behalf of the government. It has control over the administration of the civil service. Its powers include advice and approval of all acts of the Emperor in matters of state, designation of the Chief Justice of the Supreme Court, appointment of justices to the Supreme Court and of other judges, convocation of Diet sessions and submission to the Diet of government accounts.

The Prime Minister represents the Cabinet in submitting legislation, reporting on domestic and foreign affairs and in supervising the administration. All laws and Cabinet orders must be signed not only by the relevant minister but also countersigned by the Prime Minister. He may countermand measures taken by individual ministers pending submission to the Cabinet.

The Cabinet generally meets every Tuesday and Friday beginning at 10 a.m. in the Prime Minister's official residence. Extraordinary Cabinet meetings can be called as required by the Prime Minister at any time.

At Cabinet meetings the Prime Minister sits at the head of an oval table with the Chief Cabinet Secretary, who is a cabinet minister, on his left and the Minister of Justice on his right. The heads of the other ministries sit alternately on either side, their places being dictated by the order in which their ministries were established. The Director General of the Cabinet Legislation Bureau and two Deputy Chief Cabinet Secretaries (in charge of political and administrative affairs) sit at a separate table and attend only as advisers.

The Cabinet agenda is divided into six parts:

1. General business of an important nature;
2. Promulgation of laws or treaties;
3. Bills to be submitted to the Diet;
4. Cabinet orders;
5. Personnel matters;
6. Other business.

The agenda is normally discussed in advance by the Cabinet secretariat with senior civil servants in the various ministries. At noon on the day before a Cabinet meeting is due to take place the Administrative Vice-Ministers, who are the top civil servants in each ministry, meet at the Prime Minister's residence to review matters to be submitted to the Cabinet. The chair at these meetings is taken by the

Chief Cabinet Secretary and the meeting is used to thrash out any remaining interministry disagreements prior to submission to the Cabinet.

Each ministry, in addition to an Administrative Vice-Minister (*Jimujikan*), has a Parliamentary Vice-Minister (*Seimujikan*) who is appointed by the Prime Minister from among members of the Diet. Service as a Parliamentary Vice-Minister is normally a prerequisite for later appointment to Cabinet rank. But Parliamentary Vice-Ministers have minimal authority in the ministries to which they are attached and are regarded primarily as liaison officers between the ministries and Diet members. They meet every Thursday morning at the Prime Minister's residence to discuss Diet strategy.

Cabinet meetings are closed to the public and details of proceedings are supposed to remain confidential but the Chief Cabinet Secretary issues statements to the press about the deliberations, and other ministers frequently leak information to the media. As a result, most matters of major importance are decided not at formal Cabinet meetings but through informal discussions among ministers and with the Prime Minister.

Cabinet decisions are normally reached by consensus and votes in Cabinet are traditionally unanimous. The Prime Minister, who presides at Cabinet meetings, has, like other ministers, only one vote. His power to dominate the Cabinet depends partly on his personality and partly on the extent of the support or opposition to him from other faction leaders.

In fact much real power is retained by the party and exercised through its various committees. This is acknowledged by the weight given to the top party appointments. After designation by the Diet the Prime Minister normally appoints first the three top LDP officials who in many cases are more influential than the majority of cabinet ministers. The three top party posts are those of Secretary General, Chairman of the General Council and Chairman of the Policy Research Council.

The Cabinet is served by the Cabinet Secretariat, the Cabinet Legislation Bureau, the National Personnel Authority and the National Defence Council.

The Cabinet Legislative Bureau prepares legislation for submission to the Diet and co-ordinates and reviews legislation prepared in the various ministries. Similarly it deals with Cabinet Orders and submits these for approval by the Cabinet. It also liaises and negotiates as appropriate with the standing committees of the Diet.

The National Personnel Authority (NPA) is reponsible for implementing the National Public Service Law which covers the career civil service whose members are required to be independent of politics and free from corruption. It is directed by three people who are appointed by the Cabinet but whose appointments are subject to Diet approval.

The National Defence Council is a policy-making body under the chairmanship of the Prime Minister. Its other members are the Director General of the Defence Agency, the Minister of Foreign Affairs, the Minister of Finance, and the Director General of the Economic Planning Agency.

The Prime Minister's Office controls the following agencies which are not under specific Ministers of State in the Cabinet:

The Fair Trade Commission (*Kōseitorihiki-iinkai*)
The Imperial Household Agency (*Kunaichō*).

The Prime Minister's Office also supervises the following Agencies which are headed by a Minister of State in the Cabinet:

The National Public Safety Commission (*Kokkakōan-iinkai*)
The Management and Co-ordination Agency (*Sōmuchō*)
The Hokkaido Development Agency (*Hokkaidō-Kaihatsuchō*)
The Defence Agency (*Bōeichō*) which includes the Defence Facilities
    Administration Agency
The Economic Planning Agency (*Keizai-kikaku-chō*)
The Science and Technology Agency (*Kagaku-gijutsu-chō*)
The Environment Agency (*Kankyōchō*)
The Okinawa Development Agency (*Okinawa-Kaihatsuchō*)
The National Land Agency (*Kokudōchō*).

(Of these, the Defence and Economic Planning Agencies are of particular importance.)

Ministries, each headed by a Minister of State in the Cabinet, are:

The Ministry of Justice (*Hōmushō*) which is responsible for the
    Administration Commission for the National Bar Examinations,
    the Public Security Commission and the Public Security Investigation Agency (*Kōanchosachō*)
The Ministry of Foreign Affairs (*Gaimushō*)
The Ministry of Finance (*Ōkurashō*) which is responsible for the
    National Tax Administration Agency (*Kokuzeichō*)

The Ministry of Education (*Mombushō*) which controls the Agency for Cultural Affairs (*Bunkacho*)

The Ministry of Health and Welfare (*Kōseishō*) which is responsible for the Social Insurance Agency

The Ministry of Agriculture, Forestry, and Fisheries (*Nōrinsuisanshō* or *Nōrinshō* for short) which controls the Food Agency, the Forestry Agency and the Fisheries Agency

The Ministry of International Trade and Industry (MITI – *Tsūshōsangyōshō* or *Tsūsanshō*) which is responsible for the Agency for Natural Resources and Energy, the Patent Office, and the Small- and Medium-Scale Enterprise Agency

The Ministry of Transport (*Unyūshō*) which controls the Labour Relations Commission for Seafarers, the Maritime Safety Agency, the Marine Accidents Inquiry Agency and the Meteorological Agency

The Ministry of Post and Telecommunications (*Yūseishō*)

The Ministry of Labour (*Rōdōshō*) which is responsible for the Central Labour Relations Commission

The Ministry of Construction (*Kensetsushō*)

The Ministry of Home Affairs (*Jijishō* – that is, local government agency) which controls the Fire Defence Agency. (The old name of the Ministry of Home Affairs, *Naimushō*, is no longer used because of its connections with the pre-war system of thought control.)

The protocol ranking of the various ministries does not necessarily reflect their importance in the government. Apart from the Ministries of Finance and International Trade and Industry the Ministries of Agriculture, Transport and Construction are of paramount importance politically because of their control of significant government funds and patronage.

3.1.2   The Civil Service

Although the Prime Minister and the Cabinet are theoretically very powerful, the extent of their real power is limited by the generally short period(s) they spend in office and by the very busy schedule which Cabinet Ministers are forced to maintain. Parliamentary Vice-Ministers have much less authority and influence on the bureaucracy than junior ministers in the British Government. Inevitably therefore, much of the real power, especially on day-to-day matters but also on general policy issues, devolves to civil servants who, being permanent officials, acquire not only great expertise in their own spheres but also wide contacts among parliamentarians and in the industries and organisations represented by their respective ministries.

The Japanese civil service, especially the relatively small corps of about 18 000 career officials who have passed the highly competitive A-class entrance examination and who serve in the key ministries in Tokyo, is an elite body.

The Japanese civil service at national level comes under the general supervision of the Management and Co-ordination Agency (*Sōmuchō*) which is responsible for the planning and development of administrative systems and procedures. It negotiates staffing levels. It deals with data processing, office automation and computers. It is responsible for collecting and analysing statistics. It conducts audits and inspections and ensures that agreed staffing levels are adhered to.

The administration of the civil service at national level is the responsibility of an independent agency, the National Personnel Authority (*Jinjiin*). The agency is responsible for ensuring that there is impartiality in recruitment, that appointments are made on merit and that civil servants are fairly treated. It advises the government and the Diet on salaries for civil servants, whose rights to collective bargaining and strike action are restricted. The Agency has three full-time commissioners appointed by the Cabinet with the approval of the Diet.

The Japanese civil service working in central government ministries in administrative posts is recruited from graduates of the top Japanese universities. In the past almost all were graduates of Tokyo University, where they had take degrees in law or economics. In recent years more entrants have come from a few other top universities but the field is still very limited. The Ministry of Finance and the Ministry of International Trade and Industry attract the cream, not least because of the opportunities which these ministries provide for the exercise of real power but also because of the openings which the ministries find for bureaucrats at the end of their careers to enter private industry, commerce or finance in senior positions. The process of appointment to jobs in the private sector from government agencies is called *amakudari* (literally descending from heaven). When one of the number of graduates who entered a ministry in a particular year is appointed Administrative Vice-Minister (*Jimujikan*) the tradition is that all his contemporaries resign (that is, when they are in their early fifties) and after a nominal 'quarantine' period of two years, which they usually serve in a semi-governmental agency, they are found jobs at director level or as advisers to private companies.

Class A bureaucrats work very hard and long hours but, the Japanese system being largely bottom-up rather than top-down, they soon acquire considerable influence and authority even if they are normally quite junior. They are regularly reassigned to different sections, divisions or departments within different bureaux, rarely serving more than two years in any one job, and thus acquire wide experience and valuable contacts. Their powers have been eroded gradually by liberalization and the removal of subsidies and licensing requirements, but especially in Ministries such as Transport and Health and Welfare, bureaucratic controls remain significant. Moreover, bureaucrats by their control of inputs into the budget, for example, in the Ministry of Construction, retain considerable financial power. In Japan much is left to the discretion of bureaucrats and many rules are not published or specified in formal legislation. This means that bureaucrats can exercise a great deal of power through what is euphemistically called 'administrative guidance' (in Japanese *gyōseishidō*). The Administrative Vice-Minister's powers are limited by the amount he has to do and by the limited time he serves in this post. Much of his power is accordingly exercised by Directors General of bureaux (*Kyokuchō*) who may be considered to be the equivalent of a Deputy Secretary or Deputy Under-Secretary in a British department of state but who are certainly more powerful than their British opposite numbers. Considerable influence is also exercised by the more junior chiefs of divisions or sections of bureaux (*kachō*) (usually in their thirties) and even their deputies (*kachōhosa*). Comparatively junior officials think nothing of summoning businessmen considerably senior to them in age and experience to their respective ministries and giving 'guidance' on how to proceed on a particular issue.

Unfortunately, the dedication of Japanese bureaucrats to their particular ministries and to the sectional interests they represent has tended to make many bureaucrats blinkered and unable to view Japanese needs in a wider framework. This tendency is exacerbated by the pressures from Diet members who by their contracts with the personnel divisions of the ministries may try to ensure that bureaucrats, who are not thought to be pushing hard enough the particular concerns of members of the LDP, are side-tracked. This leads to a great deal of jealousy and infighting not only between ministries but also between bureaux and even divisions within the same bureau. Japanese Ministries often seem like warring fiefdoms and bureaux as petty fiefdoms struggling for power and influence where the nominal chiefs, that is, the ministers, appear to be little more than figureheads like most of Japan's Emperors and shōguns in the past. Foreign officials frequently find it necessary in making representations to ensure that the same message is conveyed separately to different parts of the Japanese government machine. This does not mean that the Japanese officials concerned do not keep adequate records but simply that because of jealousies they may keep information to themselves. It is notorious that officials of the Ministry of Foreign Affairs and the Ministry of International Trade and Industry regard one another with suspicion, if not open hostility.

It would, however, be a mistake to conclude from this account of the power of the Japanese bureaucracy that Japan is a bureaucratic dictatorship. Bureaucrats have to be responsive to the Diet and to industry pressures. The Japanese tradition of consensus building also restricts their ability to dictate courses of action. On the other hand it would be an equal mistake to think bureaucrats, even junior ones, can safely be ignored. Ministers may be persuaded that a certain course of action is required but they cannot put this into effect without the active co-operation of the bureaucracy, and the bureaucrats know hundreds of ways of delaying and frustrating fiats which they think to be against the best interests of their own organisations. Prime Minister Nakasone Yasuhiro made valiant efforts to force the bureaucracy in specific directions but he generally failed. The attempts made by various commissions to effect administrative reform and liberalization have only had very limited success so far because of the lack of co-operation from the bureaucracy, which is understandably reluctant to see its powers eroded.

In dealing with the Japanese bureaucracy infinite patience is required and pressures have to be applied both directly and indirectly in subtle ways. Movement is likely to be tortoise-like at best and forward moves may be only tactical and be followed by retreats which suggest that no progress has been made at all. But persistence and consistency must always go hand in hand with patience.

3.2 LOCAL GOVERNMENT

The Local Autonomy Law of 1947 defined the structure, organization and powers of local government and local assemblies in Japan. The structure is that of a pyramid with central government at the apex. Local authorities and assemblies may only legislate within the areas delegated to them and cannot enact rules which contravene central government laws or policies, and local assemblies may not enact by-laws which contravene the by-laws of superior authorities. The basic rules are set at the centre and local authorities must work within these ground rules. Local autonomy in Japan is thus strictly circumscribed. However, local authorities are authorized by the Local Autonomy Law to perform 'administrative affairs within [their] area in so far as such affairs are not reserved to the State'.

The country is divided into forty-seven 'prefectures' (collectively known as *tōdōfuken*). Of these one is the Tokyo Metropolitan Government which is a metropolis (*tō*) rather than a prefecture; two are metropolitan areas (*fu*), namely Osaka and Kyoto; and one is a large district (*dō*) namely Hokkaidō, the northern island of Japan which was only developed in the second half of the nineteenth century and which is still a development area. Responsibility for the development of Hokkaidō rests with the Hokkaidō Development Agency under a Minister of State in the Cabinet. The other forty-three are ordinary prefectures (*ken*). These include the prefecture of Okinawa which covers the southern island of Okinawa and the Ryūkyū islands. The Amami–Oshima islands are part of Kagoshima prefecure. Okinawa, which was under US administration until 1972 and was devastated in the fighting at the end of the Second World War, is also regarded as a development area and its development comes under the Okinawa Development Agency which is directed by a Minister of State in the Cabinet.

Each prefecture has a legislature called the prefectural assembly. Members of the prefectural assemblies are elected for four-year terms. The Tokyo Metropolitan Assembly has 130 members. Other prefectural assemblies have between 40 and 120 members depending on the population of the prefecture. Assembly members receive salaries for their services. Although there are some independent members in prefectural assemblies these tend to be dominated by the political parties operating at the national level, with the LDP in control in most rural and some metropolitan areas.

Each prefecture is headed by a Governor (*chiji*) who is elected by direct popular vote for a four-year term with the support of one or more of the major political parties. Candidates must be at least thirty years of age. The Governor, who is the chief executive of the prefecture, has one or more deputies who are appointed officials. Some of these come from the ranks of the Ministry of Home Affairs (*Jijishō*). The Governor convenes the Assembly (*Kengikai*) four times a year. He may call special sessions as required. He also retains the right to dissolve the Assembly and call for new elections if he thinks these are needed. The Governor's powers include the right to submit legislation, draft the local budget for approval by the assembly and to levy and collect local taxes as approved by the assembly. He is also responsible for all local government officials (including those on attachment from the *Jijishō* and other central government agencies) and for prefectural public enterprises. All elements of the prefectural government are responsible to him. But the police force is supervised by an independent Public Safety Commission and the school system as well as prefectural cultural and scientific activities come under an Education Commission which he appoints subject to approval by the prefectural assembly. The Governor also appoints an independent Election Commission, an Audit and Inspection Commission, a Treasurer and a Chief Accountant, but these operate independently and cannot be dismissed by him. The Governor can veto measures approved by the Assembly with which he disagrees but his veto can be overriden if there is a two-thirds majority in the assembly against his veto. The Assembly may also pass a vote of no confidence in the Governor if there is a two-thirds majority in favour of such a resolution. Demands for the dissolution of local Assemblies or the recall of Assembly members and chief executives can be submitted to the local Election Administration Commission if they bear the signatures of at least a third of the eligible voters in the area.

Prefectures normally consist of a number of geographical districts known as *gun*. These have no local government status. This is accorded to the cities (*shi*), municipalities (*chō* or *machi*) and 'villages' (*son* or *mura*). The designation of city, municipality or village is largely made on the basis of population and the terms are not synonymous with the same terms used in England. Each *shi*, *chō* and *son* has its own Assembly, its directly-elected chief executive and its own local officials. These are subject to the same rules as apply to prefectural Assemblies in respect of votes of no confidence, recall and so on. The chief executives are known as Mayors and called as appropriate *shichō*, *chōchō* or *sonchō*. Tokyo has in addition to a number of cities and municipalities twenty-three special wards (*tokubetsu-ku* or *ku* for short) which have their own assemblies and chief executives (*kuchō*). Some other large cities such as Sapporo, Yokohama, Nagoya, Kyoto, Osaka, Kōbe, Hiroshima and Fukuoka are also divided into wards (*ku*).

Local authorites are responsible for administering local public services including planning, construction and maintenance, as well as regulating and managing facilities in the the following areas:

(a) local courts and police;
(b) hospitals, welfare, burial arrangements and environmental protection;
(c) infrastructure such as local roads, bridges, transport, land development, water and sewerage, gas and electric power supplies, parks and playgrounds;
(d) education and culture, e.g. schools, laboratories, libraries, museums, sports facilities, etc.

Major areas of local goverment expenditure are education, which takes up more than a quarter of local spending; public works, which absorb about a fifth of local expenditure; health; sanitation; social welfare; and public security.

Local governments spend nearly three-quarters of Japan's total revenue. Approximately 40 per cent of this comes from central government allocations and the rest is met from local taxes and other local revenue. The fact that 40 per cent of local government revenue is provided centrally means that central government has effective control of local government expenditure. Central government produces an income and expenditure plan for local governments each year and once this has been approved by the Cabinet local governments are left with little room for manoeuvre. Poorer prefectures benefit more than richer ones in the allocation of central government funds. Part of the central government's allocations to local authorities are not earmarked for specific purposes but some allocations are made specifically for the performance of functions delegated to local governments. Local governments are permitted to do some deficit financing through the issuing of bonds on their own guarantee redeemable after two or more years.

Prefectures and municipalities are authorised to levy a local income tax (called the inhabitants' tax). This is in two parts. One part is based on total income (subject to certain deductions and allowances), the other part is a per capita tax. Prefectures can also levy corporate and business taxes as well as taxes on amusements, meals and automobiles. Prefectures and municipalities in addition levy taxes on tobacco, and municipalities on electricity and gas supplies. Some income is derived from the issuing of permits and from the sale or leasing of public land.

The structure of local government in Japan seems tidy and logical. It also appears comparatively efficient and to employ relatively fewer officials than local administrations in the USA and UK. But local autonomy is strictly circumscribed and controlled from the centre. This causes frustration and irritation among local governments. Each prefecture finds that it needs a strong liaison office in Tokyo, which has to spend most of its time negotiating with central government bodies to get necessary permissions and funds from the centre.

Among the many issues which require approval from the centre are all plans for amalgamations of villages and municipalities, which inevitably involve hard bargaining between those affected by proposed changes. The former Governor of Kumamoto prefecture in Kyūshū (Mr Hosokawa Morihiro) complained that it took months of frustrating negotiations with the Ministry of Transport in Tokyo to get agreement to the relocation of bus stops, a matter which in his view could and should have been left to the local authorities.

Governors and Mayors, although elected officials, often come up through the local bureaucracy in which they may have been placed from central government. This ensures that affairs are in the hands of experienced executives but it also tends to depoliticize and bureaucratize local administrations. Local autonomy in Japan is thus not as great as it would seem on the surface although, despite various successful moves to recentralize administration, Japanese prefectures are run in a much more democratic way than they were under the prewar system where Governors were appointed officials.

4   Law and Order

4.1   THE LEGAL SYSTEM

Japan has comprehensive legal codes based on Western models. In the nineteenth century the Japanese largely adopted French models with some German elements. In civil matters traditional Japanese concepts and practices were, however, retained. In the post-war period Anglo-American legal influences have led to some significant changes including adoption of elements of case law and common law. Laws were also adapted to take account of the basic human rights set out in the new Constitution.

Japanese law is defined in the six codes (*roppō*). The primary code is the Constitution (see Chapter 2 and Appendix 2). The other five codes are the civil code, the code of civil procedure, the penal (criminal) code, the code of criminal procedure and the commercial code. These are complemented by a vast array of statutes, Cabinet orders, local ordinances and administrative regulations with the force of law. General principles of law (*jōri*) are still important despite the growth of statutory law and precedents. Customary law is a further significant element in Japanese legal practice.

The civil code (*minpō*) was originally drafted by a French legal adviser in the nineteenth century Fontarabie de Boissonade. But French concepts were modified to ensure that traditional Japanese obligations and responsibilities were preserved. In the light of the new Constitution the code was revised to ensure that individual rights and equality of the sexes was respected. This led to amendments to the chapters on inheritance and family relations.

The code of civil procedure (*minjisoshōhō*) closely follows the German model. The code of civil procedure is divided into eight books. These are:

1.   The jurisdiction of the various courts, parties to proceedings, costs and general rules.
2.   'Procedure at first instance'.
3.   Appeals.
4.   Retrial.

5. Orders on payment, for example, of debts.
6. Rules on the execution of judgements.
7. Procedure to deal with unknown creditors.
8. Arbitration.

The commercial code (*shōhō*) was originally drafted in the late nineteenth century under the influence of a German legal adviser, Karl Friedrich Roesler. It has since frequently been revised. Article 1 of the code prescribes that where there is no specific provision in the code resort may be had to customary law and to the civil code which, for instance, sets out the general law of contracts, of torts and of property rights. The code provides for four types of commercial entity, namely the limited partnership company, the unlimited partnership company, the joint stock company, and, since 1938, the limited liability company. These are termed in Japanese *kaisha*. All individuals engaged in commercial activities are referred to in the code as *shōnin* (traders). All transactions in which a trader is engaged as a participant are commercial transations which fall under the commercial code and not the civil code. The commercial code requires that traders must inspect goods as soon as they are received and submit to the seller any complaints about quality within a prescribed period.

So long as there is a recognisable contractual relationship the civil or as appropriate the commercial code provide reasonably specific answers to any problems which may arise and such answers do not, therefore, have to be spelt out in contracts. Japanese companies generally employ numbers of law graduates who have studied the civil and commercial codes and understand the rules. Detailed rules apply to every commercial transaction, from the smallest to the largest, but considerable scope nevertheless remains for the pervasive Japanese practice of administrative guidance (*gyōseishidō*) from government officials to private businesses.

The penal or criminal code (*keihō*) was drawn up in the nineteenth century by Fontarabie de Boissonade. It was substantially revised in 1907, and again in 1947 to reflect the new Constitution. In particular the principle of equality before the law was emphasised. The criminal code is divided into two parts. The first covers general principles, the second specific crimes. Japanese criminal law recognizes that a prohibition must exist before an act can be prosecuted or punished. Under Japanese law there must also normally be an element of criminal intent, although culpability based on negligence is recognized in parts of the code, for example, in relation to fires, flooding and road traffic acts. Juveniles under twenty are subject to juvenile law and are dealt with in family courts. Insanity or mental instability are taken into account in reaching judgements on culpability. Ignorance of the law is not an excuse but may justify a reduction in punishment. An admission of guilt and remorse is not a justification but may lead to reductions in punishment. There is no crime of conspiracy in Japan.

Punishments under Japanese law are divided into three categories:

1. Death (*shikei*) (by hanging).
2. Incarceration which may be penal servitude (forced labour) (*chōeki*), imprisonment requiring custodial segregation but not forced labour (*kinko*), or penal detention of up to twenty-nine days in a special detention facility (*kōryū*).
3. Pecuniary sanctions, that is, fines (*bakkin*).

Courts may suspend sentences (*shikkōyūyo*) or may suspend execution of sentences. Prisoners may be released after serving a third of a fixed term sentence, or ten years in the case of life imprisonment. Pardons, including amnesties, can only be granted by a government decision.

The code of criminal procedure (*chizaihō*) was revised in 1948. It is in seven books:

1. General matters including jurisdiction of the courts (chapter I); disqualification and challenge of judges (II); capacity (III); defence and legal aid (IV); preliminary hearings (V); procedural acts (VI); time limits (VII); summonses, imprisonment, and preventive detention of accused persons (VIII); seizure and search (IX); viewing by the court (X); witnesses (XI); experts (XII); interpreters and translations (XIII); evidence (XIV); and costs (XV).
2. Procedure 'at first instance' covering inquiry, prosecution and procedure in court.
3. Appeals.
4. Retrial proceedings.
5. Cases stated for opinion by the court.
6. Summary proceedings.
7. Execution of judgement.

Japanese criminal procedure is adversarial; prosecuting and defence counsels are equals in front of an independent judge.

The police (see below) are mainly responsible for investigating crimes. Actions such as stopping and questioning a person without using force do not need judicial approval. Compulsory measures generally require judicial approval. Arrests (*taiho*) other than of persons caught in the act have to be authorised by a judicial order. Arrested persons and their immediate surroundings may be searched without a judicial order, but all other searches require prior judicial authorisation. Confessions obtained under compulsion, torture or threat, or after prolonged detention cannot be used as evidence, and a confession cannot be the only evidence for a conviction. Persons arrested may not be held for more than 48 hours without judicial approval and must then be referred to a public prosecutor who has a further 24 hours in which he must decide either to release the individual or to request a judicial detention order. Detention after prosecution proceedings have been instituted cannot exceed 60 days, although this may be extended for a further 30 days. In the case of suspects, detention is limited to 20 days. After formal charges have been filed an accused may apply for bail (*hoshaku*).

Under Japanese law a person cannot be compelled to give evidence which might incriminate her- or himself, or close relatives. Doctors, lawyers and others may also, with a few exceptions, refuse to report statements made to them in confidence as a professional adviser. Confessions must be voluntary and hearsay evidence is not admissible but some lawyers consider that these rules are interpreted rather more flexibly than under English law.

The Japanese Constitution provides the following important rights, namely to a speedy and public trial before an independent and impartial tribunal, to be represented by counsel, and to summon and examine witnesses. After proceedings have been completed defendants cannot be proceeded against further. Punishment must be in accordance with the law.

Normally the prosecutor presents his case first, followed by the defence case. Witnesses are then examined, first by the summoner, followed by cross-examination and parallel questioning by the court. A written record of testimony is made. The defence is allowed the last word.

The court may find an accused person guilty or not guilty, or may enter a judgement or ruling/order terminating the proceedings on procedural grounds. Both the prosecution and the defence may appeal to a higher court (see below) against a judgement, ruling or order. Some 99 per cent of cases brought before Japanese courts lead to convictions. Prosecutors do not normally bring cases to court unless they are confident of securing a conviction.

4.2　THE COURTS

At the apex of the Japanese legal system is the Supreme Court (*saikōsaibansho*) which is empowered (Article 81 of the Constitution) to decide whether laws passed by the Diet, conform with the Constitution. In this sense the Supreme Court is above the Diet although the Constitution itself states that the Diet is the supreme organ of the state. The Court itself has decided that it will only consider specific cases and if it decides that a law is unconstitutional it refuses to apply it. In fact, although the Supreme Court annually considers some 5000 cases involving constitutional points it had, according to Professor Noda Yoshiyuki (*Introduction to Japanese Law*, Tokyo 1976), only declared one legal provision unconstitutional in its first twenty-five years of operation.

The head of the judiciary is the Chief Justice of the Supreme Court, who is nominated by the Cabinet, appointed by the Emperor and ranks with the Prime Minister. The Supreme Court, which is responsible for the administration of justice and accordingly for the appointment of judges, consists of fourteen judges in addition to the Chief Justice. In principle it is only concerned with points of law and must accept the facts of the case as stated in the decison against which an appeal is referred to the court. It may sit as a full court or in divisions of five judges. The president of each division is decided by co-option. In each case before the court or a division of the court one judge is chosen as rapporteur, who has the task of drafting the judgement.

In Japan there is no separate system of civil and criminal courts.

Below the Supreme Court come the higher or superior courts (*kōtōsaibansho*). There are eight of these sitting in Sapporo, Sendai, Tokyo, Nagoya, Osaka, Takamatsu, Hiroshima and Fukuoka. The Supreme Court may also create higher court agencies (*shibu*) to deal with some cases. Each superior court has a president (*chōkan*) and chambers (*bu*) consisting of three or five judges. One judge in each chamber, the *sōkatsuhanji*, controls the business of the chamber.

The higher courts are in the main appeal courts, although some offences, for example, against state security, go straight to the higher courts. Not all appeals go directly to higher courts. District courts (see below) may first hear appeals from summary courts.

The next level is that of the district courts (*chihōsaibansho*). Each prefecture has its own district court but Hokkaidō has four district courts, making a total of fifty district courts in all. Each district court has a number of judges and assistant judges as decided by the Supreme

Court. One judge is designated the head judge of each district court which, like superior courts, are divided into chambers. Assistant judges do not in principle have full powers and cannot judge a case on their own. A court usually consists of a single judge although in serious cases and in appeals from summary courts a bench of three judges is usually formed.

Family courts (*katei saibansho*) deal with domestic matters and juvenile delinquency. They rank on the same level as district courts.

The lowest court is the summary court (*kan-i saibansho*). These courts, with their relatively quick and simple procedures, were created to speed up justice. There are 570 summary courts composed of one or more judges who may be laymen considered to have an adequate knowledge of the law for the purpose. They may draw on the experience of lay judicial commissioners (*shihōiin*) but such commissioners are neither jurors nor assessors. There is no jury system in Japan. Summary courts deal in civil cases with claims not exceeding 300 000 yen and in criminal cases with minor offences.

In addition to the various ranks of judges (known as *hanji*) the Japanese courts employ a number of different types of officials including registrars and clerks as well as sheriffs who are responsible for executing the judgements of the courts.

4.3   THE LEGAL PROFESSION

Judges form a professional corps of their own and their ranks are not filled by former prosecutors or ordinary lawyers.

The public prosecutors (*kensatsukan*) are a separate professional corps. They include prosecutors (*kenji*) and assistant prosecutors (*fuku kenji*). They come under the Prosecutor General, his deputy and superintending prosecutor who are appointed by the Cabinet. Responsibility for the proper functioning of the prosecutors lies with the Minister of Justice. However, their independence is guaranteed by law, and the Minister of Justice is not supposed to issue orders relating to individual cases. Their decisions on whether or not to prosecute can, however, be investigated by Prosecution Review Commissions. These are composed of eleven people selected by lot from among eligible voters. If more than eight commissioners so decide the commission can require the reopening of an investigation and prosecution be instituted.

The largest branch of the legal profession in Japan is that of attorney (*bengoshi*). They act for the defence in criminal cases and for claimants or defendants in civil cases. They also perform notarial acts. They thus have the functions of both barrister and solicitor. In comparison with the number of lawyers in the USA and even in Britain there are very few attorneys in Japan. Most work in the Tokyo or Osaka areas and concentrate on litigation. This means that many legal matters such as the drafting of legal documents, and patent and tax matters are dealt with by specialists in these fields. Attorneys generally receive much higher remunerations than those in the other branches of law in Japan, that is, judges and prosecutors. Attorneys who are organised in *bengoshikai* are jealous of their status and remuneration and do everything possible to limit entry into their profession. This has led them to take a restrictive attitude towards foreigners wishing to set up practices in Japan to advise Japanese on matters of foreign law.

Japanese who wish to become judges, prosecutors or attorneys must pass a national examination under the direction of a committee supervised by the Ministry of Justice. The examination (*shihōshiken*) consists of two parts. The first examination is equivalent to that of a final university examination. The second examination consists of a multiple choice test, an essay and, if successful in these, the candidate must then pass a final oral test. Less than 2 per cent of candidates for the second examination are successful. Candidates have to undertake, in addition to studying law at university, special studies at the Legal Training and Research Institute.

Custom and tradition, as well as the small number of available attorneys, mean that in Japan disputes are very often resolved by compromise and mediation by a third party. Japanese traditional attitudes are based on Confucian and Buddhist concepts of a natural and hierarchical order of society. Obedience and resignation are virtues, while duties and obligations are paramount and are generally regarded as being more important than individual rights.

Japanese rules of conduct are brought together in the obligations and counter obligations which form what the Japanese call *giri*. These include the obligations of children to parents, of the student to his teacher, and to anyone who has conferred a benefit (*onjin*). The pattern of behaviour dictated by *giri* is complex. Ruth Benedict, in her famous book *The Chrysanthemum and the Sword* (London, 1947), gives one foreigner's view of the nature of obligation in Japanese life.

The existence of such rules of conduct do not mean, however, that law is an unimportant part of Japanese life. A high proportion of Japan's senior officials and businessmen studied law at university and the Japanese are meticulous in drawing up legal contracts even if these are generally considered to be guidelines, to be modified as circumstances change.

4.4 LAW ENFORCEMENT: THE POLICE

The highly centralized police force which existed before the Second World War was broken up during the Occupation but has since been largely recentralized. At the apex of the system is the National Public Safety Commission (*Kokka-kōan-iinkai*) which is headed by a Minister of State in the Cabinet. Its function is to guarantee public control of the police. In practice the Commission exercises little authority and the main checks on the police are the press and public opinion.

The main police authority is the National Police Agency (*Keisatsuchō*) in Tokyo, under a Commissioner General. It includes bureaux responsible for administration, criminal investigation, traffic, security, and communications. It controls the National Police College, the National Research Institute of Police Science and the Imperial Guard Headquarters. The Crimininal Investigation Bureau has divisions responsible for crime prevention, juveniles, safety, pollution control and patrols. The Agency supervises all police education and training, purchases police equipment, compiles crime statistics and provides criminal identification services throughout Japan. It coordinates the movement of police officers between prefectures and generally ensures the efficiency of police services.

Under the National Police Agency there are seven regional police headquarters in Tōhoku (north-eastern Honshū, the main island), Kantō (the area around Tokyo), Chūbu (central districts around Nagoya), Kinki (Osaka/Kyoto area), Chugoku (Western Honshū), Shikoku (island off Honshū) and Kyūshū (the southern island). In addition the Agency controls the prefectural police headquarters in Tokyo and the northern island of Hokkaidō.

Each prefecture has its own police force which is autonomous in daily police operations and comes under prefectural public safety commissions. Prefectural police headquarters control their own prefectural police schools and district police stations which in turn supervise 'police boxes' popularly known as *kōban* but which are divided into *hashutsujo*, which are located in urban areas and are generally manned by at least three policemen working in shifts, and *chūzaisho*, which are established in rural areas, where the policeman is normally provided with living quarters for himself and his family. The *kōban* system ensures that there is frequent contact between the police and the local inhabitants: local policemen are known as *junsa* or more popularly *o-mawari-san* that is, honourable circulating person! Policemen manning *kōban* usually patrol the local area on foot or bicycle, for example, in urban areas, or by motorbike or mini patrol cars particularly in rural areas. They are expected to keep in touch with all local matters and to know as many as possible of the people in their area. They make use of neighbourhood associations (*chōnaikai*) and crime prevention associations in working to reduce local crime.

Officers serving in *kōban* and police in patrol cars represent some 40 per cent of the total force and are initially responsible for responding to and investigating incidents. Other police specialize in administration, criminal investigation, traffic, crime prevention and public security. The police are responsible for investigating the causes of fires and industrial accidents, control of guns and swords, drugs, smuggling, prostitution, pornography and industrial pollution. Some policemen serve in special riot police units (*kidōtai*).

The Japanese police, who number some 200 000, enjoy relatively high prestige and comparatively high pay. Police service is usually a lifetime occupation. Policemen are at least high school graduates. Entrance is by competitive examination and police recruits undergo a year's training (six months if they are university graduates). *Jūdō* and *kendō* (fencing in Japanese style) are compulsory subjects and physical fitness is emphasised.

Drug-related crimes have been increasing in Japan in recent years, but stimulants rather than narcotics have been the main problem.

Japanese controls over hand guns and other weapons are strict and Japanese police on patrol, although armed, very rarely have to draw their guns.

Three types of criminal have, however, caused particular problems for the Japanese police. These are the *yakuza* (gangsters), the *sōkaiya* (a special form of gangster who disrupts company meetings and activities to extort money), and terrorists from extreme left-wing or extreme right-wing organizations.

Of these, the largest group are the *yakuza* who are particularly active in big cities like Osaka. They form groups or *gumi* such as the notorious Yamaguchi-gumi which is organized on lines similar to the Mafia or the Chinese triads. Members are bound to secrecy and to absolute loyalty to the boss (*oyabun*). They often seem to operate almost openly. Extortion under threat is their main criminal activity but they are also involved in gun-running and drug-smuggling. They are reputed to have contacts with some right-wing politicians. They are responsible for some murders, and violent confrontations between gangs can cause problems for the police in metropolitan areas. *Yakuza* are known for their traditionally heavily tattoed torsos and for their distinctive square-shouldered business suits. They enjoy some prestige and respect because in popular mythology they claim a relationship with the masterless samurai of feudal times and the bandits who helped the poor at the expense of the landlords.

The *sōkaiya* are often members of *yakuza* gangs but they operate almost entirely as potential disrupters of shareholders' annual meetings where they cause disturbances and ask rude questions designed to frighten managements who may accordingly prefer to pay hush money. Their ability to cause disruption has been reduced by the fact that many companies now call their annual general meetings at the same time on the same day in different places.

The number of extremist terrorists in Japan is small but the Japanese police are very worried about the possibility of incidents involving the imperial family and visiting dignitaries. Accordingly, very strict security precautions are taken to ensure the safety of members of the imperial family and VIP visitors from abroad. Mortars have been used by some terrorists and this has added to the police's problems. The police also have to bear in mind the tradition of political assassination which plagued Japanese politics before the Second World War and which has resulted in a few assassinations and attempted assassinations in the post-war era.

However, crime rates in Japan are relatively low as compared with the USA and Europe, and arrest rates are high (see Table 4.1). This can be ascribed to a number of factors including social traditions, education and the relative homogeneity of Japanese society. Increased prosperity and egalitarian trends in income distribution have also helped, although prosperity is only a recent phenomenon and egalitarian trends were undermined by the asset price bubble of the late 1980s. A further factor has been Japanese policing methods, in particular the *kōban* system.

On the whole, the Japanese public's relationship with the police is good and the image of the Japanese police has improved greatly since the Second World War. Complaints of police brutality are now rare, although the large number of 'voluntary' confessions made by accused individuals have been interpreted by some observers as suggesting that the police are not always as scrupulous as they should be in extracting

Table 4.1   Crime rates in the USA and Japan, 1989

	Homicide	Rape	Robbery	Theft
Crime rate per 100 000 inhabitants				
USA	8.7	38.1	233.0	5 077.9
Japan	1.1	1.3	1.3	1 203.7
Arrest rate per 100 offences				
USA	68.3	52.4	26.0	18.0
Japan	95.9	83.6	75.9	41.7

Note: The figures for crimes and arrest rates may not be entirely accurate as definitions of crimes and reporting rates vary.

Taken from *Japan: An International Comparison* published by the Keizai Kōhō Center, Tokyo, 1993, p. 93.

confessions. Japanese traditions, however, put pressure on guilty parties to admit their faults and express remorse. The police go to great lengths to avoid confrontations. Occasionally young police officers, however, display an arrogant attitude towards, for example, traffic offenders.

5 Foreign Affairs and Defence

5.1 FOREIGN AFFAIRS

5.1.1 The Ministry of Foreign Affairs (*Gaimusho*)

The Ministry of Foreign Affairs is responsible for the conduct of Japanese foreign policy. The Minister of Foreign Affairs is usually, but not invariably, a senior politician. The senior career official in the Ministry is the Administrative Vice-Minister (*Jimujikan*). Next in seniority are two Deputy Vice-Ministers, responsible for political and economic affairs respectively, the Head of Administration (*Kambōchō*), and the official spokesmen, who also supervise the Cultural Department (*Bunkabu*).

The Minister's secretariat includes departments for research and planning as well as consular and immigration affairs. There are ten bureaux under Directors General (*Kyokuchō*):

Asian Affairs
North American Affairs
Latin American and Caribbean Affairs
European and Oceanic (that is, Australia, New Zealand and Pacific
   Islands) Affairs
Middle Eastern and African Affairs
Economic Affairs
Economic Co-operation (that is, overseas aid)
Treaties
Policy Co-ordination Bureau (*Sōgō gaikō seisaku kyoku*) (this bureau
   will replace the United Nations Bureau in 1993)
International Information Bureau (this bureau will replace the
   Information Analysis and Research Bureau in 1993)

Each bureau has a deputy director and one or more counsellors. Bureaux are divided into divisions under their own directors (*Kachō*).

The Ministry has a complement of approximately 3500. Twenty to thirty new recruits each year pass the higher foreign service examination after graduation from one of the top Japanese universities. Over half of these are law graduates of Tokyo University and the range of universities supplying recruits is very small. Middle-ranking staff enter through a foreign service specialist examination. Clerical and support staff are recruited through the examinations for such grades conducted by the National Personnel Authority (*Jinjiin*).

The Ministry is also responsible for the Foreign Service Training Institute and for the administration and staffing of Japanese Embassies, Consulates General and Consulates as well as permanent missions or delegations to international organizations.

5.1.2   Foreign Policy

The objectives of Japanese foreign policy, which can be summed up in the two words 'peace' and 'prosperity', have been defined more fully as being 'the centrality' of the United Nations, co-operation with economically advanced Western nations, and Japan's identity as an Asian nation. This means that Japan must maintain its own security and well-being while at the same time contributing to the security and prosperity of the rest of the world.

Ever since the Peace Treaty with Japan came into force in April 1952 the cornerstone of Japan's security and prosperity has been its relationship with the United States. This is based on the Treaty of Co-operation and Security signed in Washington in January 1960 as a revision to the Treaty concluded in 1952. The Treaty preamble expresses the desire of the two partners 'to strengthen the bonds of peace and friendship traditionally existing between them and to uphold the principles of democracy, individual liberty, and the rule of law'. Another objective is economic co-operation and the parties emphasise their adherence to the principles of United Nations. The Treaty commits the United States 'to act to meet the common danger in the event of armed attack on Japan'. Provision was also made for the continuance of US military bases in Japan and for prior consultation on the use of such bases and US forces in Japan for combat operations other than for the defence of Japan.

The 1960 Treaty roused a furore in Japan, although it was much more equitable than the 1952 Treaty it replaced, and the riots which accompanied ratification led to the downfall of the then LDP government of Mr Kishi Nobusuke. The treaty remains in force and although still opposed in principle by left-wing parties, it is no longer particularly controversial.

Although Japan has developed substantial defence forces of her own (see below) the Japanese, who suffered the only nuclear attacks launched in war (those on Hiroshima and Nagasaki in August 1945), have been dependant for their ultimate defence on the American nuclear umbrella. In December 1967 the then Japanese Prime Minister, Satō Eisaku, enunciated the three non-nuclear principles which remain the official basis of Japan's nuclear weapons policy. The three principles, which are backed by a Diet resolution, are that Japan will neither possess, nor manufacture, nor permit entry of nuclear weapons into the country.

The United States is not only important to Japan for defence reasons. It is also Japan's most important market and a highly significant source of supply of raw materials and manufactured goods. US/Japan relations have, however, never been easy.

Americans have accused the Japanese of having a 'free ride' in defence and not contributing adequately to their own defence.

The Japanese have also been accused of maintaining protectionist measures which restrict the amount of US exports to Japan and of dumping in and exploiting the freer American market. Fears have been expressed that Japan was 'buying up America' and threatening America's livelihood by forcing American manufacturers into bankruptcy.

For their part the Japanese have harboured anti-American feelings as a result of the Occupation and the long delays in achieving the return of Okinawa to Japan. (This was only achieved in 1972 after protracted and difficult negotiations.) They have also been critical of American exporters and managements as well as the US budget deficit. Economic friction was the basis for the Strategic Impediments Initiative negotiations which began in 1989.

Japan's relations with the former Soviet Union and now with Russia have been complicated by the problem of the northern territories. These are the islands of Etorofu and Kunashiri, the Habomai group and Shikotan island, all of which were occupied by Soviet forces at the end of the Second World War. Japan renounced her claim to the Kurile Islands in the Peace Treaty which came into force in 1952, but the Japanese claim that these islands do not constitute a traditional part of the Kurile chain. Moreover the Soviet Union was not a party to the 1952 Peace Treaty. Relations were normalized in 1956 but no agreement was reached over the disputed islands. The combined land area of the disputed islands is about 5000 square kilometres and they had a population of some 17 000 at the time of the Soviet occupation.

During discussions on the resumption of diplomatic relations, the Soviet side agreed to return the Habomai group and Shikotan if a peace treaty were concluded, but later backed off from this limited offer. Japan's relations with Russia have remained frigid. Until an agreement on these disputed islands can be reached the Japanese will continue to regard Russia with suspicion and the government will be reluctant to provide substantial aid.

Japan's relations with China are now much better. In 1952 the then Japanese government of Mr Yoshida Shigeru was forced by American pressure to conclude a peace treaty with the Chinese Nationalists in Taiwan. But following the so-called 1971 Nixon shock (when the American volte-face over relations with Communist China took place) the Japanese quickly moved to establish relations with the People's Republic of China. During a visit to Beijing (Peking) in 1972 Prime Minister Tanaka Kakuei signed a communiqué which restored Japanese relations with the Chinese mainland. Relations have not always been easy, as Chinese suspicions of Japan resulting from the Japanese attacks on China before and during the Second World War have not been entirely dissipated. However Japanese trade and investment have been growing apace and the Japanese were among the first to set aside the anger aroused by the Tiananmen Square incidents of 1989.

Japan's relations with Korea have inevitably been affected by the Korean experiences under Japanese occupation following Japanese annexation of the peninsula in 1910. Another complicating factor has been the existence of a substantial Korean community in Japan which has been the subject of discrimination and which has been divided into those with connections in the Republic of Korea and those supporting North Korea. However, after difficult and protracted negotiations a Treaty was signed with the Republic of Korea in 1965 and diplomatic relations were established. Trade with Korea has expanded fast and Korean economic development has seemed to follow the Japanese pattern.

The existence of an extremest Communist regime in North Korea had been a complicating factor in Japan's relations with the Republic of Korea in the south. The Japanese are understandably concerned about the possibility that North Korea may have, or be in a position to produce, nuclear weapons. They would like to be able to develop trade with North Korea but they have not yet managed to open diplomatic relations with the regime in Pyongyang.

Japan's relations with South East Asian countries have also not always been easy. Memories of the Japanese wartime occupation have not entirely disappeared and there have been suspicions of Japanese economic imperialism. But trade has grown vastly and Japanese investment, especially in Thailand and Malaysia, has had a significant impact on the development of ASEAN countries. Japan has taken care to develop contacts with ASEAN and to provide appropriate economic assistance. Japan has taken a lead in trying to further United Nations peace-keeping in Cambodia and is interested in the development of Vietnam.

Japan's relations with Europe until recently have been dominated by economic issues but greater emphasis is now placed on political co-operation and on the Japan–Europe element in the vital triangular relationship between the United States, Europe and Japan. The European Community is an important market for Japanese goods, and Japanese investment in Europe, particularly in Britain, has been significant.

Japan's relations with other parts of the world have not been as close as with Asian countries and the developed world of North America and Europe. But Japan has important trading relations with almost every country in the world. Particular importance has naturally been attached to relations with the Middle East, if only because of Japan's lack of indigenous energy resources. Since the first and second oil shocks of 1973 and 1979 the Japanese government have worked hard, with some success, to reduce the level of Japanese dependence on Middle-Eastern oil.

The 'centrality' of United Nations diplomacy for Japan has meant that the Japanese have made major efforts to play a significant part in UN deliberations, to provide a bridge for Asian countries and to contribute to UN agencies. Japan has served on the Security Council six times as a non-permanent member, but aspires to permanent membership if the UN charter were ever to be revised. Until the Diet passed the UN Peace Keeping Operations Law in June 1992 Japan was precluded from contributing to peace-keeping by the self-defence forces laws and by a stringent interpretation of Article 9 of the Constitution. Under the 1992 law, Japanese Self-Defence personnel may now take part in a non-combatant role under strict restrictions in UN peace-keeping operations. This has made it possible for Japanese Self-Defence Forces to be sent to Cambodia to undertake such a role there.

Arms control issues are of major importance for Japan because of the strength of Russian armed forces in the Far East, the size and growing power of Chinese forces and the dangers in the Korean Peninsula from north/south confrontation (Korea has been described as a dagger pointing at the heart of Japan). But progress on arms control has so far been primarily in Europe and the Japanese still see a threat to their security from Russian forces in the Far East with the Sea of Okhotsk still largely a Russian-controlled lake. A particularly sensitive issue for Japan is the application of arms control measures to naval forces in the Far East.

Aid to developing countries has become an increasingly important element in Japanese foreign policy and is seen by many as a way in which Japan, precluded by her constitution from sending forces overseas and taking military measures (Japan has banned exports of all arms and military equipment), can contribute to world security. Japan is now the largest world aid donor in total development assistance, contributing in 1990 some 0.31 per cent of GNP. The proportion of Japan's GNP devoted to aid is, however, well below that of some smaller countries such as Sweden and The Netherlands which in 1990 devoted 0.94 per cent and 0.9 per cent of GNP respectively. Japan's aid has, however, been growing by between 4 per cent and 5 per cent despite reductions in other parts of the budget. (In 1990 it increased by 8 per cent over 1989.)

In the past much of Japan's aid was devoted to Asian developing countries and was thought to be related to items which helped Japanese trade and investment. But in recent years more Japanese aid has been in grant form and has been going to poorer countries and multilateral institutions. The issues of human rights in developing countries and the extent to which abuses of human rights should affect aid have begun to impinge on Japanese aid policy, but despite the basic human rights enshrined in the Japanese constitution, human rights issues have hitherto generally not aroused much interest in Japan or had a great deal of influence on Japanese foreign policy decisions.

The importance of foreign trade and international finance to Japan has meant that the Japanese have given particular attention to their participation in the Group of Seven as well as in multilateral agencies such as the GATT (General Agreement on Tariffs and Trade), the Organization for Economic Co-operation and Development (OECD), the International Monetary Fund (IMF) and the World Bank. Japan has also taken a leading role in the Asian Development Bank (ADB). The Group of Seven has increasingly expanded its role from economic into political issues and the Japanese have greatly valued their inclusion in this forum as it has enabled them to be seen to be one of the world's leading powers in the political as well as the economic sphere, even though they have yet to work out quite what that role can or should be.

The Japanese have benefited from the development of freer trade and the importance of the GATT to Japan cannot be over-emphasized. While most Japanese tariffs are now low and most quotas have been phased out, Japan has not been able to play as prominent a part in the Uruguay round of GATT negotiations as her overall interests would suggest not least because of the continuing pressures for protection by Japan's small farmers, especially those producing rice, which costs many times (seven or eight times) the price of rice on the world market.

5.2 DEFENCE

5.2.1 The Defence Agency

The Defence Agency (*Bōeichō*) is responsible for the direction and administration of Japan's defence. It prepares the defence budget, procures military equipment and is responsible for military bases. It was established in 1954.

The Agency is headed by the Director General who is a Minister of State in the Japanese Cabinet. He is a member of the National Defence Council which is a Cabinet committee chaired by the Prime Minister. It is responsible for drawing up defence policy and ensuring civilian control of the forces. The Agency is largely staffed by civilian officials, but serving officers advise on technical matters.

5.2.2 Self-Defence Forces

The Japanese imperial forces were disbanded after the end of the Second World War and Japan was demilitarised. In 1950, following the outbreak of the Korean War, General Douglas MacArthur, the Supreme Commander Allied Powers (SCAP) during the Occupation of Japan, ordered the Japanese in 1950 to establish a National Police Reserve of 75 000 men to strengthen Japan's capacity to maintain order following the transfer of the bulk of American Forces from Japan to fight in Korea. In 1952 with the entry into force of the Peace Treaty, the Reserve became the National Safety Forces. In 1954, following the passage of the Self-Defence Forces Law, the forces were renamed the Ground, Maritime and Air Self-Defence Forces (*Rikujō-, Kaijō-* and *Kōkū-jieitai*).

Chiefs of Staff for each of the Self-Defence Forces (SDF) are responsible to the Director General of the Defence Agency for the organization and activities of their respective forces. Together they form the Joint Staff Council under a chairman who comes from one of the three forces and who is the highest ranking officer in the forces. The Council's function is to draw up defence plans and to co-ordinate military operations. In the event of hostilities, integrated units would be formed and the Chairman of the Joint Chiefs of Staff would assume command of the forces.

The responsibilities of the SDF are set out in Article 3 of the Self-Defence Forces Law. This states the 'The chief function of the SDF is to preserve the peace and independence of our country and to defend against direct and indirect aggression threatening the security of the nation. When need arises, the SDF will also be employed to preserve public order.' To fulfil these functions the forces may be mobilized in the event of attack or threat of attack from abroad, or on the order of the Prime Minister after obtaining Diet permission. They may also be mobilized on the command of the Prime Minister to preserve public order, but Diet approval must be obtained within twenty days of the order being given. The Maritime Self-Defence Force (MSDF) may act to protect life and property at sea. The Air Self-Defence Force (ASDF) is also authorised to respond to violations of Japanese air space. The forces may be used for disaster relief at the request of prefectural Governors or on the initiative of the Director General.

The SDF is a completely volunteer force and recruits join between 18 and 25 years of age for a minimum of two to three years. In times of economic prosperity recruitment has been difficult to maintain and the SDF has failed to achieve its authorised complement. A reserve corps of somewhat under 40 000 ex-SDF personnel was formed in 1970.

The authorised complement of the SDF in 1989 was 273 801 but the actual complement was some 249 000 or approximately 90 per cent of the establishment. Of this total some 40 000 were officers; nearly 5000 were warrant officers and the rest enlisted men.

Officers are selected from graduates of the National Defence Academy (*Bōei-daigakkō*). Officers going on to higher commands normally do a period at the National Defence College (*Bōei-kenshūjo*). Officers are given the same ranking in each of the forces with the prefix for their service before the rank/title. In training, special emphasis is placed on physical training and the SDF maintains its own physical training school while the GSDF has its own winter combat training unit.

The Ground Self-Defence Force (GSDF) is divided into twelve divisions which are grouped into five regional armies. The Northern Army is stationed in Hokkaidō, with its headquarters in Sapporo. The North-Eastern Army, stationed in the Tōhoku region of Honshū, has its headquarters at Sendai. The Eastern Army's head quarters are in Tokyo. The Central Army has its headquarters at Itami in Hyōgo prefecture, and the Western Army has its headquarters at Kumamoto in the southern island of Kyūshū. The most important of these armies has been the Northern because of the potential Russian threat to Hokkaidō. The GSDF also has two composite brigades, an armoured division, an artillery brigade, an airborne brigade, a training brigade, a helicopter brigade and eight anti-aircraft artillery groups.

The MSDF, which has its headquarters at Yokosuka, consists of approximately sixty anti-submarine surface ships, sixteen submarines, two flotillas of mine-sweepers and sixteen squadrons of land-based anti-submarine aircraft (over 200 aircraft). Its main mission is anti-submarine warfare.

The ASDF has three regional air defence forces, each with its own command headquarters. These are the Northern Air Defence Force stationed at Misawa in Aomori prefecture in Northern Honshū, the Central Air Defence Force stationed at Iruma in Saitama prefecture near Tokyo, and the Western Air Defence Force stationed at Kasuga, Fukuoka prefecture in Kyūshū. In addition, the ASDF has a separate air division stationed at Naha in Okinawa. All fighter aircraft and surface-to-air missiles in each command, as well as radar sites throughout the country are under the unified direction of the Air Defence Command at Fuchū near Tokyo. The ASDF has just over 400 operational aircraft in squadrons consisting of interceptor, support fighters, air reconnaissance, air transport and early warning units. Emphasis is placed on quick identification of aircraft encroaching on Japanese air space.

5.2.3 Defence Policy

Japanese defence policy is reviewed each year in a White Paper issued by the Defence Agency. The White Papers have emphasised Japan's responsibilities as one of the nations of the free world and Japan's close relations with the United States, but make it clear that Japanese forces are only for self defence. The government's interpretation of Article 9 of the Constitution is that Japan is only permitted to possess the minimum armaments necessary for self defence. This means that Japan is precluded from possessing offensive weapons such as long-range ballistic missiles and strategic bombers. Japanese forces may not operate in foreign territories or foreign seas and air space. The exercise of the right of collective self defence is also regarded as exceeding the provisions of Article 9. The use of the minimum necessary force for self defence is not considered to be contrary to the constitutional provision that 'the right of belligerency of the state will not be recognized'.

The White Paper reiterates that the objective of national defence is 'to prevent direct and indirect aggression, but once invaded to repel such aggression thereby preserving the independence and peace of Japan founded upon democratic principles'. For this purpose Japan has two pillars – the SDF and the security arrangements with the United States.

Japanese defence equipment is generally modern and effective. The forces are well trained, and discipline and morale are considered to be of a high standard. The SDF takes great care to maintain good relations with the Japanese public and uniform is only worn when personnel are with their own units.

5.2.4   Defence Expenditure

Japan's expenditure on defence in the 1992 fiscal year amounted to over ¥4.5518 trillion or approximately 0.94 per cent of GNP. Of this 35.9 per cent was budgeted for the GSDF; 24.2 per cent for the MSDF; 25.3 per cent for the ASDF; 10.7 per cent for the Defence Facilities Agency; and 3.9 per cent for other expenditure. Salaries, food, etc. took 41.3 per cent, 25.1 per cent was for purchases of equipment, including tanks, ships and aircraft; 16.4 per cent for education and training as well as equipment maintenance; 9.9 per cent for improvements to the environment in areas surrounding bases; 2.5 per cent for defence research; and 1.2 per cent for miscellaneous items. Japanese defence expenditure does not include some items which are included in the figures of NATO countries, and the proportion of Japanese GNP spent on defence is accordingly higher than these figures suggest. (Comparative figures for the 1989 fiscal year showed Japanese expenditure of US$28 billion, or approximately 1 per cent of GNP compared with UK expenditure of US$34 billion, or 4.2 per cent of GNP.)

6 Finance

6.1 THE MINISTRY OF FINANCE, THE ECONOMIC PLANNING AGENCY AND THE BUDGET

6.1.1 The Ministry of Finance (MOF – Ōkurashō)

The Ministry of Finance is the government agency primarily responsible for all financial matters including the budget, taxation, banking, securities business and international monetary issues. It is generally regarded as the most powerful of all Japanese government organizations and its prestige enables it to attract the élite among applicants to join the Japanese civil service. Usually 20 to 25 graduates, primarily from Tokyo University, join its higher echelons each year. At the end of their careers, usually in their early fifties, they can expect to be given senior jobs in banks or financial institutions in the private sector. A number go into politics usually in the LDP interest.

Under the Minister of Finance (MOF) who is almost invariably a senior politician, there are two Parliamentary Vice-Ministers (*Seimu-jikan*). The MOF's permanent staff is headed by the Administrative Vice-Minister (*Jimujikan*). The prime responsibility for international matters, however, rests with the Vice-Minister for International Affairs whose Japanese title is *Zaimukan*.

The main bureaux within the Ministry are:

1. The Minister's Secretariat.
2. The Budget bureau.
3. The Tax bureau.
4. The Customs and Tariff bureau.
5. The Financial bureau.
6. The Securities bureau.
7. The Banking bureau which includes the Insurance department.
8. The International Finance Bureau.

The Ministry has a range of regional branches and auxiliary organizations such as the bureaux for the mint and printing. The main external agency under MOF supervision is the National Tax

Administration (*Kokuzeichō*) with its own regional bureaux supervising district tax offices. In July 1992 a Securities and Exchange Surveillance Commission was established to monitor activities in the securities market, to try to prevent insider dealing, stock price manipulation and other irregularities. The Commission is part of the Ministry but all three Commissioners are appointed from outside the Ministry.

6.1.2   The Economic Planning Agency (EPA – *Keizai kikakuchō*)

The Economic Planning Agency (EPA) is an agency under a Minister of State in the Cabinet and is part of the Prime Minister's office. It is reponsible for producing economic forecasts and plans for the economy as a whole. It is a relatively small agency and has no power to ensure that the plans which it draws up are implemented. Moreover there are effective limits on what economic plans mean in a market economy such as exists in Japan. The agency can and does, however, attempt to explain the impact of government policies on the private sector and the economy as a whole, to identify problems and suggest remedies, to offer guidelines on economic and social development and to co-ordinate the interests of various groups. It is influential in producing a consensus of views between the government and the private sector, which generally respects the EPA's plans and forecasts.

6.1.3   The Budget

Responsibility for drafting the national budget rests with the Budget Bureau (*Shukeikyoku*) of MOF. The official fiscal year in Japan runs from 1 April to 31 March. Budget planning for the following fiscal year begins in the middle of July when the Cabinet is supposed to produce guidelines for the MOF. The Ministries each prepare their budget submissions in the light of a variety of pressures from politicians and the private sectors which the ministries represent. There is a good deal of infighting within most ministries with the aim of increasing the bureau in question's share of the Ministry's overall budget. The submissions from the ministries are reviewed by the Public Affairs Research Council of the LDP and by the various committees of the LDP which cover the areas of responsibility of the ministries. The drafts are then passed to the Budget bureau of MOF. Intensive negotiations between MOF and the various ministries are conducted in September, October and November. Finally, in December, the MOF produces its draft budget. In January the draft, subject to any final changes which may have been forced on MOF by pressures from ministries and the LDP, is submitted to the Diet for approval, hopefully by the end of March just before the new fiscal year begins.

Under Article 60 of the Constitution the budget must first be submitted to the House of Representatives. When approved by the lower house it is referred to the House of Councillors who may propose amendments which the lower house must consider. In the case of a disagreement or a failure by the upper house to take final action within thirty days, the decision of the lower house prevails. If the budget is not passed by the Diet before the end of March a temporary budget has to be submitted and approved. In many years the state of the economy requires the submission of a supplementary budget, for example, for disaster relief or capital expenditure on infrastructure projects.

6.2 TAXATION

Tax matters are the responsibility of the Tax bureau. Japanese taxes and tax law are as complicated as in most other developed countries and are administered on the basis of highly detailed legislation and regulations which are generally only fully understood by tax experts.

Official revenues are derived more from direct than from indirect taxes. The burden of local taxation is also relatively high.

The most important tax in Japan is income tax, which produces over 70 per cent of total revenue. It has to be paid by individuals, corporations and legal entities. The individual income tax is known as *shotokuzei* and corporate income tax as *hōjinzei*. In principle these are imposed on net or taxable income.

Taxable income of individuals is arrived at by adding together all the various sources of income under 10 different categories, as defined in the regulations, and subtracting from each the deductions permitted by the rules. Income from forestry and from severance pay are treated separately.

The ten categories comprise:

(i)   income from interest (*rishi shotoku*), for example, on deposit accounts and bonds;
(ii)   dividend income (*haitō shotoku*);
(iii)   income from property (*fudōsan shotoku*);

(iv) business income (*jigyō shotoku*);
(v)   remuneration (*kyūyo shotoku*), that is, salaries, but also including pensions;
(vi) severance pay (*taishoku shotoku*), that is, lump sum payments on retirement;
(vii) income from forestry;
(viii) assignment income (*jōto shotoku*) meaning capital gains;
(ix) occasional income (*ichiji shotoku*), that is, windfalls such as gambling receipts and prize money; and
(x)   miscellaneous income (*zatsu shotoku*) which includes any other income which an individual may receive.

Interest on bank deposits and some other items is subject to a withholding tax of 20 per cent (15 per cent national tax and 5 per cent local inhabitants' tax). This withholding tax covers the whole of the tax liability on such income which does not, therefore, have to be aggregated with other income in tax returns.

In the case of capital gains a maximum of ¥500 000 can be deducted from the gain made in any one year. If assets have been owned for five years or more liability is reduced to 50 per cent of the net capital gain. Capital gains arising from the sales of certain types of securities including ordinary shares and convertible debentures are taxed at a flat rate of 26 per cent (national tax of 20 per cent and local inhabitants tax of 6 per cent). Tax-payers may opt to pay tax on gains on securities at a flat rate of 1 per cent on the gross proceeds of sales made through securities companies operating in Japan. In that case the tax is deducted from the proceeds by the security company involved. Special rules may apply to capital gains deriving from the sale of real estate. (In 1988 the exemption given to sales of residences where the proceeds were used to purchase another residence was withdrawn and replaced by a complicated system under which only part of such gains is exempt from tax).

A non-resident tax-payer is taxed only on his income from Japanese sources. A non-permanent resident in Japan is taxed on his income from Japanese sources and on income from abroad remitted to or paid in Japan. An alien resident is taxed on his world-wide income. An expatriate is regarded as a permanent resident if he stays for more than five years. Where housing is provided for a director of a company he/she is generally taxed on 50 per cent of the actual rent.

Permissible deductions before the figure of taxable income is reached include:

(a) Earned income relief. On salaries of over ¥10 million per annum the relief given is a basic deduction of just over ¥2 million plus 5 per cent of taxable salary in excess of ¥10 million.

(b) Personal allowances of ¥350 000 for the taxpayer and for each dependant (for local inhabitants tax the deduction is limited to ¥300 000 per person).

Each individual must file a tax return except when income consists solely of salary from one employer not exceeding ¥15 million, then no return is required. Employers are required by law to withhold sums from salaries to cover income tax (national and local).

There are five bands for national income tax: 10 per cent, 20 per cent, 30 per cent, 40 per cent and 50 per cent. Each band applies to income in excess of the limit for the lower band. The 50 per cent rate applies to the amount by which annual income exceeds ¥20 million. No tax is payable by people earning under ¥3 million. There are three rates of local inhabitants' tax: 5 per cent, 10 per cent and 15 per cent. The 5 per cent rate applies to incomes over ¥1.2 million and the 15 per cent to annual incomes over ¥5 million. This means that on incomes of over ¥10 million the total of the marginal rate is 45 per cent and on incomes of over ¥20 million the marginal rate is 65 per cent.

Dividends are normally counted with other income and are subject to a withholding tax of 20 per cent. However, the recipient may opt to pay tax at the 35 per cent rate if he/she owns less than 5 per cent of the equity of the company in question and the dividends received do not amount to more than ¥500 000.

Employees are also liable to pay **social security premiums** of 12.2 per cent of salary.

Corporations do not have to classify their income in the same way as individuals and arrive at their income by deducting their expenses from their receipts. They pay tax on ordinary income at either 37.5 per cent or 28 per cent less various credits, for example, for experimental expenditure, equipment investment, import promotion and foreign taxes, and so on . The lower rate is paid by small businesses with a capital of ¥100 million or less and an income of less than ¥8 million. Co-operatives pay tax at a rate of 27 per cent.

Entertainment expenses which can be, and often are, very high in Japan can only be deducted from profits before taxation to a limited extent. It has been reported by the National Tax Administration that

Japanese companies spent US$48.7 billion on entertainment in the fiscal year 1991/2. Contributions/donations are in principle not deductible but some exceptions are allowed. The rules applying to depreciation are complicated. Each type of asset is accorded a 'useful' life in years varying from 65 years for ferro concrete buildings to 4 years for trucks and cars. Depreciation is generally allowed on the same basis as in the company's accounts. Special depreciation allowances are given for certain types of machinery and equipment.

Inheritance and gift taxes impose a considerable burden on Japanese families. **Inheritance tax** is levied on the increase in net assets resulting from an inheritance or bequest. **Gift tax** is also levied on the net increase in assets as a result of any donation, except that donations from a corporation are treated as income and are subject to income tax. The computation of the amount payable is complicated and involves seven steps. There is a basic allowance, on which tax is not payable, of ¥40 million per estate plus ¥8 million for each legal heir. Tax rates vary between 10 per cent and 70 per cent. The 70 per cent rate applies to estates of over ¥500 million. It is payable by the heirs on a pro rata basis. A surtax of 20 per cent is payable by a recipient of an estate if he/she is not a blood relative.

Gift tax is computed and payable annually on the total of gifts made by an individual. There is, however, an annual exemption per individual of ¥600 000. Some other limited exemptions are allowed, for example, for gifts to dependants. Gift tax and inheritance tax are not both payable on the same sums. Rates vary by rising amounts of 5 per cent from a minimum of 10 per cent on gifts up to ¥1 million to 70 per cent on gifts of over ¥70 million.

In 1989 a 3 per cent **consumption tax** was introduced. This tax, which aroused widespread opposition is an indirect tax applying to almost all domestic transactions. Financial and capital transactions as well as medical and welfare services and tuition are exempt. Automobiles are subject to a 6 per cent consumption tax. Enterprises whose taxable revenue is less than ¥30 million annually are exempt from paying the tax and reductions are made in the tax payable by enterprises earning between ¥30 million and ¥60 million. Exports and international transportation and communication services are exempt from the tax. A tax on liquor provided 3.1 per cent of government revenue in the fiscal year 1992/3. A tax on petrol (gasoline) yielded a further 3 per cent and a tax on aviation fuel 0.1 per cent. Indirect taxes met 25.9 per cent of revenue.

Property taxes are imposed on land, buildings or depreciable business assets. The tax base is the market value assessed by the municipality. Fair market value is assessed every three years. Rates vary between 1.4 per cent and 2.1 per cent. On land the rate was the property tax divided by the land value and yielded only some 0.13 per cent.

On 1 January 1992, however, a new **Land Value Tax** came into force. The rate in 1992 was 0.2 per cent, but from 1 January 1993 it is 0.3 per cent on the assessed value of all land held at the rate of assessment. A deduction of ¥1 billion, or for individuals or corporations with a capital of not more than ¥100 million of ¥1.5 billion yen, is made from assessed value for tax purposes. A further deduction of ¥30 000 per square metre is also made. Under the new law farmland in major urban areas is to be divided into two types. 'Green land', which will be land which is to be strictly preserved for farming purposes, will be exempt from land tax. Other farmland will be designated as 'development-encouraged land' and such land will, after five years, be taxed at the same rate as all other land. One purpose of the new law is to try to put a lid on the huge rises in the value of land which marked the economic bubble of the late 1980s. Another is to try to make more farmland in urban areas available for building and bring down the very high prices which have discouraged housing development. The favourable tax treatment of farmland in urban areas, including the favourable inheritance tax treatment of such land, led farmers to keep small parcels of land in cities and use these in a totally uneconomic way to cultivate rice or vegetables. The new tax does not apply to government land and land used by public corporations for welfare purposes.

6.3 FINANCIAL MARKETS

Japan has a complex financial market system which channels savings into productive investments. Much of this goes through financial intermediaries, particularly banks and associated financial institutions, as well as postal savings accounts. There is a well-developed call market which allows the banks to borrow or lend over very short periods. There is also a well-developed bill discount market which provides similar facilities for periods of one to six months. Japan has a large and sophisticated capital market.

The MOF has the primary responsibility for the supervision of all aspects of financial markets, but in the banking area this responsibility is shared with the Bank of Japan.

6.4 THE BANK OF JAPAN (BOJ – *NIHON GINKŌ*)

The Bank of Japan, established in 1882, is Japan's central bank. It issues currency, acts as a lender of last resort to the banking system and acts as the government bank. It is also responsible for monetary policy, including changes in the official discount rate, open market operations and changes in reserve requirements. It operates under the Bank of Japan Law of 1942. According to Article 1 of the Law, 'The Bank of Japan has for its object the regulation of the currency, the control and facilitation of credit and finance, and the maintenance and fostering of the credit sytem, pursuant to the national policy, in order that the general economic activities of the nation might adequately be enhanced.' The language is antiquated but it is clear that the Bank is enjoined to foster stability in the value of the currency and to maintain orderly credit conditions.

The relationship between the BOJ and the MOF is rarely easy although it is usually easier when the Governor, who is the chief executive of the Bank, comes from the MOF, as happens from time to time. The BOJ is not as independant as the Bundesbank in Germany but although the Minister of Finance is empowered to appoint and dismiss the Governor and directors and is broadly responsible for supervising the bank, it is not the servant of the MOF and there are often disagreements between MOF and the BOJ and between the BOJ and the LDP about changes in the official discount rate.

The maximum value of notes which the BOJ can issue is determined by the Minister of Finance, who must approve in not less than fifteen days any excess issue over the prescribed limit. Issues have to be backed by assets of equivalent value such as gold and silver bullion, government stock, commercial bills and loans, and foreign exchange. Notes are issued by the BOJ in denominations of ¥10 000, ¥5000 and ¥1000. Coins are issued in denominations of ¥500, ¥100, ¥50, ¥10, ¥5 and ¥1.

The Bank of Japan, as the bank for other Japanese banks, accepts deposits which earn no interest and which are used for the settlement of transactions and for remittances. Such deposits also include the reserve deposits the banks are required to keep with the BOJ. The amounts which banks must keep in their reserve deposits varies with the nature of their deposits and liabilities.

The BOJ lends to banks on bills and rediscounts, at the official discount rate, certain designated types of bills. The BOJ also trades in government securities with the main emphasis on long-term bonds. The BOJ undertakes bullion and foreign exchange trading.

The BOJ carries out payments for the MOF and government institutions. It also lends to the government without collateral. The BOJ underwrites short-term government bills although it is not permitted to underwrite government bonds with a maturity of more than one year. The BOJ, however, is responsible for issuing, redeeming and paying interest on government bonds.

The BOJ has a nominal capital of ¥100 million, of which 55 per cent is subscribed by the government and 45 per cent by the private sector. Dividends are limited to 5 per cent and surpluses are paid into the MOF's account with the Bank.

The highest decision-making body of the BOJ is the executive board which consists of the Governor, the Vice Governor and the executive directors, who are appointed by the Governor subject to the approval of the MOF. A policy board is responsible for implementing the decisons of the executive board. The policy board consists, in addition to the Governor, of representatives of the MOF and the EPA and four other appointed representatives, for example, from city banks, regional banks, commerce and industry, and agriculture.

The objectives of Japanese monetary policy are price stability, economic growth and equilibrium in the balance of payments. These objectives are not always compatible. The BOJ operates, as do other central banks, through its lending policies, open-market operations, and changes in reserve requirements. The BOJ also operates 'window guidance', that is, credit controls on increases in loans by city banks and gives 'administrative guidance' (*gyōsei shidō*) to financial institutions. Changes in the official discount rate influence the costs of raising funds by financial institutions. In order to reduce dependence by city banks on BOJ lending maximum limits have been set for such loans. The ability of the BOJ to control the money supply has inevitably been weakened by financial liberalization.

6.5 OTHER GOVERNMENTAL AND SEMI-GOVERNMENTAL BANKING INSTITUTIONS

The Post Office

Over 24 000 post offices in Japan take savings deposits from individuals.

These deposits used to be tax free and are still favourably treated for tax purposes. Interest on the first 3.5 million yen in postal deposits is treated as exempt from tax. Deposits are of various kinds, for example, ordinary, fixed amounts, fixed term and instalment (for example, for housing and educational purposes). The sums collected have been vast and the role of the post office savings accounts, whose interest rates are determined by the Minister of Posts and Telecommunications, has been criticised by the private sector as unfair competition.

The Japan Development Bank (JDB – Nihon kaihatsu ginkō)

The function of the JDB is to promote industrial development by lending funds for development, giving liability guarantees and providing capital. It has seven branches in major cities and four represenative offices in foreign countries. JDB loans are normally for periods of between one and ten years but may extend to thirty years. Many of the JDB's loans are carried out jointly with the private sector. Nearly half of the bank's loans have been in the utilities sector.

The Export–Import Bank (Yushutsunyū ginkō)

The main activities of the bank are domestic lending, direct loans, and liability guarantees. Domestic lending is intended to finance exports and the supply of technology, imports (especially of important materials), and foreign investment. The bank may also lend to foreign corporations, foreign governments and foreign banks.

The Overseas Economic Co-operation Fund (OECF) (Kaigai-keizai-kyōryoku-kikin)

The fund was established in 1961 to contribute to the stabilization and development of the economies of South East Asia and other areas. The OECF lends for development projects and development research as well as economic stabilization.

Nōrinchūkin

The central financial institution for agricultural, forestry and fishing co-operatives. It has government support and protection. It has one of the largest deposit bases of all Japanese financial institutions and one of the highest credit ratings of Japanese banks. It is limited to lending which has a connection with agriculture, forestry or fisheries.

Shōkōchūkin

A special corporation designed to facilitate the operation of co-operative societies of small businesses. *Shōkōchūkin* is only allowed to take deposits and lend to co-operatives (and their members) which contribute to its capital. The government contributed to its capital and underwrites a proportion of the bank's debentures. In 1985 the bank joined the government bond underwriting syndicate and began sales over the counter of government bonds.

Zenshinren

Not strictly a governmental or even a semi-governmental bank but it has a special status under the law and it is convenient to consider it here. It is the central institution for *shinkin* banks, which are credit co-operatives for small business enterprises. They differ from ordinary banks in that credit operations are limited to members, who must be businesses with less than 300 employees or ¥400 million in capital. They are also only permitted to operate in specific geographical areas and the amount they may lend to any one member is restricted. They and *Zenshinren* are controlled by the *Shinkin* Bank Law as revised in 1981. One of *Zenshinren*'s major functions is the efficient investment of surplus funds of *shinkin* banks.

6.6 COMMERCIAL BANKS

In terms of assets many of the top banks in the world are Japanese, but they have relatively few branches compared with, for example, National Westminster Bank in the United Kingdom and Deutsche Bank in Germany. The largest Japanese banks have fewer than 600 branches and most of the large city banks have fewer than 400.

Private clients have been less important for the Japanese banks than corporate clients and most individuals in Japan do not have cheque accounts. Instead they have ordinary accounts (*futsū yokin*) for deposits and cash withdrawals. A low rate of interest is paid, but the account can be used to pay, for example, utility bills. Customers can withdraw or pay-in cash at any branch of their bank or of any affiliated bank by using a cash card through automatic teller machines or cash dispensers, but these are not yet open 24 hours of the day, every day of the week. Customers may also have ordinary time deposit accounts (*futsū teiki yokin*) and other types of deposit accounts.

Japan can be said to have moved from being a cash society to become a plastic card society without the intermediate cheque-account stage. The use of the plastic card has grown very fast over the last ten years and in the asset price boom of the late 1980s credit card debt became a matter of major concern. The Japanese do, however, still make considerably more use of cash than is the case in other developed economies and many Japanese carry large amounts of yen on their persons. Japanese who are known to the proprietors of restaurants and places of entertainment are often not given bills but pay accounts monthly as submitted. Alternatively, they may leave their visiting card (*meishi*) as proof of their bona fides. The presentation of two identical *meishi* is generally regarded as proof of identity in such cases.

Japanese commercial banks have been subject to very strict controls and liberalization of financial markets which has been deliberately delayed by the MOF is still far from complete. Among the many controls were limits on opening branches (a Japanese bank requires MOF approval to open a new branch), strict divisions between the different types of bank and financial institutions, and limits on the amounts of interest which can be paid on specific types and sizes of deposits.

One reason for the MOF's determination to keep the banks on a tight rein has been the very significant role which the banks have played in the build-up of Japanese industry and commerce after the destruction caused by the Second World War. Substantial amounts of credit were required but if inflation was to be avoided and credits directed to the more important parts of the economy (as seen by bureaucrats) credit had, especially in the early post-war years, to be rationed and directed. The MOF needed to watch carefully to ensure that banks did not get into an overloan situation and in recent years MOF has been anxious to ensure that Japanese banks were in a position to meet the capital requirements set by the Bank for International Settlements (BIS). Japanese banks were able to count in their capital unrealised stock exchange gains but the falls in the Japanese stock exchange in 1991 and 1992 wiped out many of these gains. At the same time the bursting of the asset price bubble, especially in property, left many banks with serious losses on their loan assets.

Japanese banks can be classified as follows:

1. **City banks,** of which there are currently eleven (one of these, Daiwa Bank, is also a trust bank; and one the Bank of Tokyo, specializes in foreign exchange).

2. **Long-term credit banks** of which there are at present three.
3. **Trust banks** of which there are seven excluding the one city bank, Daiwa Bank, which also does trust business.
4. **First-tier regional banks** of which there are usually one but sometimes more in each prefecture.
5. **Second-tier regional banks** which used to be *Sōgo* or mutual banks.
6. *Shinkin banks* (see under *Zenshinren* above).
7. **Specialist and governmental banks** (see above).

The City Banks (Toshi ginkō)

City banks undertake the same kinds of operation as commercial banks elsewhere, for example, taking deposits, making loans (short-term and longer-term, although long-term lending with maturities of over one year represent only about 10 per cent of their lending), remitting funds, discounting bills, issuing and accepting letters of credit, paying dividends and safekeeping valuables, and so on. But they have been precluded under Article 65 of the Securities and Exchange Law of 1948, which followed the pattern of the Glass–Steagall Act in the United States, from undertaking securities business. They have also been precluded from doing trust banking business and they have not been allowed to float debentures to finance long-term lending. This has been preserved exclusively for the long-term credit banks. Modifications of these rules will, however, result from the more liberal framework approved by the Diet in June 1992. Under the new framework the different types of financial institution should eventually be able to participate in the business of other types of institution by setting up subsidiaries. City banks should thus be able to establish subsidiary companies to pursue trust business and to undertake securities business (except broking, which seems likely to remain the exclusive preserve of securities companies). Progress towards liberalisation is likely to be slow as the securities companies who have suffered severe losses recently are lobbying hard against any measures which might increase competition from Japanese banks.

The order of the eleven city banks varies depending on whether assets or profits are used as the basis. The city banks are:

1. Daiichi Kangyō Bank (DKB), which resulted from a merger in 1971 of the Daiichi Bank and the Kangyō Bank to form at that

time Japan's largest commercial bank. It is the main bank to a wide range of commercial and industrial companies.

2. Sakura Bank, which is the name adopted by Mitsui and Taiyō Kōbe Banks following their merger in 1990. It is the main bank for companies in the Mitsui group.

3. Fuji, the main bank of the Fuyō group of companies which, derive from the pre-war Yasuda *zaibatsu*.

4. Sumitomo Bank, the main bank used by the Sumitomo group of companies.

5. Mitsubishi Bank, the main bank for the Mitsubishi group of companies.

6. Sanwa Bank which, like Sumitomo, is regarded as a Kansai (Osaka and Kyoto area) bank. As with the Daiichi Kangyō Bank there is a Sanwa Bank group of companies but both groups are less closely knit than for instance, those in Sumitomo and Mitsubishi groups.

7. Asahi Bank, which resulted from the merger in 1991 of the Kyōwa and the Saitama banks. Saitama Bank was based primarily in Saitama prefecture and neighbouring Tokyo.

8. Tōkai Bank which has its base in Nagoya and the surrounding area.

9. Daiwa Bank, which has its main business in the Osaka area and which is the only city bank which, as a result of a special dispensation, has been allowed to do trust business as well as normal city bank business.

10. Hokkaidō Takushoku Bank (known as *Takugin*) which, as its name suggests, is primarily a Hokkaidō bank with its prime area of interest being the development of the northern island.

11. The Bank of Tokyo (BOT), which is Japan's specialist bank for foreign exchange. It has more overseas branches than any other Japanese bank and fewer domestic branches than any of the others. It is derived from the Yokohama Specie Bank, which was Japan's pre-war foreign exchange bank.

Long-term Credit Banks

These were established on the basis of a law enacted in 1952 and were designed to provide long-term capital to Japanese industry and to help its revival and development in the post-war growth period. As stated above, the long-term credit banks are the only banks which hitherto have been permitted to issue debentures and to use the funds so raised for long-term loans to industry. Debentures are limited to a maximum of twenty times the banks' capital and reserves. The long-term credit banks are only allowed to accept deposits from a specific range of qualified clients such as central government, local governments, public bodies, and their own borrowers.

The three long-term credit banks are:

1. The Industrial Bank of Japan (*Nihon kōgyō ginkō* or *Kōgin*), which has been one of Japan's strongest and most prestigious banks and which has wide interests in Japanese industry, for example, in the Nissan Motor Corporation.
2. The Long-Term Credit Bank of Japan (*Nihon chōki shinyō ginkō* or *Chōgin*), which is one of Japan's major banks.
3. The Nippon Credit Bank (*Nippon saiken shinyō ginkō*), which is the smallest of the three.

Trust Banks (Shintaku ginkō)

Trust banks engage in both normal banking business and trust business. Trust business involves the management and disposal of assets on behalf of clients. Trust banks handle investment trusts (not to be confused with British closed-ended investment trusts), loan trusts, pensions trusts and other forms of trust. The trust banks have been important in providing long-term finance through loan trusts. The trust banks have also been important as savings institutions for members of the general public. Trust banks keep their banking and trust accounts separate.

The seven Japanese trust banks are, in addition to Daiwa Bank:

1. Mitsubishi Trust and Banking Corporation.
2. Sumitomo Trust and Banking Company.
3. Mitsui Trust and Banking Company.
4. Yasuda Trust and Banking Company, which is close to Fuji Bank.
5. Tōyō Trust and Banking Company, which is close to Sanwa Bank.
6. Chūō Trust and Banking Company, which is close to Daiichi Kangyō Bank and Tōkai Bank.
7. Nippon Trust Bank, which has close connections with the Mitsubishi group of companies.

Banks in these three groups have formed the Federation of Bankers' Associations of Japan to represent their interests. The chairmanship has traditionally rotated between the Presidents of the biggest Tokyo based banks, that is, Daiichi Kangyō Bank, Sakura Bank, Fuji Bank and Mitsubishi Bank.

Regional Banks

Regional banks operate in much the same way as city banks, but while the city banks may have branches throughout the country, regional banks have their branches concentrated in their own prefectures with only a few branches outside, for example, in Tokyo and Osaka. Regional Banks, with their local roots, often have a strong local deposit base, but they are very rarely the main bank for any of the large corporations, although their services may well be used by local branches of large corporations. The larger regional banks are relatively strong institutions and are often among the wealthiest of local organizations. Some, especially the smaller regionals in less-highly-industrialised prefectures have a weaker base. Some are 'owner banks', where a particular family has a strong interest in the management of the bank. Some of the regional banks have close connections with particular city banks who may own up to 5 per cent of the shares of a regional bank. Mitsubishi Bank, for instance, has close relations with a number of banks, particularly in the Kantō area, such as Chiba, Jōyō, Ashikaga and Hachijūni banks.

Among the largest and strongest regional banks are Yokohama, Hokuriku, Shizuoka, Chiba, Ashikaga (Tochigi prefecture), Jōyō (Ibaragi prefecture), Fukuoka and Hiroshima. In other cases this is not so clear. The name may, as with the Iyō Bank in Ehime prefecture in Shikoku, derive from the name of the province which existed before the prefectures were established in the nineteenth century. Other regional banks use numbers as their names. These are based on the early numbers given to banks as they were founded in the nineteenth century. The 77 Bank has its base in Sendai in Miyagi prefecture. The Jūroku (16) Bank has its home in Gifu while the Hyakujūshi (114) Bank is based in Takamatsu (Kagawa prefecture) in Shikoku. The Hachijūni (82) Bank is the bank for Nagano prefecture. The number 82 is the sum of the two numbers of the banks from which it derives. The doyen of the regional banks is the Yokohama Bank which has close connections with the MOF. A number of regional bank presidents come from the MOF or the BOJ.

The regional banks have their own association to represent their interests.

The second-tier regional banks which were the former *Sōgo* banks are less strong and prestigious. Their strengths and weaknesses vary considerably. Where the MOF considers this necessary it may 'guide' one of the stronger regionals to take over the weaker to protect the depositors and avoid a run on the deposit insurance fund.

Many foreign banks have been permitted to open branches in Japan and nine have been allowed to have trust banking subsidiaries. the rules governing foreign banks in their operations in Japan are similar to those for domestic financial institutions.

Non-bank Financial Institutions

Among the numerous non-bank financial institutions are a series of leasing companies. Many of these are subsidiaries of banks and undertake, in addition to normal leasing operations, lending which banks are themselves discouraged or precluded from undertaking by the MOF, who do not exercise control over non-banks as they do on banks.

There are also numerous consumer credit companies (*shimpan*) which have expanded rapidly in recent years with the development in Japan of plastic credit cards.

Venture capital companies have been established by the leading banks. The recent development of small, high-technology companies has given this development a boost in recent years.

Housing finance has generally been provided by banks and their related companies (housing finance companies). The Housing Loan Corporation is a government institution which is designed to augment private financial arrangements. There is no equivalent in Japan of British building societies.

6.7 SECURITIES COMPANIES

Japanese capital markets are well developed but highly regulated. In particular, commissions are still fixed and the MOF controls access by Japanese companies to capital markets. This led especially in the 1980s to Japanese companies making great use of the Euro-markets. The apparently constant rise in Japanese stocks led companies to issue warrants with rights to purchase equities at fixed prices at a future date. These warrants were issued at minimal cost to the company. Japanese companies thus had access to very cheap finance. The falls in the Japanese stock markets in 1991/2 has altered this situation. It has also called into question the Japanese tradition of paying very low dividends on ordinary shares where the assumption has been that investors would get a more than adequate return from capital gains.

The Japanese stock market has eight stock exchanges (*Shōken torihikijo*) and the stock market has been one of the largest in the world in terms of the value of listed securities and total transactions. there are two sections. The first covers some 1250 large companies; the second some 800 smaller companies. Brief details about all the companies listed on the two sections is given in the two volumes of the *Japan Company Handbook*, published quarterly.

By far the most important stock exchange is situated in *Kabutochō* in Tokyo. This exchange accounts for around three-quarters of all transactions. The next largest is the Osaka exchange. The others in Nagoya, Kyoto, Hiroshima, Fukuoka, Niigata and Sapporo cover only a small proportion of transactions.

Securities companies are allowed to trade in securities, act as intermediaries and agents, underwrite shares and bonds, and sell and buy securities on behalf of members of the public. They may also engage in 'accumulated investment operations' in which a client pays money in instalments on a regular basis and the securities company, with the money provided, buys securities and reinvests the interest. Although securities companies have not been allowed under Article 65 of the Securities and Exchange Law to engage in banking business in Japan they have been allowed, and indeed encouraged, by MOF to do so abroad. Securities companies have to have licences to operate in Japan and have been subject to supervision of the Securities Bureau of the MOF. Since 1992 they have also become subject to the new-established Securities and Exchange Surveillance Commission.

There are over 200 securities companies in Japan, of which just over half are full members of the eight exchanges. In fact, almost two-thirds of the business of Japanese securities companies is done by the four largest companies. The largest of the securities companies, all of which are known as *Shōken gaisha*, are (in order of size):

1. Nomura.
2. Daiwa (not to be confused with Daiwa Bank).
3. Nikkō.
4. Yamaichi.

The next largest and some way down is New Japan Securities (*Shin Nihon Shōken*). A number of securities companies have as close a relationship with some of the big banks as the rules have so far permitted. For instance, Daiichi Kangyō Bank has a 4.9 per cent shareholding (the maximum permissible is 15 per cent) in Kankaku Securities.

The big four have considerable influence as they are important sources of political funds. They all have powerful research organisations of, which Nomura and Daiwa are the biggest and most prestigious.

Securities companies have not been highly regarded by top university graduates seeking jobs, as their reputation has not been high. Their reputation was particularly badly hit in 1991/2 because of their involvement with various scandals, including insider dealing.

6.8 INSURANCE COMPANIES

Insurance companies in Japan have access to very large sums of money and are accordingly major players in financial markets. There are two main groups of insurance companies whose business is limited to their own sectors. These are the life companies (*Seimei gaisha*) and casualty, fire and marine insurance companies (generally known as *Kasai gaisha*). The casualty companies do normal business but also operate savings policies which give them access to large amounts of money. The life insurance companies are normally mutual companies; the fire and marine are generally joint stock companies. Both are subject to strict and detailed regulation by the MOF which, for instance, has to approve the various types of insurance products which Japanese companies are allowed to sell. The MOF also controls the amounts which insurance companies may invest, for example, in foreign stocks.

Some of the life insurance and casualty insurance companies belong to one or other of the large groups. Among the biggest life companies are Nippon Life, Daiichi Life, Sumitomo Life, Yasuda Life, Mitsui Life, Asahi Life, Meiji Life (Mitsubishi group) and Chiyoda Life. Among the largest casualty insurance companies are Tokio Fire and Marine (Mitsubishi group), Mitsui Marine and Fire (formerly Taishō), Sumitomo Fire and Marine, Nippon Fire and Marine, Yasuda Fire and Marine, Nissan Fire and Marine, and Chiyoda Fire and Marine.

Savings Rates

An important factor in Japan's post-war economic success has been the comparatively high savings rate. This has been helped by the twice-yearly bonus system used by Japanese companies (bonuses may add 50 per cent to annual salaries) and by tax incentives, for example, on postal savings accounts. It has also been induced by the need which Japanese have felt, to save up for their old age, especially at a time when pensions have been inadequate; for housing which in the asset boom of the late 1980s became prohibitively expensive; and to meet education and health expenses where public provision has often been regarded as inadequate. Through the banks and other financial institutions these savings have been channelled into productive investment.

7 Industry and Commerce

7.1 GOVERNMENT AGENCIES

7.1.1 The Ministry of International Trade and Industry (MITI-*Tsūshō sangyōshō* or *Tsūsanshō*)

MITI is, next to the MOF, the most powerful and influential Japanese ministry. Like the MOF it attracts graduates from the top universities, especially Tokyo University, into its higher echelons.

Under the minister, who is normally a fairly senior politician, there are two Parliamentary Vice-Ministers. The Administrative Vice-Minister (*Jimujikan*) is the senior official in the Ministry. The international side is headed by a Vice-Minister for International affairs called in Japanese *Shingikan*.

In addition to the Minister's Secretariat which covers the research and statistics department there are the following bureaux:

International Trade Policy, which supervises the International Economic Affairs and the Economic Co-operation Departments;
International Trade Administration;
Industrial Policy;
Industrial Location and Environmental Protection;
Basic Industries;
Machinery and Information Industries; and
Consumer Goods.

MITI has eight regional bureaux plus specialist regional organizations covering mine safety and inspection.

MITI is also responsible for three important external agencies:

1. The Agency of Natural Resources and Energy (*Shigen enerugichō*) which has separate departments for petroleum, coal-mining (a declining industry) and public utilities.
2. The Small and Medium Enterprise Agency (*Chūshō kigyōchō*), which has departments of planning, guidance and small enterprises. The vast majority of Japanese enterprises are of small or medium size: Japanese industry is not made up entirely of the large-

scale bureaucratic companies that are often (wrongly) thought to
be typical of Japanese industry and commerce. Small companies
manufacturing parts and equiment have been vital to Japan's
economic success.
3. The Patent Office (*Tokkyōchō*).

In addition, MITI controls a number of auxiliary organizations,
including specialised training institutes. The most important of these
is the **Agency of Industrial Science and Technology (*Kōgyō gijutsuin*)**
which is responsible for various laboratories and research institutes, for
example, for meteorology, mechanical engineering, electro-technical
and chemical matters. It is also responsible for the geological survey.

JETRO (Japan External Trade Organization) comes under MITI
and is staffed from MITI. It was originally set up to provide help and
information for Japanese exporters, but as Japan's trade surplus grew
it has become increasingly concerned with promoting imports. It has
overseas offices in most major countries.

MITI has authority over a large number of public corporations and
of corporations owned jointly with private enterprise. These include the
Japan Petroleum Development Corporation, the Electric Power
Development Corporation and the Small Business Finance Corporation.

Many MITI officials serve in Embassies abroad, where they report
direct to MITI on trade issues, and in other government agencies such
as the Defence Agency.

MITI's powers and influence were at their height in the 1960s and
1970s as Japan's economy grew at a rapid rate. Observers consider that
the industrial policies promoted by MITI, through its ability to control
licences and access to funds as well as through 'administrative
guidance', contributed greatly to Japanese industrial success. As
liberalization progressed, partly but not wholly as a result of foreign
pressure (*gaiatsu*) MITI's power to influence development has been
considerably weakened. However, the power of MITI today should not
be underestimated. Japanese companies have come to respect MITI's
knowledge and ability to choose the direction which will best help the
Japanese economy. No Japanese company would wish to be in MITI's
black books. Even in the heyday of MITI power, however, the Ministry
was not all-powerful and Japanese industries were able to ignore MITI
pressures if they were determined and well-established. For instance
MITI failed to bring about the merger of Japanese automobile
manufactures into three groups which it thought would best be able

to deal with international competition. MITI's views in this respect were rejected and proved wrong. MITI has been responsible for the establishment of various cartels when Japanese enterprises have faced downturns in their markets, but it has more usually worked to promote the kind of intense competition between Japanese companies that has helped to ensure economic efficiency.

7.1.2 Japanese Trade Policy

In the early days, MITI's role in foreign trade was concentrated on ensuring that Japanese industries were developed behind high protectionist barriers. MITI was especially conscious of the fact that Japan had a long way to go to catch up with industry in other developed countries. MITI also saw the dangers to the Japanese economy which came from Japan's lack of most natural resources and indigenous energy supplies. This situation fed a mercantilist attitude which has not entirely disappeared in sections of the Japanese government, the LDP and industry. Officials have also understandably been reluctant to cede the powers which they had developed to control industry through regulations and licensing. Much was left to the discretion of officials, and codes were not always written down. Lack of clarity and administrative obstacles have acted as non-tariff barriers.

The Japanese have recognized the vital importance to them of international trade and the value of international organizations such as the GATT and OECD. Tariffs have generally come down and are among the lowest in industrialized countries. Japan retains few quotas except in agriculture, and non-tariff barriers have been greatly reduced. The main problems for exporters to the Japanese market are no longer physical but more often than not cultural (for example, language, social structure). But foreign companies have also complained about access to distribution channels which during Japan's protectionist era were tied up by domestic producers. The Americans in particular have objected to the *keiretsu* groupings (see below) which in their view tend to keep out foreign manufacturers and tie contracts to members of the same group.

Japanese international trade policy, like that of other developed countries, is influenced by pressures from sectional interests and lobbies, particularly Japan's small-scale farmers who cannot compete with imports of most products without subsidies or protection. These pressures have prevented the Japanese government from taking the kind of bold initiatives in the GATT Uruguay round which a broad assessment of Japan's national interests would suggest.

Under pressure from foreign countries whose industries have been affected by Japanese competition, the Japanese have had to enforce so-called voluntary restraint arrangements (VRAs) on sales to particular markets. These have applied at different times to many of Japan's top export items such as automobiles and electronic products. Foreign countries, in their efforts to stem the tide of imports from Japan, have taken other protectionist measures including in some cases the application of anti-dumping duties in ways which the Japanese claim are contrary to the provisions of the GATT.

Protectionism applied by foreign countries against Japanese products has been a significant factor in the decisions made by Japanese companies to invest in productive facilities abroad. But foreign protectionism has not been the only factor. Costs, including those of land and wages, as well as the need to have production close to growing markets have been important factors. Japanese foreign investment by creating jobs abroad should have helped to reduce trade friction, but in some countries, especially the USA it seems to have caused cultural friction. This has arisen from Japanese management methods and from the difficulty which many Japanese sent abroad face in adapting to local conditions and cultures. Japanese investments have also from time to time been accused of being little more than screw-driver operations, that is, assembly of parts imported from Japan or from Japanese factories in developing countries.

Economic friction seems likely to remain a major problem for Japan during much of the 1990s if only because of Japan's continuing large trade surplus. Japan's trade surplus in 1991 with the USA amounted to some US$38 billion, with the European Community to about US$27 billion, and with Asian countries to US$31 billion.

Japan's exports in 1991 amounted to some US$314 billion while imports amounted to only some US$236 billion. Japan's trade surplus in 1992 was US$107.1 billion. (The surplus on current account was US$117 billion.) Japan's largest export market was the USA, but the USA was also Japan's top source of imports. Japan's largest export category by far was machinery and equipment including automobiles, electronic equipment and ships. Japan's most important imports were fuel (oil, gas and coal); machinery and equipment (but the total was less than a quarter of the amount exported from Japan); foodstuffs; and raw materials. Japan's dependency on imports of foodstuffs was 100 per cent for maize, 95.5 per cent for soyabeans and 85.2 per cent for wheat. In industrial raw materials, Japan's dependency ratio was equally high. Imports provided over 99 per cent of Japan's needs of coal, crude oil and iron ore.

7.1.3 The Science and Technology Agency (*Kagaku gijutsuchō*)

The Science and Technology Agency, which must not be confused with the MITI Agency for Industrial Science and Technology, is an Agency under the Prime Minister's office and is headed by a Director General who is a Minister of State in the Cabinet. It is responsible for the formulation, co-ordination and carrying out of a number of programmes and research in science and technology. The Agency is responsible for the Atomic Energy Research Institute, the National Aerospace Laboratory, the National Space Development Agency, and the Japan Information Centre for Science and Technology. It includes an Atomic Energy bureau which is responsible for Japanese policies for the peaceful uses of atomic energy. The Agency's Nuclear Safety bureau draws up safety rules and enforces these to ensure the safety of Japan's nuclear power industry. The agency's main work has been in relation to atomic energy and space.

7.1.4 The Fair Trade Commission (*Kōsei-torihiki-iinkai*)

The Fair Trade Commission (FTC) is responsible for enforcing Japan's anti-monopoly law (*Dokusenkinshihō*) first enacted in 1947 during the Occupation of Japan. It was to a considerable extent modelled on US anti-trust laws. However, there have been few prosecutions for violation of the law despite American pressures for stricter enforcement in the interests of fair trade.

The FTC deals with three main areas: (a) private monopoly practices; (b) unreasonable restraint of trade, for example, through a cartel; and (c) unfair business practices including discriminatory acts, unreasonable price setting, use of coercion and unreasonable inducements, and unreasonable price restrictions. Retail price maintenance is only permitted for goods where the FTC has given its approval. Exclusive dealing arrangements are not illegal.

The FTC are required to investigate complaints brought to them by the public. The Prosecutor General must also report alleged violations brought to his notice. The FTC may take the initiative in starting an investigation. If the FTC finds a violation it first tries to persuade the party or parties concerned to cease the practice in question. If this fails it should bring a case before the courts.

The FTC has been criticised by the Americans for insufficient energy in investigating complaints and taking action against offenders.

7.2 PUBLIC UTILITIES

Electricity is provided by nine privately-owned regional power companies who hold a monopoly in their areas but whose rates are controlled by MITI. The nine companies are Hokkaidō (the northern island); Tōhoku (north-eastern Honshū); Tokyo (the area around greater Tokyo); Chūbu (central Honshū around Nagoya); Kansai (Osaka, Kyoto and the surrounding region); Chūgoku (western Honshū); Shikoku (island); and Kyūshū (the southern island). The largest of these is Tokyo Electric Power, which is the largest electricity supply company in the world.

Gas has been less important for Japanese industry than electricity but companies such as Tokyo Gas and Osaka Gas are huge privately-owned utilities whose rates are also controlled by MITI.

In order to reduce Japanese dependence on imported oil a great deal of effort has been put into the development of nuclear power which in 1988 supplied 10 per cent of Japan's electricity requirements. In 1991 Japan had fifty-three operating nuclear power plants, of which the great majority were either boiling-water reactors or pressurised-water reactors.

Oil, almost entirely imported, meets over half of Japan's energy needs. In 1991 Japan imported over 220 million kilolitres. In 1990 imports came from the United Arab Emirates (20.9 per cent), Saudi Arabia (17.8 per cent), Iran (9.8 per cent), other Middle Eastern countries (23 per cent), Indonesia (12.2 per cent) China (6.9 per cent) and others (9.4 per cent). Coal, again largely imported as Japanese production of coal in 1990 was just under 8 million tons, while imports amounted to over 110 million tons, largely from the USA and Australia, met under 20 per cent of Japan's energy requirements. Natural gas, again almost entirely imported, for example, from Brunei, met some 10 per cent of Japan's energy needs.

Water for private homes is generally supplied by municipalities, and for industry by prefectures. Sewage and drains are matters for local authorities but standards have not yet reached those of other developed countries.

Telecommunications utilities are controlled by the Ministry of Posts and Telecommunications (*Yūseishō*). The main network is run by Nippon Telegraph and Telephone (NTT – *Nihon Denshin Denwa*). NTT has been partially privatised and some limited competition has been permitted. International telecommunications were monopolised until recently by *Kokusai Denshin Denwa* or (KDD), a public company with private shareholders. Again, controlled competition has been allowed in recent years.

7.3 BUSINESS ORGANIZATIONS

There are four major business organizations in Japan, which exercise considerable power behind the scenes. This is partly due to the seniority and prestige of the participants but also to the fact that business is a major source of political funding.

Keidanren (The Federation of Economic Organizations)

Keidanren is generally regarded as the most important of the four and as the most influential non-governmental organization in Japan. Its chairman is always a respected industrial figure who is or has been president or chairman of a major industrial company. Its vice-chairmen are of equal stature. Over 100 industry-wide groups, representing all forms of industry, commerce and banking together with over 800 of Japan's major corporations belong to Keidanren.

Its main function is to unify industrial opinion and liaise with the government on policies affecting business. It thus acts as the spokesman for business interests. It also represents Japanese business in international fora. It collects and distributes funds for various educational and other charitable purposes approved by Japanese business. It has a large number of high level committees.

Nikkeiren (The Japan Federation of Employers' Organizations)

Nikkeiren concentrates on relations between management and labour. It has an important role in determining general wage policy and tactics in the annual 'struggles' over wage levels during the so-called *Shuntō* (spring struggle). It represents Japanese business in discussions about labour policies.

Keizai Dōyūkai (The Japan Committee for Economic Development)

Keizai Dōyūkai has functions which overlap with those of *Keidanren*. It consists of a large number of Japanese businessmen. It aims to promote progress and stability in the Japanese economy and stresses the social responsibilities of business. It also promotes relations between business and academia. It has taken a particular interest in economic developments in South East Asia.

Nihon Shōkō Kaigisho (The Japan Chamber of Commerce and Industry)

This is the central organization of the nearly 500 Japanese regional chambers of commerce and industry. It takes a close interest in international trade. Japanese chambers of commerce and industry are actively supported by local businessmen, and their influence in local affairs is considerable. They act as spokesmen for local business interests and the chairman of the local chamber is usually a distinguished local businessman on good terms with mayors and Governors of prefectures.

Japanese businessmen are often Rotarians and Japanese Rotary clubs are influential bodies which try to promote international friendship. Many Japanese businessmen also belong to their local Lions club, which is similarly involved in international fellowship matters and community service.

7.3.1 The Japanese Company (*Kaisha*)

Japanese management practices have been widely praised and copied. Few are, however, strictly indigenous. One of the most important, namely quality control, was imported into Japan by the Americans who sent the quality control guru Edward Deming to Japan in 1950 to teach the Japanese its basic principles. The Japanese have simply perfected what they learnt.

Large Japanese companies have been mostly lifetime employment organizations where promotion to middle ranks has been largely by seniority. This has been changing especially in the recession of 1992/3. On-the-job training is an important feature of all such companies. They are, generally speaking, 'bottom-up' organizations, but there are some exceptions especially where the president is a strong and dictatorial personality (called in Japanese a 'one-man *shachō*' – or a 'one-man President').

An important feature of Japanese companies is the emphasis placed on the achievement of a consensus within the organisation. This is achieved by endless meetings and discussions called *nemawashi*, or 'going round the roots'. When an apparent consensus has been reached it is usually confirmed by all those involved, directly or indirectly, putting their *hanko* (a personal seal used by the Japanese instead of a signature) on a statement of what has been agreed. This commits them and the organization to the agreed policy and ensures that it is carried out with full support and due diligence. This process is called the *ringi* system.

Another important aspect of modern Japanese management is the *just-in-time* system, which among other things reduces to the minimum inventory costs. It also makes the relationship between a manufacturer and his suppliers particularly close. If a supplier lets a manufacturer down by failing to deliver the correct parts of the correct quality on time he may cause a major loss to the manufacturer. This inevitably means that Japanese manufacturers want to have very close relations with the small- and medium-scale manufacturers who are so often their major suppliers.

Ranks and their titles are an import element in management in a traditionally hierarchical society. The new recruit is called a *shinnyūshain*. After a few years in which he will have been moved round every two years or so to give him or her wide experience of the company the employee may be promoted to deputy section chief (*Kachōhosa*). The next step will be to section or division chief (*Kachō*) when the employee is in his thirties. Above this are departments (*Bu*) where the head of the department (*Buchō*) is an important manager. The lowest grade of board director is that of an ordinary director (*Torishimari-yaku* or *Jūyaku*). The next grade is that of managing director (*Jōmu – torishimariyaku* – sometimes simply referred to as *Jōmu*). From this the successful may be promoted to senior managing director (*Senmu-torishimariyaku* or *Senmu*). Then come the president's deputy or deputies (*Fukushacho*). The president (*Shachō*) is the company's chief executive but many presidents regard their prime role as being the selection of the best men to serve in managerial posts. The chairman of the board (*Kaichō*) is usually promoted to this post from that of president. His job tends to be more honorific than that of the company president and he may represent the company on prestigious occasions. Presidents and chairmen, on retirement from these posts, are appointed senior advisers (*Sōdanyaku*). Lesser figures in the company may be appointed as advisers (*Komon*) on retirement. The position of company auditor (*Kansayaku*) is also an important board-level post. Japanese boards rarely have outside, non-executive directors. Some Japanese companies no longer use these titles in English. Those companies with close American connections may instead use the term vice-president for anyone from a departmental chief upwards. In that case, in order to work out the person's seniority it may be necessary to find out what he is called in Japanese. Other companies make free use of the term 'manager'.

7.4 INDUSTRY

In 1990 Japan's GDP was approximately US$2940 billion. Japan's per capita GDP was US$23 801 (as compared with US$22 062 for the United States). Manufacturing industry represented about a third of Japan's GDP and approximately the same proportion of Japan's workforce is employed in secondary industry, which includes manufacturing. Some 52 per cent of Japanese manufacturing was performed by small- and medium-scale firms (employing less than 300 workers). The remaining 48 per cent was performed by large firms.

In 1991 the ten largest Japanese manufacturing companies in terms of sales were Toyota Motor, Hitachi, Matsushita Electric Industrial Company, Nissan Motor, Toshiba, Honda Motor, NEC (Nippon Electric Company), Sony, Mitsubishi Electric and New Japan Steel, in that order. Toyota had sales of just over half those of General Motors.

Japanese manufacturing industry covers all types of manufacturing. Most of its capital equipment is modern and sophisticated. At the end of 1990 Japan had over 270 000 robots in use in industry. The definition of a robot is not yet firm and the statistics may accordingly be open to question, but the Japanese figure under any definition was far higher than that of any other industrialised country. Japanese industry is also highly computerized. Japanese industry has been particularly strong in the production of motor vehicles and components. It has also been a major manufacturer of electrical and electronic products (from integrated circuits, computers, office equipment and consumer products to heavy electrical machinery) as well as of optical equipment. It has been strong in iron and steel production, in ship-building, in the manufacture of robots and machine tools, and other machinery, for example, construction equipment.

Japanese chemical companies have a firm home base, but do not compare in size with world leaders such as Du Pont. Japan has put considerable effort into developing an aircraft industry but cannot yet compete with the giants such as Boeing or Airbus Industries. Japan has forbidden the export of defence equipment but its Self-Defence Forces are equipped with sophisticated equipment largely made in Japan. Much of this is made under licence but Japanese defence equipment manufacturers, particularly Mitsubishi Heavy Industries, are major defence equipment producers. Japanese pharmaceutical companies have developed a number of new products but are not yet in the same league as the world pharmaceutical giants of North America or Europe. The Japanese textile industry was a major factor in Japan's economic recovery after the Second World War and it is still significant, especially in the production of synthetic fibres, but the textile industry generally has been facing growing competition from developing countries.

The following examples demonstrate both the size and the strength of Japanese industry as well as the problems which it faces:

(a) *Japanese production of* **iron and steel** in 1991 amounted to over 109 million tons. Of this, nearly 20 million tons were exported, against imports of just over 7 million tons. Over a quarter of Japan's iron and steel was produced by New Japan Steel (*Shinnihon seitetsu*). Other major steel producers were NKK (*Nippon Kōkan*), Kawasaki Steel, Sumitomo companies, and Kōbe Steel. Japan's iron and steel industry has up-to-date plants and modern technology, but it has to import almost all its raw materials, including iron ore and coking coal. Its main problems are the high cost of labour in Japan, import restrictions in major markets, and growing competition from developing countries. These factors have led to some restructuring of the industry, and companies such as New Japan Steel have begun to attempt diversification.

(b) In 1991 Japan produced 9.75 million **passenger cars** (US production was about 5.5 million). Approximately 4.45 million were exported. Japan imported only about 250 000 vehicles. Toyota Motor Corporation was significantly the largest Japanese manufacturer of automobiles, producing over 30 per cent of total Japanese production. The second-largest producer was Nissan, which produced 17 per cent of the total, followed by Honda, Mazda and Mitsubishi Motors which were each responsible for some 10 per cent of Japanese production. The rest were made by Suzuki, Isuzu, Fuji Heavy Industries, and Daihatsu. Domestic competition has been acute and is unlikely to diminish. World demand for automobiles has eased and the industry has had to exercise restraint on exports in the face of protectionist pressures abroad. It has also had to move manufacture from Japan into North America, Europe and other markets.

(c) In the 1960s and 1970s Japan became the world leader in **ship-building**, but the fall in demand for tankers following the two oil crises of the 1970s and the growing competition from Korea and other developing economies forced the industry to restructure. It has since recovered, not least because of the advanced methods employed by Japanese yards, but also because of the demand for more sophisticated ships. The five largest ship-building firms are Mitsubishi Heavy Industries, Ishikawajima-Harima Heavy Industries, Hitachi Zōsen (*zōsen* = ship-building), Mitsui Engineering and Shipbuilding, and Kawasaki Heavy Industries.

(d) The Japanese **electronics** industry has also grown at a phenomenal rate during the past quarter century. MITI had rightly targeted electronics as an area for growth, and encouraged competition and innovation. The electrical and electronics industries overlap. The main electrical manufacturers, who are also involved in electronics, are Hitachi, Toshiba and Mitsubishi Electric. The four top home electric/electronic manufacturers are Matsushita Electric Industrial Company, Sanyō Electric, Sony, and Sharp. The three most important manufacturers of telecommunications equipment are NEC (Nippon Electric), Fujitsu, and Oki Electric. The main Japanese computer manufacturers, apart from IBM (Japan), are Fujitsu, NEC, Hitachi, Mitsubishi Electric, and Oki Electric. Japanese companies have made great efforts to develop and produce VLSIs and microcomputers. They have foreseen and taken advantage of the trend towards miniaturisation of electronic products and of the development of optical fibres. They are hoping that high definition television (HDTV) will provide major openings in the future but the difficulty so far has been to bring down the cost of production so that sets can be provided at a price which the public can afford. There will also be the problem of the different standards which the various areas of the world decide to adopt. Among other problems that the industry faces is the intense domestic competition between Japanese manufacturers, the cost of constantly developing and producing new products which will appeal to the consumer, protectionism abroad and wage costs at home. The latter two factors have been instrumental in persuading many of the companies to invest in production facilities abroad.

7.4.1 Research and Development (R&D)

Japanese industrial success owes much to the emphasis placed by Japanese companies on research and development. In 1990 Japan spent over US$89 billion on research and development. This amounted to 3.51 per cent of Japan's national income; 16.5 per cent of this was funded from government sources. This compares with US expenditure on research and development in 1990 of some US$156 billion, which represented 3.26 per cent of national income. However in the US case 44.4 per cent was financed by public funds. Major companies such as NEC spend as much as 10 per cent of their sales revenue on R&D. In the past, Japan was a major importer of technology; technology exports have been increasing recently but Japan is still just a net importer of technology.

One of the main reasons for Japanese success in R&D has been the ability to exploit developments commercially. Another has been the number of engineers in industry and the important status accorded to them. Japan has also made good use of the information that it collects diligently throughout the world. Companies too have been willing to co-operate in research up to the pre-commercial development phase and there is a general consensus between industries and the government on areas on which to concentrate.

Hitherto most of Japan's R&D has been spent on the commercial application of technology and of scientific developments. In recent years a greater emphasis has been placed on basic research but fears have been expressed about the possibly stultifying effects on creativity of the Japanese educational system.

7.5 COMMERCE

The Japanese trading companies generally referred to as the *Sōgoshōsha* (that is, comprehensive trading companies) play a very important role in Japanese commerce, especially in relation to exports but also to imports. They are particularly strong in commodity trading. The large trading companies are, however, now much more than exporters and importers. They are widely involved in trade between third countries and are represented, often by large offices and subsidiary companies, in all major world markets. They are increasingly involved in services, including telecommunications, and are investing in activities abroad, including manufacturing enterprises, which they consider to provide opportunities for profit.

The nine Japanese *Sōgoshōsha* in 1991 had sales of ¥119 trillion. Of this total, 44.3 per cent consisted of sales in Japan, 13.1 per cent in exports, 16.8 per cent in imports into Japan, and 25.8 per cent in offshore trade. The order in terms of sales was as follows:

Itōchū (formerly C.Itōh)
Sumitomo Corporation (*Sumitomo shōji*)
Marubeni
Mitsui and Co. (*Mitsui bussan*)
Mitsubishi Corporation (*Mitsubishi shōji*)
Nisshō Iwai
Tōmen
Nichimen
Kanematsu

As a proportion of GNP, Japanese exports in 1991 of 9.3 per cent and imports of 7.0 per cent are on the low side by world standards.

7.5.1 Distribution and Retailing

The Japanese distribution system for consumer products generally involves a series of wholesalers and sub-wholesalers which add to the costs of distribution but which are geared to the large number of small retailers still existing in Japan. These remain influential with the LDP and are active in local chambers of commerce. Such 'mom and pop' neighbourhood stores are convenient, especially for the Japanese housewife who is accustomed to daily shopping, often necessitated by the lack of home space for storage.

This situation is gradually changing and the number of small- and medium-scale supermarkets is increasing. Lack of land on the outskirts of municipal areas and strong local opposition, led by smallshop-keepers, has so far meant that Japan has few of the sort of superstores or megastores to be found in the USA and Europe. This role is filled to some extent by the large comprehensive department stores to be found in all Japanese cities. Japanese department stores sell almost every type of consumer goods from food and clothing through all kinds of household goods to furniture, electronic goods and books.

Manufacturers of automobiles and electronic goods generally have their own exclusive outlets. Pharmaceuticals and cosmetics are usually sold through salesmen working exclusively for the manufacturer.

The largest retailers in Japan in 1990 in terms of sales were the supermarket chains of Daiei, Itō-Yōkadō, Seiyū and Jusco. The main department stores were Seibu, Mitsukoshi, Takashimaya, Daimaru, Sogo, Marui, Matsuzakaya, Isetan and Tōkyū. Of these, Mitsukoshi and Takashimaya regard themselves as the leaders in quality. The major chains like Mitsukoshi and Takashimaya have large branches in major cities with multi-storey garages attached to provide parking for customers. They include restaurants and teashops on their premises and are open six days a week. They choose one day other than Sunday as their rest day. Their hours of opening, usually from 10 a.m. to 7 p.m., are controlled by the authorities. Local shops may be open seven days a week from early in the morning to late at night. Department stores also arrange cultural events and exhibitions to attract customers into their stores. The department stores are prevented from major expansion by the need under the law to obtain permission to open new stores and by the way in which the granting of permission can be held up by the objections of local retailers.

7.5.2 Services

The provision of services has become an increasingly important segment of Japanese life and tertiary industry including services occupied nearly 60 per cent of the work force in 1991. The fastest growing service sectors in 1989 (according to the *Nihon Keizai Shimbun* (newspaper)) were in holiday resorts, baby-sitting, cable television, temporary employees, telephone marketing, golf club membership broking, hairdressing and beauty care, credit cards, real-estate broking and consumer finance services. The Japanese have always attached importance to personal service and Japan can be said to be becoming increasingly a service-oriented society. While the Japanese work ethic is still strong, particularly in large enterprises and among the older generation, it has weakened among the younger generation. Instead of, or in addition to work, Japanese people take their leisure activities seriously. The businessman's favourite leisure pursuit is golf, which is very expensive in Japan. Mahjong, bowling, *pachinko* (a mindless form of pin-ball gambling) and drinking in bars are also much patronised.

7.5.3 Overseas Investment

Direct investment by Japanese companies began to grow fairly slowly in the latter part of the 1960s, and it increased rapidly in the 1980s. The main locations of Japanese investment overseas have been America, Asia and Europe. This investment has been a significant factor in Japan's economic relations with foreign countries but, despite the attention given to it, Japanese investment overseas in 1990 was less than half of US investment and was less than that of the United Kingdom.

Direct foreign investment by Japan in manufacturing industry abroad amounted (as of March 1992) to nearly US$ 94 billion, with approximately half of the total in the USA, just under a quarter in Asia and about a sixth in Europe. Electronics represented about a quarter of the total, and vehicles, iron and non ferrous metals, and chemicals about an eighth each. Japanese investment in finance, insurance and commerce, that is, in the offices and activities of Japanese banks, insurance companies and trading companies came to over US$ 106 billion, a good deal more than direct investment in manufacturing. Within Europe the United Kingdom has been the most important location for Japanese direct foreign investment receiving over US$ 26.1 billion by 1991 out of a total in Europe of over US$ 68.6 billion by the same date. In Asia Japanese investment in Hong Kong reached almost US$ 10 billion by 1991. The other Asian countries with significant Japanese investment were Singapore, Thailand, Malaysia and Indonesia. Japanese investment in Australia, mainly in mining and property, had reached over US$ 18.6 billion by 1991.

It is estimated that over 1 120 000 people were employed in Japanese overseas investments in 1990. Nearly half of these were employed in Asian countries, over 353 000 in the USA, and 120 500 in Europe.

7.5.4 Industrial, Commercial and Financial Groupings: The *Keiretsu* System in Japan

The pre-war *zaibatsu* conglomerates were broken up by the Occupation authorities. They soon coalesced after the Occupation ended in 1952 but in a considerably looser form normally referred to as *keiretsu*.

Professor Imai Kenichi of Hitotsubashi University has described (in an article which appeared in *Japan Echo*, vol. XVII, no. 3 in 1990) the *keiretsu* as being basically 'a web of relationships, ranging from tight to loose, among companies working together. It represents a configuration that is less tight than that of an integrated corporation but tighter than that of autonomous companies in a text-book free market economy.' He also explains that 'Broadly described, there are two *keiretsu* types. The major groups that are referred to as the big six might be called the *zaibatsu* type, though they lack the centralized command structure of the former *zaibatsu*. Mitsui, Mitsubishi, and Sumitomo head the list as the direct offspring of three of the giant prewar combines. The other three are the groups centred on the Fuji, Sanwa and Daiichi Kangyō banks. The *zaibatsu* type groups are loosely affiliated and highly diversified. The members have business ties with each other and use the powerful bank in each group as their main bank.'

He refers to the second group as so-called independent *keiretsu* centring on a large business, usually a manufacturer, and more specialized than the *zaibatsu* type. He instances groups round Hitachi, Matsushita Electric Industrial, Toyota, NEC, and private railway companies such as Seibu. But many of these so-called independent groups in fact have close connections with one or more of the *zaibatsu*-type *keiretsu*. NEC is normally regarded as belonging to the Sumitomo group. Hitachi has loose connections with the DKB, Sanwa and Fuyō groups (the Fuyō Group is the group surrounding Fuji Bank). Matsushita has connections with the Sumitomo group. Toyota has close financial connections with the Mitsui group through the Sakura Bank and with Tōkai Bank, which is the main city bank in the Nagoya area, where Toyota has its headquarters and main operations. Seibu has connections with the DKB Group. The Industrial Bank of Japan (IBJ) and Tōkai Bank also have groups of companies with which they have close connections. The web is highly complex and cannot be described in any detail here. The fullest survey in English of the *keiretsu* is to be found in *Industrial Groupings in Japan* published on a regular basis by Dodwell Marketing Consultants who are part of the Inchcape Group.

Companies in a *keiretsu* are connected by cross-shareholdings, by group loyalties and by informal but regular meetings of senior executives. Companies within a group may, and frequently do, compete with one another, especially on the margin. Although the Mitsubishi group is considered to be one of the most closely-knit groups, Mitsubishi Bank and Mitsubishi Trust and Banking Corporation have been known to compete against one another. Moreover Mitsubishi Bank is close to Nippon Trust Bank, which is a competitor of Mitsubishi Trust and Banking Corporation.

Members of the various groups belong to informal associations which organise regular meetings. Mitsubishi group company presidents and chairmen meet regularly on Fridays. So their group is called the *Kinyōkai* or Friday group. Mitsui group companies belong to the *Nimokukai* while Sumitomo companies belong to the *Hakusuikai*. The Fuji Bank's group is the *Fuyōkai* and includes the former Yasuda *zaibatsu* companies. Daiichi Kangyō Bank (DKB) companies belong to the *Sankinkai*. The DKB group includes the Furukawa and Kawasaki sub-groups. Sanwa Bank group companies which have only loose ties belong to either the *Sansuikai* or/and the *Midorikai/Cloverkai*.

In some of the groups a trading company plays an important central role. This is particularly the case with Mitsubishi Corporation and Mitsui and Company, and to a lesser extent Sumitomo Corporation. Itōchū and Kanematsu belong to the DKB group. Marubeni is the main trading company in the Fuyō group. Nisshō Iwai and Nichimen are connected with the Sanwa Bank group. Tōmen (*Tōyō menka*) is close to Tōkai Bank.

Banks are not allowed to hold more than 5 per cent of the shares in any single company and most cross-shareholdings are rarely more than 5 per cent. Dodwells estimate that cross-shareholding of shares was most prevalent in the Mitsubishi group but even so only some 21.9 per cent were crossheld in the fiscal year 1987. The amount of shares crossheld in the other main groups were Sumitomo 21.3 per cent, Mitsui 17.8 per cent, Fuyō 17.5 per cent, DKB Group 15.4 per cent, and Sanwa Bank Group 13.9 per cent. Despite the relatively small proportion of shares crossheld, Japanese companies have a generally stable share-ownership base because the shares held by insurance companies and other financial institutions are rarely traded.

Although appointments to senior positions in *keiretsu* companies are usually made autonomously, the views of senior people in other groups may be taken into account. Ties between companies are fostered by occasional appointments to other group companies. Finance, information and general mutual support, however, provide the main way in which group ties are cemented. This underlines the role of the main bank in each group.

It is inevitable and understandable that companies within groups will turn to other group companies when needing products made by these other companies. Personal relationships, simplicity and reliability all play a part in this. Group loyalties also mean that company employees will generally drink the beers made by the group brewery (if there is one) and drive automobiles made by the motor manufacturer in, or closest to, the group.

The Americans have criticised the *keiretsu* system as a barrier to foreign suppliers and an unfair trading practice. The Japanese are inclined to retort that a similar accusation could be made against arrangements in an integrated company which will not buy parts from outside if they are also made within the company, even if the parts from outside are cheaper and of equal quality. The *keiretsu* system is at least more flexible. There are also increasing signs of a loosening up of the structure and relationships within *keiretsu* groups.

It is not possible to list here all the major companies in each of the groups but the following are some of the most important companies in the six main groups.

Mitsubishi Group

Mitsubishi Bank, Mitsubishi Trust and Banking Corporation, Mitsubishi Corporation, Mitsubishi Heavy Industries, Mitsubishi Real Estate and almost all other companies with the name Mitsubishi in their titles (Mitsubishi Pencils is independent) belong to the Mitsubishi Group and the *Kinyōkai*. Other companies in the group include Meiji Mutual Life Insurance, Tokio Marine and Fire Insurance, Kirin Breweries, Asahi Glass, Tōyō Engineering and Nippon Yūsen Kaisha (NYK) (the first Mitsubishi Company, established in the nineteenth century by Iwasaki Yataro and which is now the leading Japanese shipping company).

Mitsui Group

Mitsui and Co. (*Mitsui Bussan*), Sakura Bank (formerly Mitsui Taiyō Kōbe Bank), and Mitsui Real Estate are key Mitsui group companies. Other important companies in the group include Mitsui Trust and Banking Company, Mitsui OSK (shipping), Mitsui Engineering and Ship-building, Mitsui Mining, Mitsui Petrochemicals, Mitsui Mutual Life Insurance, Mitsui Fire and Marine Insurance (formerly Taishō Fire and Marine), Tōray Industries, Ōji Paper, and Mitsukoshi Ltd (department store group). Mitsukoshi was the original Mitsui Company, established in the seventeenth century under the name Echigoya which sold kimono material in Edo, the old name for Tokyo. Toshiba is also usually counted as being a Mitsui group company and Toyota has close connections with the group.

Sumitomo Group

Sumitomo Bank, Sumitomo Chemicals, and Sumitomo Metal Industries are considered to be the three leading Sumitomo companies, but Sumitomo Corporation, Sumitomo Trust and Banking Corporation, Sumitomo Life Insurance, Sumitomo Marine and Fire Insurance, Sumitomo Denko (electric industries), Sumitomo Heavy Industries, and Sumitomo Rubber (which took over Dunlop) are all important Sumitomo group companies. NEC (Nippon Electric Company) is also counted as a Sumitomo group company despite its huge size and the fact that there is a separate group of NEC companies.

Fuyō Group

Fuji Bank is the central company in the group. In the financial area the main Fuyō group companies are Yasuda Trust and Banking Company, Yasuda Mutual Life Insurance, and Yasuda Fire and Marine Insurance. Marubeni is the main Fuyō group trading company. Other important Fuyō group companies include Nippon Kōkan (NKK) (steel and ship-building), Taisei Corporation (construction), Canon (optical and office machinery). Nippon Seikō (ball-bearings), Oki Electric, Yokogawa Hokushin Electric, Tōbu and Keihin private railways, Sapporo Breweries, Nisshin Flour Milling, Shōwa Denkō (chemicals), and Kubota Ltd (construction machinery).

Daiichi Kangyō (DKB) Group

Apart from DKB itself the most important company is Itōchū. In the Kawasaki sub-group are Kawasaki Steel, Kawasaki Heavy Industries and Kawasaki Kisen (shipping). In the Furukawa sub-group are Fuji Electric, Fujitsu, Furukawa Company, Yokohama Rubber, Taisei Fire and Marine Insurance, and Asahi Mutual Life Insurance. Other DKB group companies include Fukoku Mutual Life Insurance, Kanematsu (trading), Shiseidō (cosmetics), Yaskawa Electric, Shimizu Construction, and Isuzu Motors. The group has close connections with the Meiji Group which includes Meiji Seika and Meiji Milk. Companies with affiliations to DKB include Hitachi Ltd, Ebara Corporation, Asahi Chemical, and Shōwa Shell Sekiyū.

Sanwa Bank Group

This is a loose grouping round Sanwa Bank. The following are among the members of both the Sansuikai and Midorikai (Cloverkai): Nisshō

Iwai (trading), Nichimen (trading), Hitachi Ltd (which also has connections with DKB), Kōbe Steel, Daihatsu Motors, Hitachi Zōsen (ship-building), Suntory Ltd (an unlisted company making whisky, beer, soft drinks, etc.), Kansai Paint, Fujisawa Pharmaceutical Co., Ube Industries, Hankyū Corporation (private railway and department store group), Tōyō Trust and Banking Company, Teijin Ltd (textiles), Unitika Ltd (textiles). Sharp Corporation (electronics) and Kyocera (industrial ceramics) belong to Sansuikai only.

Figures 7.1 and 7.2 are taken from Dodwell's *Industrial Groupings in Japan* and illustrate the relationships in two of the main groups (Fuyō and DKB).

7.5.5 Reasons for Japan's Industrial Successes

Various factors have contributed to Japan's post-war industrial success. Some of the more important have been:

1. **Loyalty.** In Japan, loyalty has traditionally been a highly prized virtue. If a Japanese is asked what he does he is more likely to reply that he works for such and such a company than to describe himself as a manager or an engineer. Japanese people have also been brought up to believe that there is something special in being Japanese.
2. **The work ethic.** Traditionally Japanese have attached much merit to hard work. One reason for this derives from Japan's agricultural society where every tiny patch of ground had to be made to produce as much food as possible to feed a population living in a largely mountainous country. The poverty which prevailed in Japan before the Second World War and in the post-war years reinforced the work ethic.
3. **Hierarchy.** Age and seniority should in Confucian thinking be respected. Japanese society has been strictly hierarchical. This has been an important element in the paternalism which marks many Japanese companies. Promotion, at least in the first decade of an employee's career, is generally made on the basis of seniority. As the employee climbs up the ladder he earns a higher salary, status and appropriate perks.
4. **Consensus.** The importance attached in Japan to consensus means that once a decision has been approved by all concerned it is carried out quickly and efficiently.

132

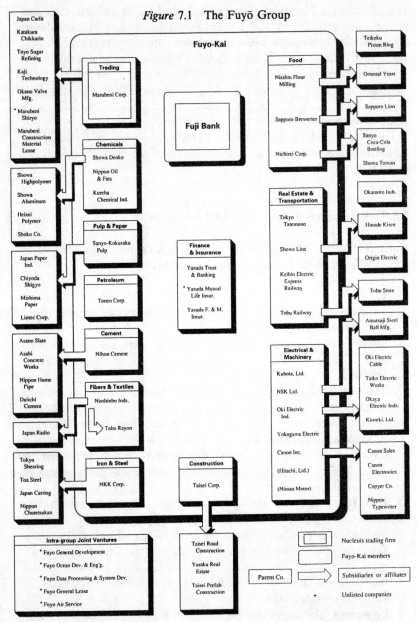

Figure 7.1   The Fuyō Group

Source: *Industrial Groupings in Japan* (Dodwell Marketing Consultants, Tokyo).

Figure 7.2 The DKB Group

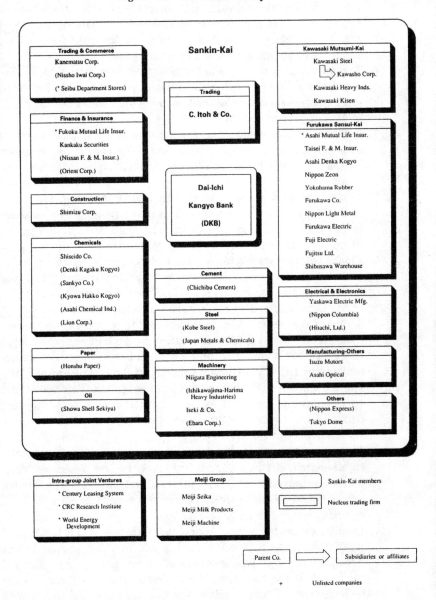

Trading & Commerce
Kanematsu Corp.
(Nissho Iwai Corp.)
(* Seibu Department Stores)

Finance & Insurance
* Fukoku Mutual Life Insur.
Kankaku Securities
(Nissan F. & M. Insur.)
(Orient Corp.)

Construction
Shimizu Corp.

Chemicals
Shiseido Co.
(Denki Kagaku Kogyo)
(Sankyo Co.)
(Kyowa Hakko Kogyo)
(Asahi Chemical Ind.)
(Lion Corp.)

Paper
(Honshu Paper)

Oil
(Showa Shell Sekiyu)

Sankin-Kai

Trading
C. Itoh & Co.

Dai-Ichi
Kangyo Bank
(DKB)

Cement
(Chichibu Cement)

Steel
(Kobe Steel)
(Japan Metals & Chemicals)

Machinery
Niigata Engineering
(Ishikawajima-Harima Heavy Industries)
Iseki & Co.
(Ebara Corp.)

Kawasaki Mutsumi-Kai
Kawasaki Steel
Kawasho Corp.
Kawasaki Heavy Inds.
Kawasaki Kisen

Furukawa Sansui-Kai
* Asahi Mutual Life Insur.
Taisei F. & M. Insur.
Asahi Denka Kogyo
Nippon Zeon
Yokohama Rubber
Furukawa Co.
Nippon Light Metal
Furukawa Electric
Fuji Electric
Fujitsu Ltd.
Shibusawa Warehouse

Electrical & Electronics
Yaskawa Electric Mfg.
(Nippon Columbia)
(Hitachi, Ltd.)

Manufacturing-Others
Isuzu Motors
Asahi Optical

Others
(Nippon Express)
Tokyo Dome

Intra-group Joint Ventures
* Century Leasing System
* CRC Research Institute
* World Energy Development

Meiji Group
Meiji Seika
Meiji Milk Products
Meiji Machine

☐ Sankin-Kai members

▭ Nucleus trading firm

Parent Co. ⟹ Subsidiaries or affiliates

+ Unlisted companies

Source: *Industrial Groupings in Japan* (Dodwell Marketing Consultants, Tokyo).

5. **Union attitudes**. In Japan unions are *labour* not trade unions. Most unions in private industry are company unions. Many senior managers have in their time served as union officials. Management and labour accordingly tend to have similar attitudes and are prepared to co-operate for the common good.

6. **Training**. Japanese companies attach great importance to on-the-job training. Workers in large companies generally remain with the same company throughout their working life and are usually ready to change jobs as needed.

7. **Attitude towards engineering and technology**. In Japan engineers and technically trained people are respected and in many companies senior posts are filled by trained engineers or technologists.

8. **Profits and market share**. The profit motive is strong, but many companies have put their main efforts into expanding market share in the belief that a significant market share will strengthen the company and in the end improve profitability.

9. **Employees and shareholders**. If asked to give their priorities in deciding policy most Japanese managements would put the interests of the company, that is, of the employees above those of the shareholder. Dividends have traditionally been kept low in the belief that shareholders would benefit from rising stock market prices. The bursting of the Japanese economic bubble has shattered this belief, but a large part of the shares of most major companies are held by friendly institutions mainly in the same *keiretsu* group and the amount of freely available stock is limited. This means that so long as the company is growing sufficiently to satisfy the financial institutions in the group the interests of the minority shareholders can be safely ignored.

10. **'Long termism'**. As major Japanese companies have a generally stable shareholder base and limited number of major shareholders, take-over bids are extremely rare and management can take a longer-term view of company policies than might be possible for a company which fears a take-over bid.

11. **Quality**. Before the Second World War Japanese goods had a poor reputation. They were often shoddy and of poor quality. Under American tutelage Japanese manufacturers have totally changed the image of their products. Great importance is attached to the maintenance of high quality. Quality circles (QCs) have been established in most companies and all employees take part in the quality process.

12. **Lean production.** Japanese companies have relentlessly pursued improvements in production methods. They have invested significantly in robots. Costs have at the same time been minimised by reducing stocks to the minimum through the 'just-in-time' (JIT) system. Suppliers of parts have to maintain strict delivery times as well as quality control.

13. **Research and development.** Japanese companies have invested heavily in research and development with the aim of keeping ahead of market demand. Improvements are constantly sought, not only in the products themselves but also in the system of manufacture.

14. **Marketing.** The successful Japanese company pays careful attention to market research and market strategy. The key to success is seen as lying in the anticipation of demand. Japanese companies are often willing to submit tenders which will have to be filled at a loss if by so doing they can gain a foothold in a market.

15. **Financing.** In the past Japanese companies have had access to cheap finance through bank loans and through the stock market (particularly via warrant issues). This is no longer the situation.

16. **Savings.** Japan's savings rates have traditionally been high. These have been boosted by post-war poverty, the need to save for housing, education and old age; government incentives, particularly through postal savings rates; and the tradition of paying two annual bonuses at year end (winter) (*seibo*) and mid-year (summer) (*chūgen*). These bonuses may amount to three or more months' salary on each occasion.

17. **Relations between government and industry.** Relations between government on the one hand and commerce and industry on the other have traditionally been close and the system of *amakudari* ('descent from heaven') by which industry and commerce take able civil servants into senior positions when they are still in their prime means that it is relatively easy to achieve a consensus between government and industry on what should be done in any given situation.

18. **Protectionist measures.** The Japanese government took strict protectionist steps while Japanese industry was growing in the post-war years and only relaxed tariff and non-tariff barriers when Japanese companies were strong and had already sewn up most of the best retail outlets.

19. **Competition.** Competition between Japanese companies was actively encouraged to ensure maximum efficiency.

20. **The human element**. Japanese managers often assert that their success stems largely from the emphasis placed in Japanese companies on man-management and good human relations through the maintenance of harmony (*wa*).

There are, however, a number of real weaknesses in the Japanese system. Some of these are:

(a) **Exploitation of traditional attitudes**. Japanese managements may think that they pay proper attention to man-management, but this can be questioned. Many appointments are made without sufficient attention being given to family and other circumstances. An employee is expected to put his company above his family. Many appointments are made without adequate notice being given.

(b) **Misuse of womanpower**. The majority of female employees in Japanese companies are used in menial tasks such as acting as receptionists and providing tea to visitors. Many qualified Japanese women are inefficiently employed and suffer discrimination at work.

(c) **Inadequate holidays and leisure time**. Japanese companies generally give very limited holidays and employees are not encouraged to take their full entitlement. There have been reports of deaths through overwork (*karōshi*).

(d) **Wasted office time**. In many offices far too much time seems to be expended on meetings designed to reach a consensus. This leads to delays in decision-making. Much time is wasted on maintaining contacts.

(e) **Bureaucratic procedures**. Many large companies have become over-bureaucratic in their procedures.

(f) **Loss of entrepreneurship**. The emphasis on consensus and loyalty can lead to a loss of the entrepreneurial spirit.

(g) **Inefficient and costly distribution systems**. Protectionism has been damaging to efficiency by protecting inefficient parts of the Japanese economy, particularly in distribution and retailing.

Japanese industry and commerce deserve respect for their successes. But Japanese super-efficiency is a myth.

7.5.6 Doing Business in Japan

Many books have been written for foreigners about how to do business in Japan. The following comments are not intended as a substitute but only as an introduction to the subject.

Three key requirements for anyone wanting to do business in Japan are **patience, persistence** and **consistency.** No one can expect to break into the Japanese market in one fell swoop. The exporter must be patient and persistent possibly over a number of years. Constant changing of tactics and channels is also damaging. Hence the need for a consistent approach.

Some important points to bear in mind are:

1. Study the market carefully and do all necessary homework before starting.
2. Ensure that brand names, trademarks, patents, copyrights and designs are properly registered and protected.
3. Never forget the importance of quality and the provision of adequate servicing.
4. Stick firmly to promised delivery times and proposed prices.
5. Follow up on all personal contacts and keep in touch afterwards.
6. Never take Japanese associates for granted.
7. In negotiations be patient, firm and straightforward. Never lose your temper.
8. Remember that most Japanese businesses are 'bottom-up' in decision-making. So do not expect to break a deadlock by reaching an understanding with the president of the company. *All* must be convinced before a deal can be counted as firm.
9. Speak clearly without using jargon even when using a good interpreter. Interpreting is a difficult task even for the expert. Remember that Japanese is often an imprecise language.
10. Try always to be polite and restrained. Mistakes in etiquette will be forgiven to anyone who is generally tactful and polite

8 Agriculture and Infrastructure

8.1 AGRICULTURE

Since the end of the Second World War the population engaged in primary industry has fallen dramatically. In 1950, it has been estimated, the proportion was 48.3 per cent. In 1991 the proportion engaged in primary industry had fallen to 6.7 per cent. And the agricultural population (in 1990) was about 4 million but only about 600 000, or just under 14.5 per cent were engaged exclusively in farming. Agriculture has for a large part become a part-time occupation and many Japanese refer to such farmers as Sunday farmers. By 1990, agriculture was only providing some 1.8 per cent of Japan's GDP.

Most farmers cultivate very small plots. In 1989, leaving aside Hokkaidō, where average plots are considerably larger because of the nature of the terrain and of the amount of land devoted to dairy farming, 1.675 million farmers had plots of less than half a hectare, and 1.16 million had plots of between a half and one hectare. Only 135 000 had plots of over 3 hectares.

The small size of Japanese farms is mainly due to the post-war land reform which destroyed the old tenant-farming system whereby large numbers of small peasants rented land from (often absentee) landlords. The peasants were enabled to purchase the land which they had cultivated for prices which were little more than nominal. Strict restrictions were placed on the amount of land that could be rented or purchased to increase the size of holdings. These restrictions have since been relaxed but the average size of holdings has not increased significantly. Holdings have also been protected by favourable treatment of farmland for inheritance tax purposes.

The small farmers have been determined to hang on to the land which traditionally they have cultivated and now own. The LDP found in the small farmers an instinctively conservative group and have made every effort to keep the farming communities happy by protecting and promoting their interests. This has meant that the rural communities provide the LDP with one of its most secure political bases.

138

Another factor that has influenced the size of Japanese farms has been the Japanese terrain and the crops which farmers have traditionally cultivated. Apart from a limited number of plains, for example, in the Kantō area, most of Japan is mountainous and the mountains rise steeply. Total agricultural land amounts to only 5.3 million hectares (less than a third of the agricultural land in the United Kingdom).

The main Japanese crop has traditionally been wet rice. This requires intensive cultivation, especially in mountainous areas where rice fields have to be terraced. Water supplies are vital and must be shared fairly. This in turn has forced small farmers to co-operate and work together.

In recent decades Japanese farmers have had access to or owned increasing quantities of farm machinery including tractors and cultivators, and Japanese agriculture can now be considered largely mechanized. However, owing to the general terrain and the size of farms most machinery has been small-scale. Even in the plains many farmers have small plots which are split into non-contiguous sections. Efforts have been made to rationalise such plots, but with only limited success.

In the early post-war years the main fertiliser available to Japanese farmers was human excrement. Now this has largely been replaced by chemical fertilisers.

Japan has had to import increasing quantities of foodstuffs to feed the Japanese population which is now over 125 million. But the farmers have demanded that Japan should do everything possible to maintain self-sufficiency at least in staple foods. In 1990 Japan was reckoned to be 70 per cent self-sufficient in all foodstuffs, with 100 per cent self-sufficiency in rice (imports have been totally banned), 98 per cent in eggs and 91 per cent in vegetables. Self-sufficiency in meat and dairy products was 72 per cent; in fruit, 67 per cent. Most wheat, barley and pulses are imported.

Japanese imports of foodstuffs in 1990 were less than those of the former West Germany, but some 25 per cent more than the United Kingdom. (Bearing in mind the difference in the population of Japan and the United Kingdom, Japan imported considerably less food per head than did the United Kingdom.) The largest supplier of foodstuffs to the Japanese market was the USA, from which in 1989 33.2 per cent of Japan's food imports came. Australia supplied 6.5 per cent and Canada 4.9 per cent. Other major suppliers were Taiwan, China, South Korea and Thailand.

Japanese production of rice, despite the decline in farm-workers, increased from about 8.6 million tonnes in 1950 to 11.6 million tonnes in 1985. The resulting over-supply and the burden of subsidies forced the government to try to persuade farmers to reduce the area under cultivation. Consumption of rice in 1990 was approximately 10.5 million tonnes.

In the 1950s rice was in short supply and rationed. All rice was procured by the government and sold at fixed prices to the public through licensed dealers. The central rice purchasing system has been continued despite the over-supply. The system of price controls and the prohibition of imports was used as a way of subsidising the farmers at a considerable cost to the tax-payer and the consumer. The consumer price of rice in Japan is now estimated to be up to seven times the world price. This and the imbalance in trade with the USA has led to increased pressure on the Japanese government to move, even if only gradually, towards some liberalization of rice imports. The farmers and the Ministry of Agriculture have, however, opposed vigorously any such move.

The Japanese diet has changed significantly since Japan became more prosperous. In particular there has been a rise in the consumption of meat and dairy products, although consumption is still low by Western standards. In 1989 it was estimated that the average calorie intake of the Japanese was 2909 kcals against the US average (1985) of 3644 kcals. Japanese eat much more cereal than Americans and considerably less sugar (just over a quarter of the American average), less than a quarter of the meat, and under a third of the dairy products. On the other hand, the Japanese consumed about five times as much fish per head as the average American and rather more vegetables.

8.1.1 Ministry of Agriculture, Forestry and Fisheries (*Nōrin Suisanshō* or *Nōrinshō*)

The Ministry is responsible for the protection and promotion of Japanese agriculture, forestry and fisheries. It has the reputation of being among the most protectionist of all Japanese government ministries.

The Ministry has made great efforts to improve the quality and quantity of Japanese agricultural production. Agricultural research stations, which can be found in all prefectures with significant agricultural communities, have developed strains of rice that can withstand cooler-than-average summers and are more resistant to disease. Japanese fruits have been developed to suit Japanese climatic conditions and Japanese tastes (for example, apples, peaches and grapes). The results of this research are passed on to farmers who are also given valuable guidance on how to improve their productivity.

The Ministry is responsible for setting standards and inspecting crops. It also supervises food markets and determines which fertilisers and farm chemicals can be used. It sets strictly limited quotas for the import of farm products which have not yet been liberalized, for example, dairy products. It fought hard against liberalization of oranges and meat, to protect Japanese producers of *mikan* (a form of tangerine) and Japan's small meat-producers who in many cases have only a few head of cattle, but was eventually forced by American pressure to agree to gradual liberalization accompanied by high, if declining, tariffs. It is debatable how far Japanese producers have suffered so far as a result of this liberalization. Certainly, the highest-quality producers have continued to be able to sell their products (*mikan* and beef) at a premium because these appeal to Japanese tastes. The lower end of the market has been more affected.

The Food Agency (*Shokuryōchō*), which is in charge of the inspection of all agricultural products comes under the Ministry. It sets the prices of many food products.

8.1.2 Agricultural Co-operative Associations (*Nōgyō kyōdō kumiai* or *Nōkyō*)

In 1947, during the Occupation of Japan, agricultural co-operatives were encouraged. Their task was to help farmers to work together and so make better use of their small plots of land, for example, through joint purchasing of seeds, fertilisers and equipment and joint selling of produce.

The co-operatives have grown from strength to strength and have done much to increase the prosperity of farmers. They now represent some of the wealthiest organizations in the country. Many have impressive buildings and are influential in local and central politics.

The co-operatives are organized in three tiers: local, prefectural and national. The national organisation is called *Zenkoku nōgyō kumiai chū-ōkai*. Within the organization are various specialist co-operatives for particular product areas. Their banking arm is *Nōrinchūkin* which has one of the strongest deposit bases of any banking institution in Japan.

8.1.3 Forestry

Nearly 70 per cent of the total area of Japan is woodland. As so much of Japan is steeply mountainous, forests are important in preventing erosion as a result of Japan's heavy rainfall.

Japan contains many varieties of trees and shrubs but most cultivated Japanese forests (about 40 per cent of total woodland) consist of evergreens (cedar, cypress and pines). Despite the extent of Japanese forests Japan only produced some 31.3 million cubic metres of wood in 1990 and had a self-sufficiency rate of 26.4 per cent. Japanese imports of lumber in 1991 amounted to nearly 36 million cubic metres.

Responsibility for the management of Japan's forests, for development of forestry and for inspection of timber products rests with the Forestry Agency (*Rinnōchō*), which comes under the Ministry of Agriculture.

8.1.4 Fisheries

Fish remains an important element in the Japanese diet, providing over 40 per cent of the average Japanese daily protein intake.

Japanese fish catches have been larger than those of the former USSR and of any other single country. The average annual catch by Japanese fishermen is over 12 million tonnes. A large part of this has come from coastal waters and the seas near Japan. The catch of larger vessels operating at a distance from Japan has decreased in recent years. One reason for the decrease has been the adoption of 200-mile fishery zones by various foreign countries and the limits imposed on Japanese fishing by Russia and North America. The catch of offshore and coastal fishing has meanwhile increased and there has been a significant growth in fish-farming. Japanese fishermen make use of trawling, drift-netting, longline angling and purse-seining.

Employment in fishing, as in agriculture, has been declining and in 1990 there were only some 371 000 people engaged in fisheries. Of these, just under 70 per cent were independent fishermen. At the end of 1990 there were 416 000 'fishing vessels', that is, more than one per fisherman. Some 95 per cent had motors and the total tonnage was just over 2.6 million tonnes.

Japanese attach a great deal of importance to fish being fresh, as much fish (especially tuna and various white fish) is consumed raw as *sashimi* or in *sushi* (raw fish on portions of packed rice). But the

Japanese like all types of fish including shellfish. Oysters are cultivated for food and for pearls.

Japan would like to see the resumption of commercial whaling and argues that stocks have now risen to the extent needed to justify this. A few Japanese fishing communities had come to rely on whaling for their living. Some Japanese regard whale meat, especially the tail, as a delicacy and an important source of animal fat.

Large Japanese fishing companies include Nippon Suisan, Taiyō Fishery, Nichiro, Kyokuyō and Hoko Fishing.

The promotion and protection of fisheries has been the main task of the Fisheries Agency (*Suisanchō*) which comes under the Ministry of Agriculture, Forestry and Fisheries. The agency deals with the improvement of fisheries resources, repair and maintenance of fishing ports, and the licensing of all inland and coastal fishing. It also carries out research into fishery resources and cultivation.

Like Japanese farmers Japanese fishermen have been greatly helped by the Co-operatives (*Gyogyō kyōdō kumiai*) which have developed in Japanese fishing ports.

8.2   CONSTRUCTION AND HOUSING

8.2.1   The Ministry of Construction (*Kensetsushō*)

The Ministry of Construction is responsible for civil engineering and public works construction. For this reason it is targeted by parliamentarians aiming to get construction projects in their constituencies.

The Ministry has five bureaux. The Planning bureau is responsible for plans covering the use of land, and building works at central, regional and local level. It is also responsible for supervising the Japanese construction industry. The City bureau deals with urban planning and renewal including improvements, development, conservation and construction. The Rivers bureau is responsible *inter alia* for the construction of dams and river embankments to prevent flooding. It also deals with similar problems in coastal areas. The Road bureau deals with road construction and maintenance. The Housing bureau is in charge of housing projects. The Ministry of Construction supervises the Housing and Urban Development Corporation (*Jūtaku toshi seibikōdan*) and the Japan Highway Public Corporation (*Nihon dōrōkōdan*).

8.2.2 Housing

The Housing and Urban Development Corporation is a non-profit making body charged with speeding up the supply of housing and residential land. It has been responsible for the construction of housing units in urban areas, both for sale and for rent. Rents are set to ensure that the corporation covers its costs of construction and funding, and are thus not subsidized.

Housing in Japan is expensive and much of it cramped by European and North American standards. Many workers live in apartments which were described by Sir Roy Denman of the European Commission as 'rabbit hutches'. But improvements have been made and the better flats, termed in Japanese 'mansions', can be luxurious if still on the small side. The government aims to increase the average space in Japanese homes from some 89 square metres to 100 square metres by the year 2000.

In 1988 61.4 per cent of Japanese people lived in housing which they owned outright or were purchasing with a mortgage; 37.2 per cent lived in rented accommodation (25.7 per cent were in private rented accommodation). Many companies in Japan provide apartments and dormitories for staff, especially if and when their jobs require them to move to another location inside Japan. Many move as temporary bachelors (*tanshin funin*) because of housing problems and the need for continuity in childrens' education. Japanese posted abroad receive help in meeting rental costs.

In 1988 over 37 per cent of Japanese owning a family house and over 71 per cent of those owning an apartment were repaying housing loans at an average rate of ¥70 000 to ¥80 000 a month. In addition they paid an average of over ¥12 000 yen in service/maintenance charges. Rental costs were lower. Average rentals were ¥49 000 for a house; ¥38 300 for housing from the Housing and Development Corporation; ¥21 200 for company housing and ¥20 500 for municipal or prefectural housing.

Land costs have been very high and remain high despite the pricking of the asset price bubble in 1991 and 1992. It has been estimated that land cost twice as much as the costs of construction in the suburbs of Tokyo. Residential land in Tokyo costs much more than in any other city. In 1990, say the cost of land in Tokyo was 100, the cost in the Osaka area was 54.7. In Chiba prefecture, in the neighbourhood of Tokyo, the figure was 35.6, and in Saitama, also near Tokyo, 31.2. As a result, workers in Tokyo have had to move some way out in order to be able to afford housing and this has meant very long commuting times. The average daily commuting time in Tokyo was over 1 ½ hours and many commute for much longer periods in rush-hour trains which are crammed to capacity. Dormitory suburbs, called in Japan 'bed-towns', surround Tokyo in a wide belt through the Kantō plain.

One reason for the high prices for residential land and the distances people have to commute is the existence in many urban areas of pockets of agricultural land. Farmers do not want to sell for development because of the capital gains and inheritance tax burden which they would have to accept, and the government is unwilling to take on the farm lobby in an attempt to find ways round this problem.

8.2.3   Parks

Japanese cities are in general not well provided with parks, although there are exceptions. It has been estimated that there are some 30 square metres of park space in London per inhabitant. The comparable figure for Tokyo is 2.5 square metres, although the average for Japanese cities is 5.4 square metres. The government aims to increase this by the year 2000 to 10 square metres per person.

8.2.4   Public Drains and Sewers

Most Japanese cities still lack adequate public sewerage facilities and many dwellings rely on septic tanks which have to be emptied from time to time by special trucks. At present public sewerage is provided for only some 40 per cent of Japanese dwellings. The government aim to increase this to 70 per cent by the year 2000.

8.2.5   Roads

The Japanese road system was neglected before the Second World War, priority being given to the railways. Until the early 1960s many Japanese main roads were only partly paved and were too narrow for anything but small vehicles. The economic development of the 1960s, 1970s and 1980s forced the government to improve the road system. Toll roads were built at great cost in cities such as Tokyo and Osaka and toll highways (expressways) were constructed between the main centres of population. Some are still under construction. Construction of these highways was expensive and time-consuming because of the nature of the Japanese terrain and the need for precautions against the earthquakes which are prevalent in the Japanese islands. Japanese engineers proved very capable in tunnelling and bridge-building. But Japanese road-building has been unable to keep up with the growth in traffic and most urban roads are overcrowded. Traffic jams are endemic and in many places notices warn motorists that they face jams (*jūtai*) of many kilometres in length. Sometimes these are described as *shizenjūtai* or natural jams! Road construction is financed through a special road improvement account funded by taxes on petrol, automobile sales, etc. Tolls can be an expensive item when travelling by car over even relatively short distances.

8.2.6 Construction Industry

Japan has a large and well-developed construction industry. Approximately a third of investment in construction is spent on engineering works and two-thirds on building. About a third of construction projects are government-funded. In large projects, prime contractors make use of numerous sub-contractors. Over 5 million workers are employed in the industry which, particularly during the boom in the late 1980s, suffered an increasing labour shortage. Japanese workers were reluctant to take on jobs which were dirty (*kitanai*), dangerous (*kiken*) and difficult (*kitsui*) referred to as the three 'ks'. The industry was accordingly forced to employ increasing numbers of foreigners. Many of these from Iran, Pakistan and elsewhere in Asia were illegal immigrants, having arrived, for example, as 'tourists'.

The construction industry has expanded abroad and undertakes projects in North America and Europe as well as in parts of Asia. Very few foreign construction companies have been successful in bidding for projects in Japan, both because of the difficulty of getting on the lists of companies with approval to bid and because, it is widely alleged, of the way in which Japanese construction companies ensure through the so-called *dangō* system that contracts go to a Japanese bidder selected by the industry and who puts in the bid at an 'acceptable' price.

Among the many large Japanese general construction companies (there are over seventy on the first section of the Japanese stock exchange) are such well-known names as Kajima, Taisei, Shimizu, Obayashi, Tobishima, Kumagai-gumi, Takenaka Kōmuten, and Hazama. Well-known house-construction companies include Misawa Homes, Daiwa House, and Sekisui House.

8.3   TRANSPORT

Japan has a sophisticated and efficient transport network. Much of it, however, is overcrowded and overregulated. Further improvements and liberalization are required to ensure its continued efficiency.

8.3.1   The Ministry of Transport (Unyūshō)

The Ministry of Transport is the government agency responsible for supervising all forms of transportation in Japan. It also draws up transport policies. It is thus responsible for the regulation of shipping and inspection as well as registration of ships. It grants licences for the construction of ships and arranges subsidies when appropriate. It administers ports and harbours. It regulates motor vehicles. It supervises and regulates the railways. It is also responsible for the aviation industry, including aircraft safety and international aviation policy, as well as the administration of airports.

The Ministry controls the Maritime Safety Agency (*Kaijōhōanchō*) which deals with criminal activities in coastal waters and is responsible for lighthouses and other facilities for the safety of shipping. A separate agency is responsible for investigating marine accidents. Another agency under the Ministry's aegis is the Meteorological Agency (*Kishōchō*)

8.3.2   Road Transport

In Europe and North America about 90 per cent of passenger traffic is by motor vehicle. In Japan about two-thirds of passenger traffic is transported by buses and cars. In 1990 there were some 60 million motor vehicles in Japan. This provided an average of one automobile per household. The first expressway opened in 1963. By 1989 there were 4406 kilometres of expressway in Japan. This is expected to grow to some 14 000 kilometres by the year 2000. Traffic accidents have been growing and over 11 000 people were killed on Japanese roads in 1989. The Ministry of Transport enforces strict, comprehensive and detailed standards for motor vehicles. Japanese cars must be fitted with catalytic converters and various safety equipment. Vehicles have to pass periodic inspections (*shaken*) which are both stringent and expensive.

Japan has a good and wide network of buses both within cities and in the countryside. There are also nationwide express bus services.

Truck transport has grown hugely and some 50 per cent of Japanese freight travels by road. In 1988 freight transport by road amounted to nearly 250 billion tonne-kilometres as compared with just over 780 passenger kilometres in the case of cars.

8.3.3 Railways

Railways are more important in Japan than in any other developed country. In 1988 rail transport was responsible for over 360 billion passenger kilometres, and Japan had nearly 27 500 kilometres of railway track.

Until 1987 there were two rail systems in Japan. These were the Japan National Railways (JNR) and Japanese private railways which were mainly commuter lines operating from Tokyo, Osaka and Nagoya. JNR was also responsible for the *Shinkansen* (bullet train) lines which are new express lines built to a wide gauge (old Japanese lines are all narrow guage). There were over 2000 kilometres of such new lines in 1988. These are due to be expanded, but costs are high. The Tōkaidō line extends via Osaka and Hiroshima as far as Fukuoka in Kyūshū. There is a separate Tōhoku line as far as Morioka in Iwate prefecture in the northern part of Honshū and the Jōetsu line goes as far as Niigata on the Japan Sea coast. In 1992 a branch line from the Tōhoku network was opened as far as Yamagata, but this is different from the others in that it follows the line of the old railway and is not a separate new line. Railway tunnels connect Honshū with Kyūshū and Honshū with Hokkaidō. The latter, called the Seikan Tunnel, is longer than the Channel Tunnel. There is also a railway (and road) bridge to Shikoku (between Okayama and Kagawa prefectures) and two other bridge connections are under construction.

Following the 'privatisation' of JNR in 1987 seven regional companies have been established. 'Privatisation' meant the lifting of various governmental restrictions and the ending of many overmanning practices. It thus allowed the new companies to diversify and renew their rolling stock. East Japan Railway and Central Japan Railway have been the most profitable. The regional companies in Kyūshū, Shikoku and Hokkaidō, however, have made losses, although they were able to produce nominal profits as a result of financial aid given to them by the government on 'privatisation'. None of the companies has yet been sold to the public and the government has been saddled with the huge burden of debt accumulated by the former JNR.

Before the 'privatisation' of JNR private railway companies, which on some lines were in direct competition with JNR were able to offer cheaper and better services. The new regional companies have become more competitive and the private railways have in their turn been forced to improve their services. One problem for them is the strict controls of the Ministry of Transport over the fares which they can charge.

The Japanese are frequent travellers and despite the relatively high fares on *Shinkansen* trains, which speed up and down the Tōkaidō line every few minutes, most trains are full.

8.3.4 Underground Railways

Tokyo, Osaka and Nagoya have extensive and efficient underground railway services with many different lines. These provide the most reliable method of travel within the metropolises. Trains run frequently and are clean. Fares are reasonable. They are almost always well filled. They are generally overcrowded during the morning rush hour.

Other cities with underground railways include Kyoto, Sapporo, Sendai, Yokohama and Fukuoka. Some cities, such as Hiroshima and Matsuyama, still operate trams.

8.3.5 Shipping

Japan has the third largest shipping industry in the world. It is only exceeded by ships under the flags of convenience of Liberia and Panama. Its merchant fleet in 1988, including both ocean-going and coastal fleets, amounted to over 32 million tonnes. Japanese shipping companies were badly hit by the fall in demand for tankers following the two oil crises of the 1970s and by growing competition from the shipping of newly-industrialized economies. This has forced Japanese shipping companies to rationalize.

Japanese shipping lines have friendly relations with European shipping lines and belong to the conference systems. They are opposed to the US regulations designed to protect and promote otherwise uneconomic US shipping.

The major Japanese shipping lines operating tankers, bulk carriers and container ships are Nippon Yūsen Kaisha (NYK) (which has been developing cruise liners), Mitsui OSK, Kawasaki Kisen and Navix, which is the name adopted when Yamashita-Shinnihon and Japan Line merged in 1989.

8.3.6 Airlines

Domestic air services grew greatly in the 1980s. By 1988 Japanese airlines were flying over 41 billion passenger kilometres on internal routes. The main operators were Japan Airlines (JAL – *Nihon kōkū*), All Nippon Airways (ANA – *Zennikkū*) and Japan Air Systems (formerly Toa Domestic Airlines (TDA)). There are airports in most prefectures and reasonably frequent services to, for example, Tokyo and Osaka. Connections between prefectures are more infrequent and often non-existent. The Ministry of Transport keeps a tight control on fares and on services. While on some internal lines there is limited competition this does not extend to fares or the level of cabin service which the airlines can offer to passengers.

The main Japanese international carrier is JAL, although ANA has been permitted to offer services on a number of international routes, for example, to London, Hong Kong, etc. The Ministry of Transport, which is responsible for Air Service agreements with foreign countries, does all it can to limit competition from foreign airlines and to keep up international air fares to ensure the profitability of Japanese carriers. JAL has had difficulties because of overmanning; labour relations within the company have often given problems.

There are various Japanese 'international airports' but many of these only provide services to neighbouring countries such as Korea. Most international airlines wish to serve primarily Tokyo and Osaka. Narita Airport, Tokyo's distant and inconvenient international airport in Chiba prefecture, is overcrowded and the authorities have encountered violent opposition to their efforts to expand the airport and build an additional runway. The old international airport at Haneda, which is much nearer to central Tokyo, is now only used for domestic flights, foreign VIP flights and flights to and from Taiwan (to ensure that there is no conflict with the Chinese government in Beijing). Osaka Airport is equally crowded and the problem caused to local residents by airport noise means that flights have to be restricted. A new airport being built in Osaka Bay should be ready in 1994 but difficulties over construction have caused delays.

Japanese travelling abroad increased greatly in the 1980s. Japanese departures in 1988 numbered nearly 8.5 million. Foreigners visiting Japan amounted to almost 2.5 million in the same year. About half of Japanese air travellers went to destinations in Asia but the number travelling to North America and Europe has been increasing steadily.

9 Employment, Health and Welfare

9.1 EMPLOYMENT

The employment system in Japan has much in common with systems in other developed countries but also includes features which, if not peculiar to Japan, play a more important role there than in other countries.

9.9.1 Population

On 1 October 1990 the population of Japan was stated to be 123.61 million. According to the 1985 census the population then was 121.05 million. This means that in this 5-year period Japan's population was rising annually by 0.4 per cent. But the Japanese birth-rate has been declining sharply. The net reproduction rate of 1.75 in 1986 had fallen to 1.53 by 1990. The annual number of live births of approximately 1.27 million (in 1990) is likely to increase to about 1.36 million in the year 2000 owing to an earlier 'baby boom'. But the Japan Center for Economic Research estimates that the Japanese population will peak at about 126.7 million in 2005 and will then begin to decrease by some 670 000 each year. Among the various reasons for the fall in the net reproduction rate are increasing prosperity and the growing numbers of women in employment, combined with relatively cramped housing and the perceived costs of education and maintenance of children.

Japan is likely to continue to have a high population density. This is estimated at 322 people per square kilometre which is the fourth highest after Bangladesh, South Korea and The Netherlands. (Japan is mountainous, The Netherlands comparatively flat; this means that Japan is in most areas more densely populated than The Netherlands.) The population of Tokyo is estimated at 11.85 million but the urban area around the Tokyo metropolis is also crowded and there is little countryside left in the vicinity of Tokyo. The population of Osaka is some 8.73 million.

The Japanese population is ageing fast. In 1989 people over 65 represented some 11.6 per cent of the population. By the year 2005 the over-65s will be some 14 per cent of the inhabitants of Japan. This implies an increasing burden of tax and social security contributions for those in full-time employment. By the year 2020 the costs could be as high as 53.5 per cent of national income.

The average age of retirement has been rising, but it is still generally around 60. In enterprises surveyed by the Ministry of Labour in 1989, some 57.6 per cent applied a mandatory retirement age of 60, but 20.7 per cent still enforced retirement at 55 and 17 per cent at ages between 55 and 60.

In 1990 Japan had a working population of 63.69 million; 6.7 per cent were employed in primary; 33.9 per cent in secondary and 59.4 in tertiary industry. In 1989 women represented 40 per cent of the Japanese work force; 58.5 per cent of these were married women whereas the proportion of married women in 1965 was only 38.6 per cent.

Japan has for many years enjoyed practically full employment. According to Japanese statistics the number of unemployed in Japan in May 1991 was 1.36 million, or 2.1 per cent of the working population. Even if the statistical base is not the same as in European countries (and there is a good deal of underemployment especially in service industries) unemployment in Japan has been very low. Underemployment is largely disguised by the retention of staff in large companies, who traditionally do not lay off workers in a recession or dismiss workers who are no longer giving adequate service. Such people are often referred to as *madogiwa-zoku* (people who sit by the window and have nothing much to do except read a newspaper). A figure of one million 'unemployed' employees of such companies is often mentioned.

The low rate of unemployment and the fact that job opportunities have exceeded the number of job-seekers has meant that there has been a shortage of labour in Japan. The recent bursting of the asset price bubble has temporarily altered the position, but observers expect that when the economy again turns up there will once more be a shortage of labour in Japan, particularly in construction.

9.1.2 Ministry of Labour (*Rōdōshō*)

The Ministry of Labour is responsible for administering Japan's labour laws and formulating labour policies. It deals with unemployment and employee accident compensation. It is responsible for various training programmes and for improving the conditions of employment of women and minors. Attached to the Ministry are the Central Labour Relations Commission (*Chūō-rōdō-iinkai*) which deals with disputes in private industry and the Public Corporation and National Enterprise Labour Relations Commission (*Kōkyō kigyōtai to rōdō iinkai*) which covers disputes in public corporations.

9.1.3   Conditions of Employment

Labour Laws

Some of the more important labour laws in Japan are:

The Labour Standards Law.   This dates from 1947 and was a major component of the reforms introduced during the Occupation. It covers a wide range of issues and has been amended frequently. It deals with minimum wages, maximum working hours, rest and holidays, employment rules for women and minors, plant safety and health, and aspects of training. Under the law employers may only establish work regulations after consultation with representatives of the employees and with the approval of the Ministry of Labour.

The Minimum Wage Law.   This was enacted in 1959 and established a procedure for setting minimum wages on a regional and industry-by-industry basis following agreement between employers and unions or worker representatives.

The Vocational Training Law.   Enacted in 1958, this provided the basis for the development of facilities to improve industrial skills as one means of alleviating Japan's growing labour shortage.

The Employment Measures Law.   Enacted in 1947, this set a framework to stabilize employment and the achievement of full employment. Provisions covering the employment of middle-aged and elderly workers were added in 1973.

The Employment Security Law.   Enacted in 1947, this was designed to provide employment safeguards and prohibit exploitation of workers. It regulates job placement services and under its provisions public employment security offices were established to help workers to find jobs. Private agencies are generally forbidden from charging fees for finding employment except with Ministry permission, for example, for artists. The law forbids discrimination on grounds of race, sex, religion, social position, past employment or union membership.

The Labour Relations Law.   Dating from 1946 this granted almost all workers the right to organize unions, to take part in collective bargaining and to take collective action including strikes. Only firemen, the police and prison guards were excluded from the law. Strikes in public utilities such as gas and electricity were prohibited for thirty days after the Ministry of Labour had been notified that a dispute existed. Later, under other laws, government employees and employees of public corporations had their right to take strike action forbidden or limited.

The Labour Relations Adjustment Law.   This was also enacted in 1946 and prohibits practices which would prevent or obstruct workers from exercising their rights under the Labour Relations Law. Unfair labour practices forbidden by the law include refusal to recognize unions or to engage in collective bargaining. To administer these laws, tripartite commissions were established at national and prefectural level. These may offer conciliation (*assen*), mediation (*chōtei*) and arbitration (*chūsai*).

The Ministry of Labour maintains regional offices for the enforcement of laws relating to labour standards and practices.

Normal Employment Practices

The three main principles governing employment in Japan can be said to be lifelong employment (*shūshin koyō*), the seniority system (*nenkō joretsu*) and union organisation by enterprises rather than by trades. In fact, the first two of these principles have begun to break down to some extent and in any case never applied fully outside the larger companies.

The principle of employment for life conforms with the importance attached to loyalty and the relations between the leader (*oyabun*) and his followers (*kobun*) under Japanese interpretatons of Confucian principles. It has also become an essential element of paternalism in Japanese companies. It ensures that employees are closely identified with a firm and its success which enhances teamwork. It does, however, have certain disadvantages. It means that companies lose flexibility in employment and it encourages employees to take a safety first attitude. It also means that companies cannot seek new talent at a senior level from outside the company. Instead of dismissing staff large companies apply various pressures on employees to retire voluntarily.

The seniority system that provides for promotion and wage rises according to seniority and length of service has resulted in greater equality of treatment in salaries and perks for employees and thus obviates the huge disparities found in some American and European companies between the salaries of juniors and top management. It keeps employees bound to their firms so that they can enjoy annual increases on the ladder of rising salaries. It also reduces jealousies between employees of differing seniority. It does, however, discourage the ambitious and able younger staff who find promotion blocked by seniors who may be inadequate for the job and who lack incentives to do better.

Enterprise unionism has been an important element in ensuring the success of Japanese companies in a competitive climate. The union becomes identified with the success of the enterprise and labour relations are as a result much smoother. Frequently senior directors have served at one stage in the enterprise union. The main argument against the system is that it encourages a cosy relationship between management and the union which in its turn may not do enough to fight for the rights and benefits due to union members. As an enterprise union it cannot look to other unions for much if anything in the way of help in the event of a dispute. In 1989 Japan lost about 175 000 man-days as a result of industrial disputes. The comparable figure for the USA was well over 4 million.

Working Hours

In 1988 the average number of hours worked on a contractual basis by Japanese employees in companies with over thirty employees was 41 hours 28 minutes. Under a revision to the Labour Standards Law agreed in 1987 the statutory contractual limit of 48 hours was reduced to 46 hours. In 1991 it was reduced by Cabinet order to 44 hours. The aim is to reduce this to 40 hours in due course and to make the five-day week universal. The number of hours worked in Japanese companies has been coming down and over 50 per cent of all companies and nearly 80 per cent of workers in Japan are now on a five day week.

Many companies, however, operate regular overtime arrangements and office workers frequently 'work' twelve or more hours a day. Some of this 'working' time is spent socializing with colleagues, but a great deal of time is spent in meetings and attempting to reach a consensus by what is termed in Japan *nemawashi* or 'going round the roots'. Few employees, especially those in positions of any kind of authority, take their full entitlement of holidays. The employees fear that if they are absent on leave they will be considered to be lacking in conscientious application to their duties and that this will tell against them when promotion is being discussed. As a result, most employees rarely take more than half their leave entitlement. There is also a strong tradition in many if not all major companies that juniors, even if they do not have any real work left to do, should not leave the office until their immediate boss leaves.

Wages and Salaries

Execpt for day labourers almost all Japanese employees are paid monthly, usually by direct transfer to bank accounts. In many households the wife holds the purse-strings and the husband is given an allowance by her to cover his day-to-day costs including his contribution to socializing with his colleagues.

Starting salaries (*shoninkyū*) for new employees (*shinnyū shain*) vary slightly depending on the educational achievements of new employees. They also vary between different types of enterprise. Women usually start at some 3 per cent less than male colleagues. Each year an increase is granted depending on length of service. As a result, the salaries of those in their late forties will be twice as much as those in their early twenties whatever promotion they have or have not had. In 1992 the average monthly wage in enterprises employing thirty or more was ¥392 608 (¥288 805 in regular wages and ¥103 803 in bonuses).

It has been the regular practice in Japanese companies to pay two annual bonuses, in December (winter) and in June (summer). These normally amount to between two and four months' average salary on each occasion. They may, in particularly profitable companies or when circumstances are very favourable, amount to considerably more. These bonuses, which are the subject of negotiation with the unions and which do not include a personal and discretionary element, are often saved or used to meet special expenditure on such items as cars, refrigerators and so on. Bonuses brought average total salaries up to over ¥5 million a year.

Perks and allowances for senior employees include fairly lavish entertainment expenses. These cover the cost of taking clients out to golf, restaurants and geisha houses. These activities are all very expensive in Japan. Senior directors are generally provided with company cars, including chauffeurs. The provision of a company car without the provision of a chauffeur is not a normal perk of employment in Japan. All employees can expect help towards commuting costs and in some cases the full cost is met by the company. Many companies provide company housing at subsidised rents and help towards the payment of mortgage interest.

On retirement all employees are entitled to a retirement gratuity based on the number of years in company employment. The sums can be considerable and can go a long way to paying off a mortgage. Company pension schemes have been growing in numbers but have not yet reached the same level of development as in Europe and North America and some employees have had to regard their retirement gratuity as their main reward for their long service.

Status of Women

Equality of opportunity and non-discrimination in the workplace are enshrined in Japanese laws. But in practice women are rarely given the kind of responsibility and opportunities for promotion which their male colleagues of comparable seniority and experience can expect, and reports suggest that sexual harassment is not uncommon in many Japanese offices. The traditional view remains that women should devote themselves to their homes after marriage, and if a man marries a female colleague in the same firm she will normally have to retire from that firm. Under the provisions of the Labour Standards Law women are entitled to six weeks' maternity leave. The law also limits the amount of overtime which women are allowed to work. Holiday work and late-night work are banned for women employees. These rules provide opportunities for employers to discriminate legitimately against women workers. Clerical and office work, including acting as receptionists and serving tea to visitors and male staff, are common occupations for women. They are also employed in large numbers in retailing and in light factory work. Even if women have not achieved important positions in industry and commerce they have had somewhat more success in the professions and in the Diet.

Part-time and Temporary Workers

Women account for some 25 per cent of the part-time work force in Japan. Part-time workers represented just over 13 per cent of Japan's working population in 1989. Part-time employees and temporary workers are the first to be laid off in a recession. Companies accordingly try to limit the number of their permanent employees who generally receive 50 per cent higher remuneration than temporaries.

Employment Contracts

In theory, each employee is supposed to have a contract of employment. In practice, written contracts are rare and an oral understanding is usually regarded as sufficient. In the event of a dispute a contract is assumed to exist. Contracts of over one year are forbidden under the Labour Standards Law. In theory staff can be dismissed with thirty days' notice or payment in lieu, but dismissal except for clearly dishonest conduct is regarded as contrary to Japanese practice and is, if at all possible, avoided.

9.1.4 Foreign Workers

Foreigners may only undertake paid work in Japan if they have been granted the necessary resident status by the immigration authorities. This is generally limited to foreigners carrying out commercial activities or teaching, or with special skills. The increasing shortage of labour in Japan in the last few years has, however, resulted in an increasing number of foreigners working illegally in Japan, especially in construction but also in bars and other similar activities known in Japan as *mizu-shōbai* (literally, 'the water trade'). This led to a revision in 1990 of the Immigration Control Law. The amendment increased the number of categories of work which foreigners are permitted to undertake in Japan and imposed stiff penalties on employers of and brokers for illegal foreign workers. In 1990 nearly 30 000 illegal workers were detected. In November 1991 it was estimated that there were 216 399 foreigners in Japan who had overstayed their visas. Many of these illegal workers have been Iranians, Pakistanis and Filipinos.

Immigration controls are operated by the Ministry of Justice. All foreigners must have a valid passport (or, in the case of seamen, a 'pocket ledger') in order to enter Japan. Visas, which may be renewable, are limited to a maximum of three years. Nationals of countries with which Japan has concluded visa abolition agreements do not require entry visas but do require work permits if they wish to undertake paid employment. Permanent residence is rarely granted to foreigners. Naturalisation in Japan is difficult to achieve.

The largest community of foreigners resident in Japan are the Koreans, estimated at some 650 000. Many of these are second or third generation Koreans who may not even speak Korean and have no real connections with Korea. They are still subject to discrimination, for example, in relation to housing and social security benefits.

9.1.5 Disadvantaged People (*burakumin*)

Another group which suffers discrimination in employement in Japan is the *burakumin* (literally 'village people'). These are alleged to be the descendants of former slaves and outcasts who were engaged in such occupations as tanning and butchery, occupations which Buddhists, who theoretically at least should not take life, are not permitted to undertake. The *burakumin*, often referred to as the *eta* (outcasts) or as *suiheisha* (levellers), regard all these names as abhorrent and foreigners are advised, if at all possible, not to use the words. If reference has to be made to such unfortunate people it is better to mention the *dōwa* (harmony) movement. It has been estimated that there are upwards of 2 million living in various dōwa-*chiku* (i.e. *dōwa* areas) in Japan, primarily but not exclusively in the Kansai and Shikoku. Many of the unemployed belong to this class of unfortunates, who try to disguise their origin if they possibly can. Investigations carried out before marriage are often designed to discover whether either party to the marriage has connections with this group.

9.1.6 Japanese Unions

Most unions in Japan, being enterprise or company unions, have a relatively low profile. In 1992 it was estimated that there were about 12.54 million workers organized in unions in Japan, but these only represented 24.4 per cent of Japanese employees.

About 8 million, or roughly two-thirds of, workers in unions belong to *Rengō* (the Japanese Labour Union Confederation). *Rengō* was formed in 1987 when the two groups of private-sector unions, *Dōmei* and *Chūritsu rōren*, which were regarded as organizations which took generally moderate positions and supported the Democratic Socialist Party (DSP), amalgamated. Another small moderate group *Shinsanbetsu* joined *Rengō* in 1988. Finally, in 1989 *Sōhyō* which primarily represented workers in the public sector (and which supported the Japan Socialist Party (JSP), including many Marxists among its leaders) was dissolved and many of the public-sector unions in *Sōhyō* joined *Rengō*.

Rengō which has no unified association with any single political party but it has been close to the JSP put up candidates for the Upper House elections in 1989 and did comparatively well. In the elections in 1992 all the *Rengō* candidates failed.

Rengō plays a leading part in the wage negotiations that are held every spring to decide on the annual wage rise for leading companies. The negotiations are part of the 'spring struggle' (*shuntō*) which is frequently marked by short but annoying strikes in the public sector, for example, on the railways.

One of the most prominent of the left-wing public sector unions is *Nikkyōsō*, the union which represents a majority of primary and middle school (junior high school) teachers.

Unions are not as important or influential in Japan as in other developed economies.

9.2 HEALTH AND WELFARE

The Japanese have one of the highest life expectancies in the world. Japanese medical practice is well developed, although there are some weaknesses. Social security provisions are extensive although not as fully comprehensive or generous as in some European countries. Increasing concern is being expressed in Japan about the growing burden of health insurance and pensions in an ageing society.

9.2.1 The Ministry of Health and Welfare (*Kōseishō*)

The Ministry of Health and Welfare is the Japanese government agency responsible for all health, welfare and social security issues. It consists of nine bureaux covering public health, environmental sanitation, medical affairs, pharmaceutical matters, social affairs, children and families, health insurance, pensions, and relief for war victims. It draws up and administers public health policies. It supervises the import of food and drink products as well as pharmaceuticals to ensure that these are safe. (It has the reputation of being meticulous to a point where some of its actions appear protectionist, in practice, if not in intent.) It regulates drugs and medicines and is the ministry responsible for relations with and promotion of Japan's pharmaceutical industry. It operates port quarantine services, over ninety national hospitals and over 150 public sanatoria, the national centres for cancer and for cardiovascular disease, the institutes of public health, of hygiene science, of mental health, of nutrition, of hospital administration, of population problems, and of leprosy research. And it supervises the Social Insurance Agency (*Shakai hokenchō*) which manages the national health insurance scheme and government pension programmes.

9.2.2 Health Insurance and Health Costs

All Japanese people are covered by one of a number of health insurance schemes. National Health Insurance (*Kokumin kenkō hoken*), managed by municipalities or the National Health Insurance Assciation, covers over 45 million people. It applies to people such as the self-employed, farmers, housewives, children and old people who do not belong to other health insurance schemes. Workers in enterprises with less than five employees and foreign residents may also be included in this scheme. The average annual contribution by the insured was ¥57 855 in 1989 (the average for a household was ¥142 539).

Employees of small- and medium-scale businesses (with more than five employees) belong to a different, government-managed health insurance plan which covers some 35 million people. Employees of large firms usually belong to non-governmental plans established by an employer or jointly by a number of employers as health insurance associations. These cover some 31.5 million people. Employees contribute 3.5 per cent of their monthly pay as their share of health insurance costs under such schemes to cover themselves and their families. Employers contribute about a further 4.5 per cent.

Health insurance does not meet the full cost of health care. The proportion borne by the insured under schemes other than National Health Insurance was increased in 1984 to 10 per cent for the insured employee and 30 per cent for dependants. Those insured under the National Health Insurance scheme pay 30 per cent of the costs of treatment.

It has been estimated that in 1988 insurance payments met 55.1 per cent of the total cost of medical fees; 12.4 per cent was, on average, met by the patient. National government contributions covered 26.7 per cent of costs and local government 5.9 per cent.

Under a system introduced in 1973, medical care was provided virtually without charge for people over 70 and to bedridden people over 65. Under a revised system introduced in 1983, elderly people have to pay a small proportion of the cost of medical treatment. Since 1987 elderly patients have had to pay ¥800 per month for out-patient treatment and ¥400 a day for in-patient treatment in hospitals.

The total cost of health care in Japan in 1987 amounted to 6.8 per cent of national income. This is considerably lower than in the USA but it is nevertheless, bearing in mind the size of the Japanese GNP, a very large amount. According to *The Economist* in June 1990 the total cost in 1989 was ¥23.6 trillion (at that time US$ 156 billion).

9.2.3 Medical Care

Although the Ministry of Health and Welfare supervises a number of national hospitals, the main providers of health care are private hospitals, numbering some 10 000, and private clinics numbering over 80 000. Clinics may have no in-patient accommodation or may have up to nineteen beds. In all, Japan had in 1990 some 1.7 million beds or in relation to Japan's total population, one bed for every 74 people.

In 1988 there were a total of 1048 mental hospitals containing over 260 000 beds. There were a further 90 000 beds for mental patients in clinics.

Hospitals and clinics are remunerated by the insurers on a fee-for-service basis. This has led to a proliferation of diagnostic tests, not all strictly necessary. Japanese doctors who are well provided with modern equipment do not hesitate to make full use of all the latest gadgets. They do not, however, have to do so for fear of malpractice suits, as these are practically unknown in Japan.

The average length of stay in hospital was estimated by *The Economist* in June 1990 as 40 days. The mean length of stay in hospital of mental patients was over 500 days.

The astonishingly long stay in hospital by ordinary patients is partly a result of the lack of facilities outside hospitals for rest and recuperation as well as to traditional attitudes. But the way in which fees are met in Japan has also been an important factor in lengthening the time the Japanese spend in hospital, which is considerably longer than in Europe or North America. Another factor has been that most doctors, who treat patients in their own clinics and only make home calls in emergencies, dispense their own drugs and naturally profit thereby. They receive a price set by the government for the drugs which they dispense but can expect to receive the drugs from the suppliers at discounted prices. This has meant that the Japanese consume record quantities of drugs which often do not mix well. This in turn leads to some damaging side effects. There were some 122 000 qualified pharmacists in Japan in 1988.

Fortunately for the insurance companies and the government, Japanese people prefer not to go to hospital if they can avoid it. According to *The Economist*, admission rates are only some 6.4 per cent compared with Western rates of some 18 per cent. One reason for Japanese reluctance to go into hospital is the inadequate provision for nursing services in Japan, although there were over 365 000 'clinical nurses' in Japan in 1988. Physiotherapy services are also generally considered to be inadequate.

The Ministry is responsible for the organization and administration of health centres which undertake mass health screening and give general advice on health matters, but do not normally provide medical treatment.

Japanese doctors belong to one of the best-paid occupations in Japan. They are well looked after by the Japan Medical Association (JMA) which is an effective lobbying group. It is largely due to their pressure that oral contraceptives ('the pill') are still only permitted to be prescribed for certain gynaecological conditions and are not generally used as a means of contraception. The ostensible argument is the possible harmful side effects from use of the pill. It is also argued that use of the pill would lead to a further reduction in the net reproduction rate in Japan. But the real reason is generally thought to be that doctors make a good profit from carrying out abortions. There is no pro-life lobby in Japan opposed to abortion.

Japanese surgeons have a high reputation, but so far transplant operations have been rare.

Japan had some 212 000 doctors in 1990, or approximately one doctor for every 584 people. This is a slightly lower proportion than in the USA and most Western European countries.

Japanese Western-style medicine, which is predominant in Japan today, was modelled on the German pattern. Medical training consists of two years of pre-medical courses and four years of professional courses. On graduation candidates for the profession have to pass the national medical examination and then generally go on for a further two years of clinical training.

Chinese herbal medicine (*kampō*) is still practiced in Japan and many Japanese make use of *kampō* drugs. Some 100 to 200 drugs, mainly of vegetable origin, are used in Japan. One form of treatment which has been much favoured in Japan is moxibustion. It is regarded by some elderly people as beneficial to general health. In moxibustion cones of moxa are applied to the skin at specific points and then ignited. It causes a feeling of intense but bearable heat. Chinese acupuncture is also used quite frequently in Japan.

Dentistry in Japan follows general Western methods. Dental care has improved considerably in recent years and the use of gold fillings, which seemed at one stage to exemplify Japanese dentistry, has declined. In 1988 there were some 50 000 dental clinics and nearly 70 000 dentists in Japan.

9.2.4 Life Expectancy and Prevalance of Diseases in Japan

In 1990 the average life expectancy for Japanese males at birth was 75.86 and for females 81.81. Life expectancy has generally increased by some thirty years in the past half century. This is due to improved public health, nutrition and medical services, which have led to vast reductions in deaths from tuberculosis and infectious diseases. The average death rate was 6.4 per 1000 in 1989.

Major causes of death in Japan in 1990 were cancer (223.7 of every thousand deaths), heart diseases (168.9), cerebro-vascular diseases (118.4), pneumonia and bronchitis (76.4), accidents (33.2), senility (23.2), suicide (19.9), nephritis (17.0), cirrhosis of the liver (16.9) and diabetes (9.6). Cancer of the stomach, probably because of aspects of Japanese diet, has been the most common form of cancer in Japan but cancers of the bowel and rectum have been increasing as the Japanese eat more meat and animal fats. Cancer of the lung has also been increasing. Hitherto lung cancer has been less prevalent in Japan than in Europe and North America despite the high level of smoking, especially by Japanese men. The number of cases of lung cancer in Japan is now increasing. In 1991 it was estimated that 60 per cent of Japanese men and 14 per cent of Japanese women were regular smokers.

People living in northern Japan, perhaps because of the fact that on average they have consumed larger quantities of salt (for example, through *shōyu* (soy sauce), have had a greater tendency to suffer from strokes than those in other parts of Japan.

The prevalence of diabetes among politicians is put down by some to their high consumption of sake, the generally sweet Japanese rice wine. Average annual consumption of alcohol in Japan amounted in 1988 to 6.4 litres (pure alcohol equivalent) which was somewhat less than in the USA and less than half the average consumption in France.

Pollution-related diseases have decreased with the adoption of stricter standards for air and water.

In the 1970s exhaust emissions which caused photochemical smog in the summer made living in cities very unpleasant. But Japanese exhaust emission controls are now strictly enforced and photochemical smog is much rarer. Asthma and bronchial diseases were particularly common in places like Yokohama and Kawasaki where factories belched out noxious fumes and oil was refined, sending out sulphur dioxide. Air pollution is still a problem in industrial areas but it is less than it was.

The most infamous case of water pollution in Japan was that due to the release of mercury into the waters round the Kyūshū fishing port of Minamata. A number of serious cases involving mental disorders, numbness and loss of sensation, including loss of sight and hearing, occurred. The disease came to be called Minamata disease. This was followed by other cases of mercury poisoning in Niigata. Another disease which appeared in Toyama prefecture and which came to be called *itai-itai* (literally, 'it hurts') was ascribed to cadmium poisoning. Chronic arsenic poisoning also occurred in the neighbourhood of arsenic mines. These incidents led to much stricter controls on factory emissions and on water quality. In 1973 a pollution-related Health Damage Compensation Law was enacted.

Interest in environmental/green issues has been growing in Japan. As a result, managers and politicians have been forced to pay more attention to environmental problems.

Among diseases specific to Japan, or more common in Japan that elsewhere, is encephalitis-B, which is carried by mosquitoes and appears in the hot Japanese summer. Various forms of hepatitis are found in Japan.

Polio has largely been eliminated by the use of the Sabin-type live polio vaccine, and so has tuberculosis, as a result of the use of the BCG vaccine.

In 1991, 238 new cases of AIDS (acquired immune deficiency syndrome) were confirmed in Japan. The incidence was 2.5 times greater than in the previous year.

9.2.5 The Pharmaceutical Industry

The Japanese pharmaceutical industry is fragmented. Its main market has been in Japan, and Japanese forms have not so far had outstanding success in developing new drugs. The Ministry controls the prices of drugs supplied under the health insurance schemes and generally cuts back prices every two years. In 1990, an average cut of 9.2 per cent was enforced.

Japanese firms are now looking to expand abroad and in order to find appropriate new drugs are increasing their R&D expenditure. This amounted to 6.9 per cent of net sales of all Japanese pharmaceutical companies in 1988; major companies have been spending as much as 10 per cent of net sales on R&D. Some firms have also been buying companies abroad, while foreign companies have been developing their ties with Japanese companies in order to maintain and expand their market shares in Japan. In the past, Japanese companies, with an eye to protecting their share of the domestic market, supported the maintenance of special testing of drugs before they could be used in Japan. Now, with their eye on foreign markets, they are favouring the development of uniform drug licensing arrangements.

Among major Japanese pharmaceutical companies are Tanabe, Takeda, Yamanouchi, Fujisawa, Eisai, Chūgai and Sankyō.

9.2.6   Other Insured Benefits

Sickness and Injury Allowances

When someone who is insured under any of the schemes approved by the government is sick or injured he or she is entitled to receive 60 per cent, in the case of a person with dependants, or 40 per cent, if there are no dependants, of his or her salary (worked out according to a set of rules). The allowance starts after three days of incapacity and is limited to a period of eighteen months. It is reduced or stopped if the employee continues to be paid by the employer. It also ceases if the insured becomes eligible for an invalidity allowance or disability pension under the Employees' Pension Insurance scheme (see below).

Childbirth

When an insured woman cannot work because she is giving birth to a child she is entitled to 60 per cent or 40 per cent, depending on whether she has dependants or not, of her standard remuneration. The allowance is paid for 42 days before the child is born and 56 days after the birth. During the nursing period an insured woman or the wife of an insured person may receive a daily allowance of ¥2000. A lump sum of ¥200 000 is paid on the delivery of the baby.

Funeral Expenses

When an insured person or dependant dies a sum of ¥100 000 is paid towards the funeral expenses.

9.2.7 Pensions

There are two major public pension schemes as well as four schemes for various groups of government employees. The two main schemes are the Employees' Pension Insurance and the National Pension (*nenkin*).

Employees' Pension Insurance

The Employees' Pension Insurance scheme applies compulsorily to all employees in the private sector. Activities excluded from compulsory coverage are those carried out on an individual basis including farming, fishing and professional work, for example lawyers and accountants, actors and so on.

Contributions and benefits take into account salaries and length of service. The minimum qualifying period is twenty-five years. Pensions are payable from the age of 60 whereas under the National Pension (see below) the basic pension is only payable from the age of 65. When this is paid it is set against benefits under the Employees' Pension Insurance scheme. Pensions are generally calculated according to a formula based on average monthly salary × 7.5 divided by 1000 × number of months in insured work. If an employee continues to work after the age of 60 his pension is reduced while working and no pension is payable if he earns more than ¥250 000 a month. Additional sums are payable for dependants. Bereaved spouses are entitled to a pension of 75 per cent of the pension due to the insured. Benefits are linked to the cost of living. The contribution rate is 14.5 per cent of salary. Half is paid by the employer and half by the employee.

National Pension

When the National Pension was first established it was intended to cover only those who were not included in the Employees' Pension scheme. But in 1985 the National Pension arrangements were revised to ensure that everyone will receive a basic pension. Those enrolled in the Employees' Pension Insurance are automatically included in the National Pension. There are three categories of people covered by the scheme. These are:

(i)   Class I, people only insured in the National Pension.
(ii) Class II, people covered under the Employees' Pension Insurance or by Mutual Aid associations.
(iii) Class III, dependent spouses of those insured under Class II.

The annual basic pension payable to insured people who had contributed for forty years was, in 1991, ¥702 000. If contributions have not been paid for the full 40 years or if the pension is taken before the age of 65 the amount is reduced proportionately. Invalidity benefits are provided to those who have contributed for at least two-thirds of the period necessary to qualify for a National Pension. Benefits at the basic rate are paid to a surviving spouse and provision is made for the support of bereaved children. Lump sum benefits may also be paid to surviving dependants who are not entitled to a survivor's pension. Those insured in Class I contribute ¥8400 and month. Insured people in Classes II and III are covered by contributions to the Employees' Pension Insurance. One-third of the total cost of the National pension is met by contributions from the state.

9.2.8   Employment Insurance

Employment Insurance is a scheme run by the Ministry of Labour. The act covering the scheme was revised in 1984. The aim is not only to provide unemployment benefits but also to increase employment opportunities and to help with retraining. All businesses employing more than five people must belong to the scheme. Other smaller businesses may join on a voluntary basis. The insured are divided into three categories, namely, those working more than 33 hours a week; part-time workers who do less than 33 hours a week; and day labourers. Contribution rates are 1.45 per cent of salary, of which the employer pays 0.9 per cent and the employee 0.55 per cent. the rates are slightly higher for agricultural, forestry and construction workers. To obtain unemployment benefit an insured person must have contributed for over six months prior to becoming unemployed. The rate of benefit varies between 60 per cent and 80 per cent of salary, calculated on a daily basis, and subject to a maximum of ¥12 000 per day. The period during which the allowance is payable varies between 90 and 300 days, depending on how long the insured was employed before losing his or her job. The period is also shorter for part-time workers. There are various other allowances towards training costs.

Workmen's Accident Compensation Insurance

Workmen's accident compensation insurance, which is also administered by the Ministry of Labour, covers some 41 million workers in Japan and is applicable to all undertakings which have employees. The costs of the scheme are met largely from contributions from employers. Benefits include medical compensation, temporary disability compensation and funeral expenses. Payments are made on a sliding scale. The Labour Welfare Corporation, financed by the scheme, provides services to help injured people return to work. These include the supply of artificial limbs. It also supplies relief services for injured workers and their families.

9.2.9 Social Welfare Benefits

Children's Allowances

Children's allowances are means-tested and only paid when a person has (or is looking after) children under 6 years of age. The amount is ¥2500 a month for the second child aged under 6, and ¥5000 for third or subsequent children aged under 6. The costs are met partly by employer contributions and partly by national and local subsidies.

There are some 850 000 one-parent families in Japan. Such households receive special child-dependency allowances. The amount of the allowance is related to the number of children in the household. The annual allowance for households with one dependent child is ¥430 290. A further ¥60 000 is paid for the second child and ¥24 600 for a third and subsequent children.

Livelihood Assistance

Livelihood protection, or public assistance, is available on a means-tested basis to ensure a minimum standard of living to poor people without adequate incomes. Seven different types of aid are available. These cover living expenses, housing, essential education expenses beyond those provided free by the state, medical expenses (for example, to cover the proportion which individuals and dependants must bear under the National Health Insurance scheme), maternity costs, funeral expenses, and help in finding employment. The 1989 budget provided a sum of ¥1.1 trillion for livelihood assistance. The basic monthly payment under this scheme for a family of three living in Tokyo came to ¥136 444.

Assistance for the Physically Handicapped

In 1987 there were 2.41 million people in Japan with physical handicaps and 353 000 mentally-handicapped people. The disabled have access to special medical examinations and advisory services. They can also get help with medical expenses and the provision of special equipment. Welfare workers pay regular visits to such people in their homes. Disability pensions are also paid to disabled people over the age of 20 at rates varying (in 1989) between ¥55 500 and ¥69 375 depending on the extent of their disability. Severely disabled people who are confined to their homes and who do not qualify for a pension receive a special monthly allowance of ¥22 250. In addition, households looking after disabled people under 20 years of age receive special monthly allowances of between ¥28 400 and ¥42 600 depending on the extent of the disability.

New public buildings in Japan have to have facilities for the disabled, including ramps for wheelchairs, special toilets and lift (elevator) controls which are within reach of those in wheelchairs. Provisions for the blind include studs on floors and on pavements, especially near street crossings. Many street crossings which are controlled by lights also play specific tunes indicating when it is safe to cross in a particular direction.

10 Education and Culture

10.1 EDUCATION

The Japanese education system has ensured high standards of general and technical education. It has major strengths but some weaknesses which have caused concern in Japan. Japan is well-endowed with cultural riches and Japanese museums and galleries are among the finest in the world. There are large numbers of religious organizations in Japan; none is dominant. The Japanese media are strong and free; journalists are numerous, but sometimes seem tame. Leisure facilities have developed fast.

10.1.1 The Ministry of Education (*Mombushō*)

The Ministry of Education is responsible for the administration of the Japanese public educational system, for determining educational standards and for promoting cultural activities. It gives guidance to local boards of education and controls the curricula and the textbooks used in schools. It is also responsible for teacher training. The national universities as well as other national tertiary education institutes come under its jurisdiction. It deals with student exchanges and gives scholarships for selected foreign students. It is also responsible for the supervision of museums and other cultural institutes.

The Agency for Cultural Affairs (*Bunkachō*), which is attached to the Ministry, is the government body dealing with cultural work including the promotion of cultural events. It is responsible for the preservation of national treasures (*kokuhō*) and important cultural properties (*jūyōbunkazai*), which have been carefully listed.

10.1.2 The School System

Education normally begins in kindergarten (*yochien*) which may last for up to three years. Children may begin kindergarten at the age of 3 and stay until they are 6, but most children go to kindergarten from the age of 5. There were some 15 000 kindergartens in Japan in 1991. Of these some 60 per cent were private and the remaining 40 per cent were public. In 1991 there were some 100 000 kindergarten teachers in Japan.

Attendance at kindergarten is not compulsory and parents pay fees whether the kindergarten is public or private. At public kindergartens costs amount to some ¥95 000 a year, while at private kindergartens the cost is more than double. To this must be added extra expenses, for example, for private lessons, amounting to some ¥75 000 per annum on average, and the cost of school meals, which add up to some ¥11 000.

Japanese kindergartens are more than play schools and children at kindergarten learn the rudiments of reading and arithmetic. They also have their first lessons in living with other children and relating to adults outside the home. This is an important part of the process of assimilation to the Japanese environment with its emphasis on consensus. About 70 per cent of children attend kindergarten for at least one year.

Elementary school (*shōgakkō*) lasts for six years (from 6–11 years of age). This is compulsory and free in the public schools to which the vast majority of Japanese children go. There were in 1991 only about 170 private elementary schools in Japan out of a total of nearly 25 000. The number of primary school teachers was about 453 000.

The curriculum fixed by the Ministry of Education is a detailed one. The number of hours devoted to each subject varies from year to year but in all six years roughly a quarter is devoted to the Japanese language and one fifth to arithmetic. Other subjects which feature strongly in the curriculum are physical education, social studies (including history), science, music and art/handicrafts. Classes tend to be large. Discipline is strict and all children have to help in cleaning classrooms and school premises before returning home. Some school outings are arranged. Parent/teacher associations (PTA) are actively promoted in the schools and teachers attempt to keep in touch with parents by periodic home visits.

Although primary school education is free, parents are expected to pay additional amounts, for example, for travel (about ¥52 000 a year on average), extras (not far short of ¥100 000) and meals (around ¥35 000). Schools are co-educational and textbooks are free.

Junior high (or middle) schools (*chūgakkō*) cater for the 12–14-year-old group and provide the next stage in compulsory free education, which lasts for three years. In 1990 there were over 11 000 such schools, of which the vast majority were in the public sector (only 608 were privately run). There were some 308 000 teachers in these schools.

The system is similar to that at elementary schools, but more excursions are arranged and the cost to parents of extras such as travel amounted in 1989 to about ¥104 000 per pupil per annum plus ¥92 000 for other extras and nearly ¥30 000 for meals. Textbooks are provided free. The Japanese language, mathematics and science take a large and roughly equal share of teaching time. Educational pressures build up and there is more homework. At this stage parents and teachers decide on which high school the child should aim to enter. The competition to get into the more successful high schools leading to the top universities becomes intense. Schools in this age group are also co-educational.

Senior high schools (*kōtōgakkō*), which may be single-sex schools, provide three further years of education for the 15–17/18-year-old group of children. Attendance at such schools is not compulsory but almost all children (nearly 95 per cent) go on to senior high schools of one form or other (see below). Of the 5 503 senior high schools (as of May 1991) 4170 are public. Some 349 000 teachers were provided for these schools.

Even at public high schools limited fees averaging about ¥60 000 per annum are levied and the average cost of extras brought the cost per pupil at public senior high schools (including the cost of textbooks and school equipment) to some ¥241 000 per annum, plus extras costing a further ¥54 000. Charges at private high schools are higher, although the cost of some 50 per cent of the salaries of teachers at such schools is met by a state subsidy. In order to graduate from high school a student must earn 80 or more credits; each credit consists of 35 class hours (each of 50 minutes). The number of credits for Japanese language is around 17, for mathematics 19 (including algebra, geometry, differential and integral calculus, probability and statistics), science 22 (including physics, chemistry, biology and earth science), English 18. Credits for other subjects include contemporary society (4), Japanese history (4), world history (4), geography (4), ethics, politics and economics, music, fine arts, crafts, and calligraphy. About 2.2 per cent of those enrolling in high schools failed to graduate in 1989.

About 38 per cent of children graduating from junior high schools elect to go on to vocational high schools for three years or to technical colleges for five years instead of to the more academic senior high schools. Subjects studied in vocational schools included agriculture (3 per cent of students), industrial subjects (9 per cent), business studies (10 per cent), home economics (2 per cent) and nursing (1 per cent).

Special education schools cater for the physically and/or mentally handicapped.

In 1989, 30.7 per cent of those graduating from senior high schools went on to universities offering either four-year or two-year courses (see below). Special training schools attracted some 30 per cent and about 35 per cent took up employment

Public funding of education came to just over 4 per cent of GNP or 6 per cent of GDP. Just over 17 per cent was spent on high schools and 25 per cent on higher education.

The school year begins on 1 April each year and ends on 31 March of the following year. Primary, middle and most high schools operate three terms. A few high schools, however, have adopted a two-term year (from April to September and October to March). Saturday morning school, which was the norm, is likely to be phased out as the five-day week is generally adopted in Japan. The Ministry of Education requires schools to operate for 210 days a year but most prefectural boards of education require 240 days attendance.

Teaching methods stress the acquisition of knowledge, memorisation and the achievement of competence by the tackling of numerous problems and examples. Children are trained to develop their memories from the beginning of elementary schooling. This is a necessary part of learning Chinese characters (*kanji*), of which they are expected to know the 881 basic *kanji* (*kyōiku kanji*) by the time they leave elementary school. By the time they finish middle school they should know the remaining characters in the *tōyō kanji* prescribed for general use. This requires a knowledge of some 2000 characters in addition to the two syllabaries (*hiragana* and *katakana*). The syllabaries are normally learnt in the first year of elementary education. Surprisingly, considering the difficulty of the Japanese language, illiteracy is very rare.

Competition in class is not encouraged as this might lead to loss of face by the less successful. It is also contrary to the Japanese tradition that an individual should not stand out obviously among his or her contemporaries. There is a Japanese saying that the nail which stands out will be hammered down.

Pupil performance is generally assessed by teachers and grades 1–5 are allotted for each subject. A grade 1 mark means a failure and pupils unable to achieve better grades may be required to repeat a year.

The Ministry of Education vets and approve all textbooks for use in schools. In 1988, 1100 were approved by the Ministry. Local boards of education select from these the books to be used in the schools under their jurisdiction. The Ministry also rigorously controls the curriculum.

The Ministry's exercise of its control over textbooks and the curricula has aroused controversy. In particular, the way in which the Ministry has vetted history textbooks and especially the words used to describe Japanese aggression in China and other parts of Asia led to accusations against the Ministry from China and South East Asia in the 1980s that the Japanese authorities were trying to rewrite history to suit Japanese taste rather than reflecting the realities of what happened. Concern has also been expressed about the emphasis now placed on the teaching of morals in schools, on the grounds that this smacks of a return to pre-war patterns. This has been accompanied by a revival of the use in schools of the flying of the national flag and singing of the national anthem. While the Ministry of Education and the LDP contain a number of conservatives with regressive views, the extent of their ability to influence the way in which education operates in Japan should not be exaggerated. The media are likely to ensure that abuses are publicised.

Standards of achievement, for example, in mathematics and science, are high. One Western observer (Richard Lynn, *Educational Achievement in Japan*, Macmillan, 1988) has estimated that 'by mid-adolescence Japanese teenagers are at least one standard deviation ahead of their contemporaries in the West. This lead represents approximately three years of schooling, so that the average Japanese 12-year-old is approximately at the same academic level as the average 15-year-old in the West.' This may be exaggerated but the difference is significant. Another important feature of Japanese education is the high output of technically-qualified people. The Japanese do not regard technical achievements as of any less importance than academic qualifications.

But the Japanese education system faces a number of problems. The demand for places in the top state and private high schools and universities exceeds the supply of places. This is largely because the best jobs in the civil service, industry, commerce and banking tend to be filled only by graduates of the most prestigious institutions. This is an important factor in the strong motivation of parents and pupils. Competition to pass the rigorous entrance examinations is intense and the examinations have become increasingly difficult. Hence the Japanese phrase (*shiken jigoku*) ('examination hell').

In order to pass these examinations Japanese children have to spend long hours not only on homework but also in attending various cramming schools (*juku* and *yobikō*) at weekends (usually Saturday afternoons) and on two or even three evenings each week. Costs of *juku* are high, depending on the subjects taught and the qualifications and successes of the teachers. The average fees are probably about ¥100 000 a year. Mothers stay at home to supervise homework and keep their children hard at work. Such mothers are called *kyōiku mama* ('education mums').

Students who are unsuccessful in passing into their chosen university may decide either to go to one of the less prestigious private universities (see below) or to do a year's extra study at a *yobikō*, costing over ¥1 million. Such students are described as *rōnin* (this is the term used for the masterless samurai in pre-modern Japan, that is, a samurai who had lost his position because of the death or disgrace of his master).

Among the consequences of 'examination hell' are:

(a) The children of parents who can afford the better *juku* and are prepared to spend the time needed to ensure the success of their children do better than those from less well-endowed families.
(b) Because of the pressures, individuality is suppressed.
(c) Children become repressed and introverted, inducing in extreme cases suicide or attempted suicide.
(d) Examinations, which are largely multiple choice because of the numbers involved, do not really test ability in the broadest sense.
(e) Successful candidates relax after passing the university entrance examination and students in many non-technical subjects coast through university to graduation as very few are permitted to fail once they have been allowed into a university.
(f) Bullying in schools has become an increasing problem. The culprits are often those who have been unsuccessful in the examination rat-race.
(g) Truancy has increased as a result of parental pressure and bullying.

Japanese teachers' salaries are higher than those of civil servants of equivalent grades but lower than those in industry and commerce. Teachers' status is generally high. Lynn has commented on 'the high levels of professionalism of Japanese teachers'. Candidates for a licence to become a teacher have to graduate from the education faculties of universities or from faculties which are authorized to run training courses for teachers. A majority of elementary school and middle school teachers belong to the teachers' union, *Nikkyōsō*. This is a left-wing union with a Marxist ideology, but the union has not had much success in instilling left-wing ideas into teaching.

In Japanese schools a good deal of time is spent on the teaching and study of the English language. Unfortunately, much of this effort is wasted. The emphasis has been placed on grammar and vocabulary and insufficient time is allowed for practice in listening and speaking.

The Japanese authorities have been aware of the problems in their school system for many years and various efforts have been made at reform with a view to encouraging individual initiative, giving children more time for play and sports, reducing the role of the *juku*, mitigating 'examination hell', ensuring equality of opportunity without adding to costs and bureaucratic control, eliminating serious bullying, improving language teaching and developing appreciation of cultural values. These efforts have only had very limited success so far. Organizations involved in these efforts include the Ad Hoc Council on Education (*Rinji kyōiku shingikai*) established under Prime Minister Nakasone in 1984, and the Education System Research Council (*Bunkyō seidō chōsakai*) under the LDP's Policy Affairs Research Council (*Seimu chōsakai*).

10.1.3 Universities

Japan has a large number of universities of greatly varying prestige and competence. There is a clear hierarchy among universities, with the main government universities which formed Japan's eight pre-war imperial universities at the top of the league. The university with the highest prestige is Tokyo University, followed by Kyoto University. Another highly prestigious government university is Hitotsubashi University in Tokyo which was originally the Tokyo School of Commerce. It specialises in economics, law, social science and commerce. Some of the top private universities also attract élite students. The best known of these are Keiō University and Waseda University in Tokyo and Dōshisha in Kyoto. Sophia University, which is a Jesuit foundation, has grown in stature and attracts high-quality students. The Gakushūin, which was the peers college, also retains its prestige, not least because it was attended by the Emperor and his sons. Some of these universities, including Keiō and Gakushūin, are the apex of a private educational system beginning at kindergarten and going on up the scale to university.

In 1989 there were 2065 universities in Japan of which 504 were national institutions, 61 were local public universities and 1500 were private. There were also 462 junior colleges (*tanki daigaku* or short-term universities), 42 colleges of technology, 742 special training schools and 434 miscellaneous schools. The vast majority in these latter categories were private institutions. They have to be approved by the Ministry and are subject to inspection.

Only about a quarter of Japanese university students are women.

The most popular field of study at university is social science which includes law and economics, subjects which are regarded as useful when applying for jobs in the civil service and business. The next most popular subjects are engineering and the humanities. Only 3 per cent of university students study science.

Tuition fees at state universities average about ¥300 000. Fees at private universities are generally much higher, depending on the prestige of the institution. Fees for medical, dental and veterinary students are the highest of all. Most university students either live at home or in dormitories attached to the university. There is some limited financial support for able students who cannot afford the costs. This includes interest-free loans of up to ¥50 000 a month and some low-interest scholarships. Some 450 000 students in 1990 took advantage of these arrangements.

In order to graduate from a four-year university course a student requires 124 credits, of which 76 relate to his chosen specialist field of study, 8 to foreign languages, 4 to health and physical education and 36 to general education. The general education credits are normally taken in the first two years of a university course. Considerable flexibility is allowed in the selection of subjects for study.

Teaching generally consists of lectures to large classes. Academic staff teach for between 8 and 15 hours each week and students attend classes for about 15–20 hours each week.

Students are assessed at the end of each term and must normally pass in all subjects before proceeding to the next year's course. There are examinations at the end of each session and grades 1 to 5 are allocated on the basis of the examination and on course work. There is no final grading at graduation and thus no comparable system to the British grades of honours degrees. A student normally passes and graduates or fails and redoes the work until he passes. Very few fail to graduate in the end and university students reckon that they have a much easier time than they had at high school. In 1989, 377 000 students graduated from Japanese universities, of whom 80 per cent entered employment and 7 per cent started graduate courses. Of those entering employment,

36 per cent took up jobs in commerce, 26 per cent in engineering, 19 per cent in sales and 10 per cent in teaching.

In 1989, 302 Japanese universities had post-graduate schools. Of these, 87 only offered masters programmes and the remaining 215 offered doctoral programmes. The vast majority of national universities have postgraduate schools but only just over half the rest have such facilities.

Most students at junior colleges (*tanki daigaku*) lasting two, or occasionally three, years are women. These colleges train teachers for kindergarten and elementary schools and women who enter commercial firms in clerical posts. The main subjects studied at junior colleges are humanities, social science, home economics and education.

Colleges of technology, which offer courses in engineering or marine studies covering five years or so, are few in number (62) and take less than 1 per cent of entrants into higher education. But some 10 per cent of students at these colleges go on to study technology at university.

Special training schools provide high-level technical training in specialist fields. They had about 750 000 students in 1990.

Miscellaneous schools cover a wide variety of subjects including driving, nursing and so on.

Relations with industry are on the whole good, but industrial companies do not do much commissioning of research at universities and do not normally develop the same close links as some firms in Britain do with particular institutions. Industry generally likes to do much of its own training.

Standards of research vary greatly between universities. Some Japanese research is of a high level, both in social sciences including history and in scientific and technical subjects.

10.2 CULTURE

10.2.1 Cultural Organizations

The most important government cultural organization is the Cultural Agency (*Bunkachō*) under the Ministry of Education (see above).

The Japan Foundation (*Kokusai kōryū kikin*) is a public corporation which comes under the supervision of the Ministry of Foreign Affairs. It is responsible for administering international exchanges in cultural fields. It arranges and provides funds for exchange programmes involving scholars and artists; organizes exhibitions; helps to fund research on Japan; and tries to promote the study of the Japanese language. It has a number of small offices abroad. Its headquarters are in Tokyo. The President of the Foundation is normally a senior retired ambassador. While its director general also comes from the Foreign Ministry its staff are separately recruited. Its funds come mainly from a government endowment. It aims to emulate the British Council but its resources and its overseas offices are considerably smaller.

The National Theatre (*Kokuritsu gekijo*) was built with government funds. It is located next to the Supreme Court in Tokyo. It puts on performances of traditional Japanese drama. The larger theatre normally houses performances of *Kabuki*. When the puppet drama (*Bunraku*) company from Osaka is in town they perform in the smaller theatre. Their performances are also called *Jōruri*.

Japan has a number of national museums. The Tokyo National Museum is at Ueno Park. The main building was designed by the English architect Josiah Conder and built in 1882, but it was damaged in the earthquake of 1923 and the present buildings are of a later date. It houses many objects owned by the imperial household as well as treasures deposited with or loaned to the museum by Japanese temples, including the Hōryūji in Nara. There are also national museums in Kyoto and Nara with fine Japanese collections of their own. The museum in Nara has an outstanding collection of Buddhist sculpture. It is used for the annual displays of items from the Shōsōin, the imperial storehouse in the precincts of the Tōdaiji in Nara, which was built in wood in the eighth century (the Nara period) and contains objects donated by the Empress Kōmyō in 756 AD in memory of her husband the Emperor Shōmu.

The Tokyo National Museum of Modern Art, also in Ueno Park, houses paintings and prints by modern Japanese artists. The National Museum of Western Art at Ueno Park, in a building designed by Le Corbusier, houses the Matsukata Collection which includes many Impressionist and Post-impressionist paintings.

In recent years the number of museums and art galleries established by prefectures and municipalities has grown enormously. Most are well-designed modern buildings with good lighting and exhibition space. The collections vary in quality depending on local wealth and resources. Archaeological museums provide valuable educational opportunities and groups of school children visit such museums on a regular basis.

There are a large number of excellent private museums established by foundations and wealthy individuals in Tokyo, Osaka and other cities. Some of these are devoted to Western art such as the Bridgestone Gallery in Tokyo, or have a mixture of Western and Japanese galleries such as the Ohara Museum at Kurashiki. Among the outstanding private museums in Tokyo are the Idemitsu, Nezu, Gotō and Suntory galleries. Some, such as the Idemitsu, also have a gallery in Osaka. There are particularly fine galleries in Hiroshima (owned by the Bank of Hiroshima), in Atami (established by the MOA Foundation, a religious organization), at Hachioji in the Fuji Museum (established by Soka Gakkai, the Buddhist organization). The Japan Folk Craft Museum (*Mingeikan*) in Komaba, Tokyo, is devoted to preserving Japanese traditional crafts and the works of famous artists of the *mingei* movement. Various cities have museums/galleries devoted to the works of individual artists.

Japanese department stores often organize good art exhibitions as a means of attracting customers to their stores.

Many new concert halls have been built in recent decades. Japanese orchestras and musicians performing Western music are among the best in the world. Tokyo and Osaka are particularly well served.

10.2.2 Leisure Facilities

In recent years facilities for sport and leisure have expanded vastly. One of the most popular sports in Japan is baseball and major baseball matches are top events. Rugby football is played by a number of universities and clubs. Some also have rowing clubs. Skiing in the winter is increasingly popular and many ski resorts have been developed in the Japan Alps and in Hokkaidō. In summer, water sports including swimming and sailing attract large numbers of young people.

Martial arts (*budō*) including *jūdō*, *aikidō* and *kendō* are practised by young and old, but do not attract the same publicity as baseball. Japanese-style wrestling known as *sumo* is a cult sport. There are six 15-day tournaments (*basho*) each year. Two of these are held in Tokyo at the *Kokugikan* and one each in Osaka, Nagoya and Fukuoka. The *sumo* champions are trained in 'stables' (*heya*). Top champions are known as *yokozuna*. The next grades are *ōzeki*, *sekiwake*, *komusubi* and *maegashira*.

The businessman's sport is golf, and golf clubs have sprung up in country districts especially but not exclusively in the neighbourhood of Japanese cities, where many golf practice ranges can be found. The cost of joining the more prestigious golf clubs can be enormous and a trade in golf-club membership has developed. A hole-in-one can be expensive in Japan because winners are not only expected to stand drinks but also to give presents to their friends and colleagues. Many golfers take out hole-in-one insurance policies.

The indoor game most popular with the working man is the mindless pinball pursuit called *pachinko* which has become an addiction for some. Pachinko parlours can be found in all towns and in many country districts. Bowling is also popular with some men. Older men and women play gate ball, a form of croquet. The businessman prefers mahjong.

Japanese chess (*shōgi*) and *go* are more games for the connoisseur. Players of these games are awarded grades (*dan*); the highest grade for professional players is the ninth. The central *go* association is the *Nihon kiin*.

10.2.3 Religious Organizations

Article 20 of the Japanese Constitution guarantees freedom of religion for all. The same article stipulates 'No religious organization shall receive any privileges from the State, or exercise any political authority.' This article was designed to prevent the revival of state Shintō which had been used before the Second World War to promote extreme Japanese nationalism.

As explained in Chapter 1, the two main religions in Japan are Buddhism and Shintō. There are many forms of both Buddhism and Shintō in Japan. Before the Meiji Restoration of 1868 they were often to a considerable extent merged, and Buddhist and Shintō deities were combined. Even today many Japanese households have both a *Butsudan* (Buddhist tabernacle) and a *Kamidana* (Shintō shrine) in their houses. Japanese will go to Shintō shrines in their childhood and may be married in Shintō shrines by Shintō rituals (the *san san kudō* involving the drinking of sake in special cups). But most funerals follow Buddhist rights and most bodies are cremated.

Shintō places of worship are called shrines (*jinja*) and are distinguished by *torii*, a kind of simple gateway which marks the entrance to the shrine. Buddhist places of worship are called temples (*tera*). The

'Chinese' reading of this word is *ji*, thus temples are referred to by their name with the suffix *ji* added.

As described in Chapter 1, **Buddhism**, which reached Japan from China via Korea in the sixth century AD is of the Mahayana (greater vehicle) type. Most Japanese Buddhist sects originated in China but have had Japanese characteristics added. There are currently thirteen principal Buddhist sects in Japan but also many sub-sects. There are about 80 000 temples and some 150 000 Buddhist priests and nuns who can be distinguished by their shaven heads and robes.

The main sects that a foreigner may come across are Tendai, Shingon, Zen, Jōdo, Shinshū (a derivative of the Jōdo or 'pure land' sect) and Nichiren (a purely Japanese sect). Shingon is a form of Tantric or esoteric Buddhism. Jōdo and Shinshū are Amidist sects which emphasise the importance of Amida Buddha, one of the Buddha's manifestations known for his sense of mercy. The Amidists make use of the *nembutsu*, calling on the name of Amida (Amithaba) in the phrase *namu Amida Butsu*. Nichiren, who preached in the thirteenth century, stressed the importance of the Lotus Sutra known in Japanese as the *Myōhō renge kyō*. Nichiren Buddhism developed nationalist overtones and in contrast to the tolerance of other Buddhist sects in Japan has displayed intolerance towards other sects. One form of Nichiren Buddhism is Nichirenshōshū. Sōka gakkai is a lay organization which regards itself as belonging to Nichirenshōshū although the two have quarrelled. Kōmeitō (the clean government party) derives from Sōka gakkai.

Buddhists, other than followers of Sōka gakkai, have no clear political aspirations. Sometimes, as in Kyoto the temples that benefit greatly from tourism band together, for example, in opposition to a tax on entry tickets for famous temples or to the building of a large hotel which will, in their view, damage the Kyoto skyline.

Some temples have close historical connections with the imperial family and come within the orbit of the Imperial Househiold Agency. But since the Meiji Restoration the Emperors have not been practising Buddhists.

There were 81 835 recognized **Shintō** shrines in 1987. Most of these were organized under the Association of Shintō Shrines (*jinja honchō*). Shintō has many forms. It is polytheistic but Shintō gods (*kami*) may be better described as spirits. In farming communities it was primarily a fertility cult and the local *kami* might be thought to be in a rock, a tree or a mountain. The *kami* are not represented by images and the central item in a shrine may simply be a mirror. A cardinal feature of Shintō is the emphasis on ritual purity or cleansing.

Shintō was closely associated with the development of the Yamato people who came to dominate Japan in prehistoric times. The origins of Japan and the Japanese people are described in Japan's first 'history', the *Kojiki* (see Chapter 1) to the gods Izanagi and Izanami and to their daughter Amaterasu-omikami-no-mikoto (the sun goddess).

Following from this, Shintō came to be closely associated with the imperial family. Shintō ceremonies mark the enthronement of a new Emperor, and the Emperor still performs various Shintō rites such as planting and harvesting rice and may be regarded as a priestly king. The imperial shrines at Ise are very ancient and are regarded as the holiest of all Japanese shrines. Perhaps the next in importance is Taisha (literally, 'big shrine') at Izumo near Matsue in Tottori prefecture. The tombs of the various Emperors which are administered by the Imperial Household Agency are all marked by shrines.

Shintō also takes on elements of ancestor worship through the enshrinment of famous men in Japanese history. The Emperor Meiji (reigned 1867–1912) is one of these, and the Meiji shrine in Tokyo attracts vast numbers of visitors from all over Japan. Other heroes with their own shrines in Tokyo include Admiral Tōgō and General Nogi who made their reputations in the Russo-Japanese War of 1904/5. Sugawara Michizane (see Chapter 1) is revered as the god of learning and there are many *Tenjin* shrines dedicated to him.

The shrine to the war dead in Tokyo, the Yasukuni shrine, includes the names of convicted war criminals in its scrolls. On the anniversary of the end of the Second World War politicians anxious to appease right-wingers visit the shrine, some in their official capacities. This has aroused controversy in Japan and abroad. Some people object on the grounds that it is contrary at least to the spirit of Article 20 of the Constitution. A non-religious memorial to the war dead is at Chidorigafuchi by the imperial palace moat, not far from the Yasukuni shrine.

There are many other famous shrines in Japan. These include a number to the war god Hachiman. These shrines are known as Hachimangu, for example, at Kamakura.

Merchants often pray at *Inari* shrines which are marked by statues of foxes and red *torii*.

Whatever their beliefs or religion large numbers of Japanese people visit one or more Japanese shrines on New Year's Day if only for the ladies to display their best kimonos. People queue in thousands to visit the Meiji shrine and many will buy a talisman as a souvenir of their visit. Children of seven, five and three (*shichi, go, san*) years are taken to shrines to be blessed in November.

Christianity was first introduced into Japan in the sixteenth century by Portuguese Jesuits. Christians were persecuted and Christianity banned during the Tokugawa or Edo period (1600–1868) and it was only in 1873 that the anti-Christian laws were abrogated. Before the Second World War Christians faced difficulties because of the nationalist demands of state Shintō. Today there are about one million Christians in Japan. Just under 40 per cent are Catholics and the remainder belong mainly to Protestant sects including Anglicans and Baptists. The largest groups are, however, the *Nihon Kirisuto Kyōdan* (Japanese Christian Church) and the *Iesu no Mitama Kyokai Kyodan* (Spirit of Jesus Church). Although the number of Christians in Japan is small their influence has been greater than their numbers would suggest.

Japan also has a large number of **new religions** (*shinkō shūkyō*), although some of which will fall into this category are not really new. For instance, *Tenrikyō* was founded in 1838 and *Kurozumikyō* in 1814. Most of the new religions draw on aspects of Buddhism, Shintō and Christianity in one way or another. Some are very much the formations of charismatic individuals. The founder of *Tenrikyō*, Nakayama Miki, was thought of as a living god (*ikigami*) during her lifetime. Her aim was to restore the harmony between man and heaven. *Tenrikyō* has been very successful in making converts and collecting money. Its headquarters are in the city of Tenri near Nara. It has a particularly fine library.

In addition to *Sōka gakkai* (see above) another offshoot of Nichiren Buddhism is the *Risshō Kōseikai. Konkokyō* owes much to Taoism. Among the better-known new religions, largely of post-war origin, are *Oyama Nezunomikoto Shinshikyōkai,* claiming half a million followers; *Shinnyyōen*, claiming 2 million followers; and *Mahikari, Agonshū, Shinreikyō* and *Sekai kyūseikyō* (religion for the salvation of the world) which is also know as MOA after the name of the founder Okada Mokichi. It believes that one way towards salvation is through beauty in art. This has enabled it to build up fine collections in its two museums at Atami and Hakone.

10.2.4   The Media

Japan has a highly developed system of newspapers, journals, broadcasting and television.

Newspapers

According to statistics produced by the Japan Newspaper Publishers Association, Japan had in October 1989 124 daily newspapers with a combined circulation of 71.5 million. Most of Japan's newspapers are delivered to homes and are published seven days a week in morning and evening editions except that there are no evening papers on Sundays. Newspapers attract some 25 per cent of total advertising expenditure.

The three largest national dailies are the *Yomiuri*, with a morning circulation in 1989 of 9.65 million; the *Asahi*, with a circulation of just over 8 million; and the *Mainichi* with a circulation of 4.4 million. The other national dailies are the *Sankei* and the *Nihon Keizai*. The *Nihon Keizai* is the economic daily which is read by all businessmen.

All these newspapers are serious journals with wide coverage of national and international news. All claim to be independent and unattached to any political party. The *Yomiuri* is regarded as more populist than the others. The *Asahi* and the *Mainichi* have been considered 'leftist' at times while the *Sankei* is thought to be the most conservative. The *Nihon Keizai* (*Nikkei*) has the best economic coverage and takes a generally moderate position on most issues.

The national dailies have many foreign correspondents and give reasonable coverage to international news. Within Japan the newspapers have large numbers of correspondents who are attached to particular Ministries and agencies. These are organized in exclusive journalist groups (*kisha clubs*). The exclusivity of these and the close relationship which develops with the providers of news has aroused criticism among foreign correspondents in Japan.

The English-language papers in Japan have no political influence and little significance, but they can be a useful source of information for foreigners if they are interpreted with care. *The Daily Yomiuri*, *The Mainichi Daily News* and *The Asahi Evening News*, while taking news from the wire service also carry translations into English of pieces from the Japanese papers. The main English language daily with the best general coverage is *The Japan Times*. Japanese people often read these papers to get English language practice.

Kyōdō and Jiji are Japan's two main news agencies.

Magazines

Japan has numerous weekly magazines of varying quality. The weeklies produced by the main newspapers tend to be populist, although *Aera* produced by the *Asahi* regards itself as a magazine for the intellectual. Some of the monthlies, in particular *Bungei Shunjū* and *Chūō Kōron*, whose edition may run to 500 pages or more, are influential and serious magazines with significant circulations. Other important economic economic journals are *Tōyō Keizai*, *Diamond*, and *Nikkei Business*.

Books

In 1988 over 38 000 titles were published in Japan. The country's publishing industry is well developed, bookshops are numerous and the Japanese read a great deal despite the development of TV. One reason for this may be the amount of time that many Japanese have to spend commuting. The most popular books are *manga* books. *Manga* books contain serial stories in cartoon form. Many tell erotic or horror stories.

Broadcasting and Television

The Japan Broadcasting Corporation (NHK or *Nihon Hōsō Kyōkai*) was to some extent modelled on the BBC. It is a public broadcasting network funded by licence fees. In addition to radio broadcasting it runs two TV channels. One of these is termed educational (*kyōiku*).

There are five main commercial networks, each connected with one of the national newspapers. These are TV Asahi, NTV (*Yomiuri* group), TBS (*Mainichi* group), Fuji (*Sankei* group) and TV Tokyo (*Nihon Keizai*). Each prefecture has its own local stations which are usually connected with one or other of the mainstream companies. TV commercials used up nearly 29 per cent of Japanese advertising expenditure in 1990.

Satellite and cable television have been developing rapidly in the 1990s and 99.3 per cent of all Japanese households have TV sets, almost all of which are colour.

Opinions vary about the quality of Japanese TV programmes. To foreign observers TV games seem to occupy too much time and appear very childish, but the historical TV dramas put out by NHK attract many viewers.

Appendix 1

THE CONSTITUTION OF JAPAN

We, the Japanese people, acting through our duly elected representatives in the National Diet, determined that we shall secure for ourselves and our posterity the fruits of peaceful cooperation with all nations and the blessings of liberty throughout this land, and resolved that never again shall we be visited with the horrors of war through the action of government, do proclaim that sovereign power resides with the people and do firmly establish this Constitution. Government is a sacred trust of the people, the authority for which is derived from the people, the powers of which are exercised by the representatives of the people, and the benefits of which are enjoyed by the people. This is a universal principle upon which this Constitution is founded. We reject and revoke all constitutions, laws, ordinances, and rescripts in conflict herewith.

We, the Japanese people, desire peace for all time and are deeply conscious of the high ideals controlling human relationships, and we have determined to preserve our security and existence, trusting in the justice and faith of the peace-loving peoples of the world. We desire to occupy an honored place in an international society striving for the preservation of peace, and the banishment of tyranny and slavery, oppression and intolerance for all time from the earth. We recognize that all peoples of the world have the right to live in peace, free from fear and want.

We believe that no nation is responsible to itself alone, but that laws of political morality are universal; and that obedience to such laws is incumbent upon all nations who would sustain their own sovereignty and justify their sovereign relationship with other nations.

We, the Japanese people, pledge our national honor to accomplish these high ideals and purposes with all our resources.

Chapter I. The Emperor

Article 1. The Emperor shall be the symbol of the State and of the unity of the people, deriving his position from the will of the people with whom reside sovereign power.

Article 2. The Imperial Throne shall be dynastic and succeeded to in accordance with the Imperial House Law passed by the Diet.

Article 3. The advice and approval of the Cabinet shall be required for all acts of the Emperor in matters of state, and the Cabinet shall be responsible therefor.

Article 4. The Emperor shall perform only such acts in matters of state as are provided for in this Constitution and he shall not have powers related to government.

The Emperor may delegate the performance of his acts in matters of state as may be provided by law.

Article 5. When, in accordance with the Imperial House Law, a Regency is established, the Regent shall perform his acts in matters of state in the Emperor's name. In this case, paragraph one of the preceding article will be applicable.

Article 6. The Emperor shall appoint the Prime Minister as designated by the Diet.

The Emperor shall appoint the Chief Judge on the Supreme Court as designated by the Cabinet.

Article 7. The Emperor, with the advice and approval of the Cabinet, shall perform the following acts in matters of state on behalf of the people:

(1) Promulgation of amendments of the constitution, laws, cabinet orders and treaties.

(2) Convocation of the Diet.

(3) Dissolution of the House of Representatives.

(4) Proclamation of general election of members of the Diet.

(5) Attestation of the appointment and dismissal of Ministers of State and other officials as provided for by law, and of full powers and credentials of Ambassadors and Ministers.

(6) Attestation of general and special amnesty, commutation of punishment, reprieve and restoration of rights.

(7) Awarding of honors.

(8) Attestation of instruments of ratification and other diplomatic documents as provided for by law.

(9) Receiving foreign ambassadors and ministers.

(10) Performance of ceremonial functions.

Article 8. No property may be given to, or received by, the Imperial House, nor can any gifts be made therefrom, without the authorization of the Diet.

Chapter II.   Renunciation of War

Article 9. Aspiring sincerely to an international peace based on justice and order, the Japanese people forever renounce war as a sovereign right of the nation and the threat or use of force as means of settling international disputes.

In order to accomplish the aim of the preceding paragraph, land, sea, and air forces, as well as other war potential, will never be maintained. The right of belligerency of the state will not be recognized.

Chapter III.   Rights and Duties of the People

Article 10. The conditions necessary for being a Japanese national shall be determined by law.

Article 11. The people shall not be prevented from enjoying any of the fundamental human rights. These fundamental human rights guaranteed to the people by this Constitution shall be conferred upon the people of this and future generations as eternal and inviolate rights.

Article 12. The freedoms and rights guaranteed to the people by this Constitution shall be maintained by the constant endeavor of the people, who shall refrain from any abuse of these freedoms and rights and shall always be responsible for utilizing them for the public welfare.

Article 13.   All of the people shall be respected as individuals. Their right to life, liberty, and the pursuit of happiness shall, to the extent that it does not interfere with the public welfare, be the supreme consideration in legislation and in other governmental affairs.

Article 14.   All of the people are equal under the law and there shall be no discrimination in political, economic or social relations because of race, creed, sex, social status or family origin.

Peers and peerage shall not be recognized.

No privilege shall accompany any award of honor, decoration or any distinction, nor shall such award be valid beyond the lifetime of the individual who now holds or hereafter may receive it.

Article 15.   The people have the inalienable right to choose their public officials and to dismiss them.

All public officials are servants of the whole community and not of any group thereof.

Universal adult suffrage is guaranteed with regard to the election of public officials.

In all elections, secrecy of the ballot shall not be violated. A voter shall not be answerable, publicly or privately, for the choice he has made.

Article 16.   Every person shall have the right of peaceful petition for the redress of damage, for the removal of public officials, for the enactment, repeal or amendment of laws, ordinances or regulations and for other matters; nor shall any person be in any way discriminated against for sponsoring such a petition.

Article 17.   Every person may sue for redress as provided by law from the State or a public entity, in case he has suffered damage through illegal act of any public official.

Article 18.   No person shall be held in bondage of any kind. Involuntary servitude, except as punishment for crime, is prohibited.

Article 19.   Freedom of thought and conscience shall not be violated.

Article 20.   Freedom of religion is guaranteed to all. No religious organization shall receive any privileges from the State, nor exercise any political authority.

No person shall be compelled to take part in any religious act, celebration, rite or practice.

The State and its organs shall refrain from religious education or any other religious activity.

Article 21.   Freedom of assembly and association as well as speech, press and all other forms of expression are guaranteed.

No censorship shall be maintained, nor shall the secrecy of any means of communication be violated.

Article 22.   Every person shall have freedom to choose and change his residence and to choose his occupation to the extent that it does not interfere with the public welfare.

Freedom of all persons to move to a foreign country and to divest themselves of their nationality shall be inviolate.

Article 23.   Academic freedom is guaranteed.

Article 24. Marriage shall be based only on the mutual consent of both sexes and it shall be maintained through mutual cooperation with the equal rights of husband and wife as a basis.

With regard to choice of spouse, property rights, inheritance, choice of domicile, divorce or other matters pertaining to marriage and the family, laws shall be enacted from the standpoint of individual dignity and the essential equality of the sexes.

Article 25. All people shall have the right to maintain the minimum standards of wholesome and cultured living.

In all spheres of life, the State shall use its endeavors for the promotion and extension of social welfare and security, and of public health.

Article 26. All people shall have the right to receive an equal education correspondent to their ability, as provided by law.

All people shall be obligated to have all boys and girls under their protection receive ordinary education as provided for by law. Such compulsory education shall be free.

Article 27. All people shall have the right and the obligation to work.

Standards for wages, hours, rest and other working conditions shall be fixed by law.

Children shall not be exploited.

Article 28. The right of workers to organize and to bargain and act collectively is guaranteed.

Article 29. The right to own or to hold property is inviolable.

Property rights shall be defined by law, in conformity with the public welfare.

Private property may be taken for public use upon just compensation therefor.

Article 30. The people shall be liable to taxation as provided by law.

Article 31. No person shall be deprived of life or liberty, nor shall any other criminal penalty be imposed, except according to procedure established by law.

Article 32. No person shall be denied the right of access to the courts.

Article 33. No person shall be apprehended except upon warrant issued by a competent judicial officer which specifies the offense with which the person is charged, unless he is apprehended, the offense being committed.

Article 34. No person shall be arrested or detained without being at once informed of the charges against him or without the immediate privilege of counsel; nor shall he be detained without adequate cause; and upon demand of any person such cause must be immediately shown in open court in his presence and the presence of his counsel.

Article 35. The right of all persons to be secure in their homes, papers and effects against entries, searches and seizures shall not be impaired except upon warrant issued for adequate cause and particularly describing the place to be searched and things to be seized, or except as provided for by **Article 33.**

Each search or seizure shall be made upon separate warrant issued by a competent judicial officer.

Article 36. The infliction of torture by any public officer and cruel punishments are absolutely forbidden.

Article 37. In all criminal cases the accused shall enjoy the right to a speedy and public trial by an impartial tribunal.

He shall be permitted full opportunity to examine all witnesses, and he shall have the right of compulsory process for obtaining witnesses on his behalf at public expense.

At all times the accused shall have the assistance of competent counsel who shall, if the accused is unable to secure the same by his own efforts, be assigned to his use by the State.

Article 38. No person shall be compelled to testify against himself.

Confession made under compulsion, torture or threat, or after prolonged arrest or detention shall not be admitted in evidence.

No person shall be convicted or punished in cases where the only proof against him is his own confession.

Article 39. No person shall be held criminally liable for an act which was lawful at the time it was committed, or of which he has been acquitted, nor shall he be placed in double jeopardy.

Article 40. Any person, in case he is acquitted after he has been arrested or detained, may sue the State for redress as provided by law.

Chapter IV. The Diet

Article 41. The Diet shall be the highest organ of state power, and shall be the sole law-making organ of the State.

Article 42. The Diet shall consist of two Houses, namely the House of Representatives and the House of Councillors.

Article 43. Both Houses shall consist of elected members, representative of all the people.

The number of the members of each House shall be fixed by law.

Article 44. The qualifications of members of both Houses and their electors shall be fixed by law. However, there shall be no discrimination because of race, creed, sex, social status, family origin, education, property or income.

Article 45. The term of office of members of the House of Representatives shall be four years. However, the term shall be terminated before the full term is up in case the House of Representatives is dissolved.

Article 46. The term of office of members of the House of Councillors shall be six years, and election for half the members shall take place every three years.

Article 47. Electoral districts, method of voting and other matters pertaining to the method of election of members of both Houses shall be fixed by law.

Article 48. No person shall be permitted to be a member of both Houses simultaneously.

Article 49. Members of both Houses shall receive appropriate annual payment from the national treasury in accordance with law.

Article 50. Except in cases provided by law, members of both houses shall be exempt from apprehension while the Diet is in session, and any members apprehended before the opening of the session shall be freed during the term of the session upon demand of the House.

Article 51. Members of both Houses shall not be held liable outside the House for speeches, debates or votes cast inside the House.

Article 52. An ordinary session of the Diet shall be convoked once per year.

Article 53. The Cabinet may determine to convoke extraordinary sessions of the Diet. When a quarter or more of the total members of either House makes the demand, the Cabinet must determine on such convocation.

Article 54. When the House of Representatives is dissolved, there must be a general election of members of the House of Representatives within forty (40) days from the date of dissolution and the Diet must be convoked within thirty (30) days from the date of the election.

When the House of Representatives is dissolved, the House of Councillors is closed at the same time. However, the Cabinet may in time of national emergency convoke the House of Councillors in emergency session.

Measures taken at such session as mentioned in the proviso of the preceding paragraph shall be provisional and shall become null and void unless agreed to by the House of Representatives within a period of ten (10) days after the opening of the next session of the Diet.

Article 55. Each House shall judge disputes related to qualifications of its members. However, in order to deny a seat to any member, it is necessary to pass a resolution by a majority of two-thirds or more of the members present.

Article 56. Business cannot be transacted in either House unless one-third or more of total membership is present.

All matters shall be decided, in each House, by a majority of those present, except as elsewhere provided in the Constitution, and in case of a tie, the presiding officer shall decide the issue.

Article 57. Deliberation in each House shall be public. However, a secret meeting may be held where a majority of two-thirds or more of those members present passes a resolution therefor.

Each House shall keep a record of proceedings. This record shall be published and given general circulation, excepting such parts of proceedings of secret session as may be deemed to require secrecy.

Upon demand of one-fifth or more of the members present, votes of the members on any matter shall be recorded in the minutes.

Article 58. Each House shall select its own president and other officials.

Each House shall establish its rules pertaining to meetings, proceedings and internal discipline and may punish members for disorderly conduct. However, in order to expel a member, a majority of two-thirds or more of those members present must pass a resolution thereon.

Article 59. A bill becomes a law on passage by both Houses, except as otherwise provided by the Constitution.

A bill which is passed by the House of Representatives, and upon which the House of Councillors makes a decision different from that of the House of Representatives, becomes a law when passed a second time by the House of Representatives by a majority of two-thirds or more of the members present.

The provision of the preceding paragraph does not preclude the House of Representatives from calling for the meeting of a joint committee of both Houses, provided for by law.

Failure by the House of Councillors to take final action within sixty (60) days after receipt of a bill passed by the House of Representatives, time in recess except, may be determined by the House of Representatives to constitute a rejection of the said bill by the House of Councillors.

Article 60. The budget must first be submitted to the House of Representatives.

Upon consideration of the budget, when the House of Councillors makes a decision different from that of the House of Representatives, and when no agreement can be reached even through a joint committee of both Houses, provided for by law, or in the case of failure by the House of Councillors to take final action within thirty (30) days, the period of recess excluded, after the receipt of the budget passed by the House of Representatives, the decision of the House of Representatives shall be the decision of the Diet.

Article 61. The second paragraph of the preceding article applies also to the Diet approval required for the conclusion of treaties.

Article 62. Each House may conduct investigations in relation to government, and may demand the presence and testimony of witnesses, and the production of records.

Article 63. The Prime Minister and other Ministers of State may, at any time, appear in either House for the purpose of speaking on bills regardless of whether they are members of the House or not. They must appear when their presence is required in order to give answers or explanations.

Article 64. The Diet shall set up an impeachment court from among the members of both Houses for the purpose of trying those judges against whom removal proceedings have been instituted.

Matters relating to impeachment shall be provided by law.

Chapter V. The Cabinet

Article 65. Executive power shall be vested in the Cabinet.

Article 66. The Cabinet shall consist of the Prime Minister, who shall be its head, and other Ministers of State, as provided for by law.

The Prime Minister and other Ministers of State must be civilians

The Cabinet, in the exercise of executive power, shall be collectively responsible to the Diet.

Article 67. The Prime Minister shall be designated from among the members of the Diet by a resolution of the Diet. This designation shall precede all other business.

If the House of Representatives and the House of Councillors disagree and if no agreement can be reached even through a joint committee of both Houses, provided for by law, or the House of Councillors fails to make designation within ten (10) days, exclusive of the period of recess, after the House of Representatives has made designation, the decision of the House of Representatives shall be the decision of the Diet.

Article 68. The Prime Minister shall appoint the Ministers of State. However, a majority of their number must be chosen from among the members of the Diet.

The Prime Minister may remove the Ministers of State as he chooses.

Article 69. If the House of Representatives passes a non-confidence resolution, or rejects a confidence resolution, the Cabinet shall resign en masse, unless the House of Representatives is dissolved within ten (10) days.

Article 70. When there is a vacancy in the post of Prime Minister, or upon the first convocation of the Diet after a general election of members of the House of Representatives, the Cabinet shall resign en masse.

Article 71. In the cases mentioned in the two preceding articles, the Cabinet shall continue its functions until the time when a new Prime Minister is appointed.

Article 72. The Prime Minister, representing the Cabinet, submits bills, reports on general national affairs and foreign relations to the Diet and exercises control and supervision over various administrative branches.

Article 73. The Cabinet, in addition to other general administrative functions shall perform the following functions:

(1) Administer the law faithfully; conduct affairs of state.

(2) Manage foreign affairs.

(3) Conclude treaties. However, it shall obtain prior or, depending on circumstances, subsequent approval of the Diet.

(4) Administer the civil service, in accordance with standards established by law.

(5) Prepare the budget, and present it to the Diet.

(6) Enact cabinet orders in order to execute the provisions of the Constitution and of the law. However, it cannot include penal provisions in such cabinet orders unless authorized by such law.

(7) Decide on general amnesty, special amnesty, commutation of punishment, reprieve, and restoration of rights.

Article 74. All laws and cabinet orders shall be signed by the competent Minister of State and countersigned by the Prime Minister.

Article 75. The Ministers of State, during their tenure of office, shall not be subject to legal action without the consent of the Prime Minister. However, the right to take that action is not impaired hereby.

Chapter VI. Judiciary

Article 76. The whole judicial power is vested in a Supreme Court and in such inferior courts as are established by law.

No extraordinary tribunal shall be established, nor shall any organ or agency of the Executive be given final judicial power.

All judges shall be independent in the exercise of their conscience and shall be bound only by this Constitution and the laws.

Article 77. The Supreme Court is vested with the rule-making power under which it determines the rules of procedure and of practice, and of matters relating to attorneys, the internal discipline of the courts and the administration of judicial affairs.

Public procurators shall be subject to the rule-making power of the Supreme Court.

The Supreme Court may delegate the power to make rules for inferior courts to such courts.

Article 78. Judges shall not be removed except by public impeachment unless judicially declared mentally or physically incompetent to perform official duties. No disciplinary action against judges shall be administered by any executive organ or agency.

Article 79. The Supreme Court shall consist of a Chief Judge and such number of judges as may be determined by law; all such judges excepting the Chief Judge shall be appointed by the Cabinet.

The appointment of the judges of the Supreme Court shall be reviewed by the people at the first general election of members of the House of Representatives following their appointment, and shall be reviewed again at the first general election of members of the House of Representatives after a lapse of ten (10) years, and in the same manner thereafter.

In cases mentioned in the foregoing paragraph, when the majority of the voters favors the dismissal of a judge, he shall be dismissed.

Matters pertaining to review shall be prescribed by law.

The judges of the Supreme Court shall be retired upon the attainment of the age as fixed by law.

All such judges shall receive, at regular stated intervals, adequate compensation which shall not be decreased during their terms of office.

Article 80. The judges of the inferior courts shall be appointed by the Cabinet from a list of persons nominated by the Supreme Court. All such judges shall hold office for a term of ten (10) years with privilege of reappointment, provided that they shall be retired upon the attainment of the age as fixed by law.

The judges of the inferior courts shall receive, at regular stated intervals, adequate compensation which shall not be decreased during their terms of office.

Article 81. The Supreme Court is the court of last resort with power to determine the constitutionality of any law, order, regulation or official act.

Article 82. Trials shall be conducted and judgement declared publicly.

Where a court unanimously determines publicity to be dangerous to public order or morals, a trial may be conducted privately, but trials of political offenses, offenses involving the press or cases wherein the rights of people as guaranteed in Chapter III of this Constitution are in question shall always be conducted publicly.

Chapter VII. Finance

Article 83. The power to administer national finances shall be exercised as the Diet shall determine.

Article 84. No new taxes shall be imposed or existing ones modified except by law or under such conditions as law may prescribe.

Article 85. No money shall be expended, nor shall the State obligate itself, except as authorized by the Diet.

Article 86. The Cabinet shall prepare and submit to the Diet for its consideration and decision a budget for each fiscal year.

Article 87. In order to provide for unforeseen deficiencies in the budget, a reserve fund may be authorized by the Diet to be expended upon the responsibility of the Cabinet.

The Cabinet must get subsequent approval of the Diet for all payments from the reserve fund.

Article 88. All property of the Imperial Household shall belong to the State.

All expenses of the Imperial Household shall be appropriated by the Diet in the budget.

Article 89. No public money or other property shall be expended or appropriated for the use, benefit or maintenance of any religious institution or association, or for any charitable, educational or benevolent enterprises not under the control of public authority.

Article 90. Final accounts of the expenditures and revenues of the State shall be audited annually by a Board of Audit and submitted by the Cabinet to the Diet, together with the statement of audit, during the fiscal year immediately following the period covered.

The organisation and competency of the Board of Audit shall be determined by law.

Article 91. At regular intervals and at least annually the Cabinet shall report to the Diet and the people on the state of national finances.

Chapter VIII. Local Self-Government

Article 92. Regulations concerning organization and operations of local public entities shall be fixed by law in accordance with the principle of local autonomy.

Article 93. The local public entities shall establish assemblies as their deliberative organs, in accordance with law.

The chief executive officers of all local public entities, the members of their assemblies, and such other local officials as may be determined by law shall be elected by direct popular vote within their several communities.

Article 94. Local public entities shall have the right to manage their property, affairs and administration and to enact their own regulations within law.

Article 95. A special law, applicable only to one local public entity, cannot be enacted by the Diet without the consent of the majority of the voters of the local public entity concerned, obtained in accordance with law.

Chapter IX. Amendments

Article 96. Amendments to this Constitution shall be initiated by the Diet, through a concurring vote of two-thirds or more of all the members of each House and shall thereupon be submitted to the people for ratification, which shall require the affirmative vote of a majority of all votes cast thereon, at a special referendum or at such election as the Diet shall specify.

Amendments when so ratified shall immediately be promulgated by the Emperor in the name of the people, as an integral part of this Constitution.

Chapter X. Supreme Law

Article 97. The fundamental human rights by this Constitution guaranteed to the people of Japan are fruits of the age-old struggle of man to be free; they have survived the many exacting tests for durability and are conferred upon this and future generations in trust, to be held for all time inviolate.

Article 98.   This Constitution shall be the supreme law of the nation and no law, ordinance, imperial rescript or other act of government, or part thereof, contrary to the provisions hereof, shall have legal force or validity.

Article 99.   The Emperor or the Regent as well as Ministers of State, members of the Diet, judges, and all other public officials have the obligation to respect and uphold this Constitution.

Chapter XI.   Supplementary Provisions

Article 100.   This Constitution shall be enforced as from the day when the period of six months will have elapsed counting from the days of its promulgation.

The enactment of laws necessary for the enforcement of this Constitution, the election of members of the House of Councillors and the procedure for the convocation of the Diet and other preparatory procedures for the enforcement of this Constitution may be executed before the day prescribed in the preceding paragraph.

Article 101.   If the House of Councillors is not constituted before the effective date of this Constitution, the House of Representatives shall function as the Diet until such time as the House of Councillors shall be constituted.

Article 102.   The term of office for half the members of the House of Councillors serving in the first term under this Constitution shall be three years.

Members falling under this category shall be determined in accordance with law.

Article 103.   The Ministers of State, members of the House of Representatives, and judges in office on the effective date of this Constitution, and all other public officials, who occupy positions corresponding to such positions as are recognized by this Constitution shall not forfeit their positions automatically on account of the enforcement of this Constitution unless otherwise specified by law. When, however, successors are elected or appointed under the provisions of this Constitution, they shall forfeit their positions as a matter of course.

Appendix 2

TREATY OF PEACE WITH JAPAN

San Francisco, 8th September, 1951

Whereas the Allied Powers and Japan are resolved that henceforth their relations shall be those of nations which, as sovereign equals, co-operate in friendly association to promote their common welfare and to maintain international peace and security, and are therefore desirous of concluding a Treaty of Peace which will settle questions still outstanding as a result of the existence of a state of war between them;

Whereas Japan for its part declares its intention to apply for membership in the United Nations; to seek to create within Japan conditions of stability and well-being as defined in Articles 55 and 56 of the Charter of the United Nations and already initiated by post-surrender Japanese legislation; and in public and private trade and commerce to conform to internationally accepted fair practices;

Whereas the Allied Powers welcome the intentions of Japan set out in the foregoing paragraph;

The Allied Powers and Japan have therefore determined to conclude the present Treaty of Peace, and have accordingly appointed the undersigned Plenipotentiaries, who, after presentation of their full powers, found in good and due form, have agreed on the following provisions:

CHAPTER I.—PEACE

ARTICLE 1

(*a*) The state of war between Japan and each of the Allied Powers is terminated as from the date on which the present Treaty comes into force between Japan and the Allied Power concerned, as provided for in Article 23.

(*b*) The Allied Powers recognise the full sovereignty of the Japanese people over Japan and its territorial waters.

CHAPTER II.—TERRITORY

ARTICLE 2

(*a*) Japan, recognising the independence of Korea, renounces all right, title and claim to Korea, including the islands of Quelpart, Port Hamilton and Dagelet.

(*b*) Japan renounces all right, title and claim to Formosa and the Pescadores.

(*c*) Japan renounces all right, title and claim to the Kurile Islands, and to that portion of Sakhalin and the islands adjacent to it over which Japan acquired sovereignty as a consequence of the Treaty of Portsmouth of 5th September, 1905.

199

(*d*) Japan renounces all right, title and claim in connection with the League of Nations Mandate System, and accepts the action of the United Nations Security Council of 2nd April, 1947, extending the trusteeship system to the Pacific Islands formerly under mandate to Japan.

(*e*) Japan renounces all claim to any right or title to or interest in connection with any part of the Antarctic area, whether deriving from the activities of Japanese nationals or otherwise.

(*f*) Japan renounces all right, title and claim to the Spratly Islands and to the Paracel Islands

ARTICLE 3

Japan will concur in any proposal of the United States to the United Nations to place under its trusteeship system, with the United States as the sole administering authority, Nansei Shoto south of 29^0 north latitude (including the Ryukyu Islands and the Daito Islands), Nanpo Shoto south of Sofu Gan (including the Bonin Islands, Rosario Island and the Volcano Islands) and Parece Vela and Marcus Island. Pending the making of such a proposal and the affirmative action thereon, the United States will have the right to exercise all and any powers of administration, legislation and jurisdiction over the territory and inhabitants of these islands, including their territorial waters.

ARTICLE 4

(*a*) Subject to the provisions of paragraph (b) of this Article, the disposition of property of Japan and of its nationals in the areas referred to in Article 2, and their claims, including debts, against the authorities presently administering such areas and the residents (including juridical persons) thereof, and the disposition in Japan of property of such authorities and residents, and of claims, including debts, of such authorities and residents against Japan and its nationals, shall be the subject of special arrangements between Japan and such authorities. The property of any of the Allied Powers or its nationals in the areas referred to in Article 2 shall, insofar as this has not already been done, be returned by the administering authority in the condition in which it now exists. (The term "nationals" whenever used in the present Treaty includes juridical persons.)

(*b*) Japan recognises the validity of dispositions of property of Japan and Japanese nationals made by or pursuant to directives of the United States Military Government in any of the areas referred to in Articles 2 and 3.

(*c*) Japanese owned submarine cables connecting Japan with territory removed from Japanese control pursuant to the present Treaty shall be equally divided, Japan retaining the Japanese terminal and adjoining half of the cable, and the detached territory the remainder of the cable and connecting terminal facilities.

CHAPTER III.—SECURITY

ARTICLE 5

(*a*) Japan accepts the obligations set forth in Article 2 of the Charter of the United Nations, and in particular the obligations

(i) to settle its international disputes by peaceful means in such a manner that international peace and security, and justice, are not endangered;

(ii) to refrain in its international relations from the threat or use of force against the territorial integrity or political independence of any State or in any other manner inconsistent with the purposes of the United Nations;

(iii) to give the United Nations every assistance in any action it takes in accordance with the Charter and to refrain from giving assistance to any State against which the United Nations may take preventive or enforcement action.

(b) The Allied Powers confirm that they will be guided by the principles of Article 2 of the Charter of the United Nations in their relations with Japan.

(c) The Allied Powers for their part recognise that Japan as a sovereign nation possesses the inherent right of individual or collective self-defence referred to in Article 51 of the Charter of the United Nations and that Japan may voluntarily enter into collective security arrangements.

ARTICLE 6

(a) All occupation forces of the Allied Powers shall be withdrawn from Japan as soon as possible after the coming into force of the present Treaty, and in any case not later than 90 days thereafter. Nothing in this provision shall, however, prevent the stationing or retention of foreign armed forces in Japanese territory under or in consequence of any bilateral or multilateral agreements which have been or may be made between one or more of the Allied Powers, on the one hand, and Japan on the other.

(b) The provisions of Article 9 of the Potsdam Proclamation of July 26, 1945, dealing with the return of Japanese military forces to their homes, to the extent not already completed, will be carried out.

(c) All Japanese property for which compensation has not already been paid, which was supplied for the use of occupation forces and which remains in the possession of those forces at the time of the coming into force of the present Treaty, shall be returned to the Japanese Government within the same 90 days unless other arrangements are made by mutual agreement.

CHAPTER IV.—POLITICAL AND ECONOMIC CLAUSES

ARTICLE 7

(a) Each of the Allied Powers, within one year after the present Treaty has come into force between it and Japan, will notify Japan which of its pre-war bilateral treaties or conventions with Japan it wishes to continue in force or revive, and any treaties or conventions so notified shall continue in force or be revived subject only to such amendments as may be necessary to ensure conformity with the present Treaty. The Treaties and conventions so notified shall be considered as having been continued in force or revived three months after the date of notification and shall be registered with the Secretariat of the United Nations. All such treaties and conventions as to which Japan is not so notified shall be regarded as abrogated.

(*b*) Any notification made under paragraph (a) of this Article may except from the operation or revival of a treaty or convention any territory for the international relations of which the notifying Power is responsible, until three months after the date on which notice is given to Japan that such exception shall cease to apply.

ARTICLE 8

(*a*) Japan will recognise the full force of all treaties now or hereafter concluded by the Allied Powers for terminating the state of war initiated on 1st September, 1939, as well as any other arrangements by the Allied Powers for or in connection with the restoration of peace. Japan also accepts the arrangements made for terminating the former League of Nations and Permanent Court of International Justice.

(*b*) Japan renounces all such rights and interests as it may derive from being a signatory Power of the Conventions of St. Germain-en-Laye of 10th September 1919, and the Straits Agreement of Montreux of 20th July, 1936, and from Article 16 of the Treaty of Peace with Turkey signed at Lausanne on 24th July, 1923.

(*c*) Japan renounces all rights, title and interests acquired under, and is discharged from all obligations resulting from, the Agreement between Germany and the Creditor Powers of 20th January, 1930, and its Annexes, including the Trust Agreement, dated 17th May, 1930, the Convention of 20th January, 1930, respecting the Bank for International Settlements and the Statutes of the Bank for International Settlements. Japan will notify to the Ministry of Foreign Affairs in Paris within six months of the first coming into force of the present Treaty its renunciation of the rights, title and interest referred to in this paragraph.

ARTICLE 9

Japan will enter promptly into negotiations with the Allied Powers so desiring for the conclusion of bilateral and multilateral agreements proving for the regulation or limitation of fishing and the conservation and development of fisheries on the high seas.

ARTICLE 10

Japan renounces all special rights and interest in China, including all benefits and privileges resulting from the provisions of the final Protocol signed at Peking on 7th September, 1901, and all annexes, notes and documents supplementary thereto, and agrees to the abrogation in respect to Japan of the said protocol, annexes, notes and documents.

ARTICLE 11

Japan accepts the judgments of the International Military Tribunal for the Far East and of other Allied War Crimes Courts both within and outside Japan, and will carry out the sentences imposed thereby upon Japanese nationals imprisoned in Japan. The power to grant clemency, to reduce sentences and to parole with respect to such prisoners may not be exercised except on the decision of the Government or Governments which imposed the sentence in each instance, and on the recommendation of Japan. In the case of persons sentenced by the International Military Tribunal for the Far East, such power may not be exercised except on the decision of a majority of the Governments represented on the Tribunal, and on the recommendation of Japan.

ARTICLE 12

(*a*) Japan declares its readiness promptly to enter into negotiations for the conclusion with each of the Allied Powers of treaties or agreements to place their trading, maritime and other commercial relations on a stable and friendly basis.

(*b*) Pending the conclusion of the relevant treaty or agreement, Japan will, during a period of four years from the first coming into force of the present Treaty

   (1)   accord to each of the Allied Powers, its nationals, products and vessels
      (i)   most-favoured-nation treatment with respect to customs duties, charges, restrictions and other regulations on or in connection with the importation and exportation of goods;
      (ii)   national treatment with respect to shipping, navigation and imported goods, and with respect to natural and juridical persons and their interest–such treatment to include all matters pertaining to the levying and collection of taxes, access to the courts, the making and performance of contracts, rights to property (tangible and intangible), participation in juridical entities constituted under Japanese law, and generally the conduct of all kinds of business and professional activities;

   (2)   ensure that external purchases and sales of Japanese state trading enterprises shall be based solely on commercial considerations.

(*c*) In respect to any matter, however, Japan shall be obliged to accord to an Allied Power national treatment, or most-favoured-nation treatment, only to the extent that the Allied Power concerned accords Japan national treatment or most-favoured-nation treatment, as the case may be, in respect of the same matter. The reciprocity envisaged in the foregoing sentence shall be determined, in the case of products, vessels and juridical entities of, and persons domiciled in, any non-metropolitan territory of an Allied Power, and in the case of juridical entities of, and persons domiciled in, any state or province of an Allied Power having federal government, by reference to the treatment accorded to Japan in such territory, state or province.

(*d*) In the application of this Article, a discriminatory measure shall not be considered to derogate from the grant of national or most-favoured-nation treatment, as the case may be, if such measure is based on an exception customarily provided for in the commercial treaties of the party applying it, or on the need to safeguard that party's external financial position or balance of payments (except in respect to shipping and navigation), or on the need to maintain its essential security interests, and provided such measure is proportionate to the circumstances and not applied in an arbitrary or unreasonable manner.

(*e*) Japan's obligations under this Article shall not be affected by the exercise of any Allied rights under Article 14 of the present Treaty; nor shall the provisions of this Article be understood as limiting the undertakings assumed by Japan by virtue of Article 15 of the Treaty.

ARTICLE 13

(a) Japan will enter into negotiations with any of the Allied Powers, promptly upon the request of such Power or Powers, for the conclusion of bilateral or multilateral agreements relating to international civil air transport.

(b) Pending the conclusion of such agreement or agreements, Japan will, during a period of four years from the first coming into force of the present Treaty, extend to such Power treatment not less favourable with respect to air-traffic rights and privileges than those exercised by any such Powers at the date of such coming into force, and will accord complete equality of opportunity in respect to the operation and developments of air services.

(c) Pending its becoming a party to the Convention on International Civil Aviation in accordance with Article 93 thereof, Japan will give effect to the provisions of that Convention applicable to the international navigation of aircraft, and will give effect to the standards, practices and procedures adopted as annexes to the Convention in accordance with the terms of the Convention.

CHAPTER V.—CLAIMS AND PROPERTY
ARTICLE 14

(a) It is recognised that Japan should pay reparations to the Allied Powers for the damage and suffering caused by it during the war. Nevertheless it is also recognised that the resources of Japan are not presently sufficient, if it is to maintain a viable economy, to make complete reparation for all such damage and suffering and at the same time meet its other obligations.

Therefore,

1. Japan will promptly enter into negotiations with Allied Powers so desiring, whose present territories were occupied by Japanese forces and damaged by Japan, with a view to assisting to compensate those countries for the cost of repairing the damage done, by making available the services of the Japanese people in production, salvaging and other work for the Allied Powers in question. Such arrangements shall avoid the imposition of additional liabilities on other Allied Powers, and, where the manufacturing of raw materials is called for, they shall be supplied by the Allied Powers in question, so as not to throw any foreign exchange burden upon Japan.

2.—(I) Subject to the provisions of sub-paragraph (II) below, each of the Allied Powers shall have the right to seize, retain, liquidate or otherwise dispose of all property, rights and interest of—

(a) Japan and Japanese nationals,
(b) persons acting for or on behalf of Japan or Japanese nationals, and
(c) entities owned or controlled by Japan or Japanese nationals, and

which on the first coming into force of the present Treaty were subject to its jurisdiction. The property, rights and interests specified in this sub-paragraph shall include those now blocked, vested or in the possession or under the control of enemy property authorities of Allied Powers, which belonged to, or were held or managed on behalf of, any of the persons or entities mention in (a), (b) or (c) above at the time such assets came under the controls of such authorities.

(II) The following shall be excepted from the right specified in sub-paragraph (I) above:

(i) property of Japanese natural persons who during the war resided with the permission of the Government concerned in the territory of one of the Allied Powers, other than territory occupied by Japan, except property subjected to restrictions during the war and not released from such restrictions as of the date of the first coming into force of the present Treaty;

(ii) all real property, furniture and fixtures owned by the Government of Japan and used for diplomatic or consular purposes, and all personal furniture and furnishings and other private property not of an investment nature which was normally necessary for the carrying out of diplomatic and consular functions, owned by Japanese diplomatic and consular personnel;

(iii) property belonging to religious bodies or private charitable institutions and used exclusively for religious or charitable purpose;

(iv) property, rights and interest which have come within its jurisdiction in consequence of the resumption of trade and financial relations subsequent to 2nd September, 1945, between the country concerned and Japan, except such as have resulted from transactions contrary to the laws of the Allied Power concerned;

(v) obligations of Japan or Japanese nationals, any right, title or interest in tangible property located in Japan, interests in enterprises organised under the laws of Japan, or any paper evidence thereof; provided that this exception shall only apply to obligations of Japan and its nationals expressed in Japanese currency.

(III) Property referred to in exceptions (i) through (v) above shall be returned subject to reasonable expenses for its preservation and administration. If any such property has been liquidated the proceeds shall be returned instead.

(IV) The right to seize, retain, liquidate or otherwise dispose of property as provided in sub-paragraph (I) above shall be exercised in accordance with the laws of the Allied Power concerned, and the owner shall have only such rights as may be given him by those laws.

(V) The Allied Powers agree to deal with Japanese trademarks and literary and artistic property rights on a basis as favourable to Japan as circumstances ruling in each country will permit.

(b) Except as otherwise provided in the present Treaty, the Allied Powers waive all reparations claims of the Allied Powers, other claims of the Allied Powers and their nationals arising out of any actions taken by Japan and its nationals in the course of the prosecution of the war, and claims of the Allied Powers for direct military costs of occupation.

ARTICLE 15

(*a*) Upon application made within nine months of the coming into force of the present Treaty between Japan and the Allied Power concerned, Japan will, within six months of the date of such application, return the property, tangible and intangible, and all rights or interests of any kind in Japan of each Allied Power and its nationals which was within Japan at any time between 7th December, 1941, and 2nd September, 1945 unless the owner has freely disposed therof without duress or fraud. Such property shall be returned free of all encumbrances and charges to which it may have become subject because of the war, and without any charges for its return. Property whose return is not applied for by or on behalf of the owner or by his Government within the prescribed period may be disposed of by the Japanese Government as it may determine. In cases where such property was within Japan on 7th December, 1941, and cannot be returned or has suffered injury or damage as a result of the war, compensation will be made on terms not less favourable than the terms provided in the draft Allied Powers Property Compensation Law approved by the Japanese Cabinet on 13th July, 1951.

(*b*) With respect to industrial property rights impaired during the war, Japan will continue to accord to the Allied Powers and their nationals benefits no less than those heretofore accorded by Cabinet Orders No. 309 effective 1st September, 1949, No. 12 effective 28th January, 1950, and No. 9 effective 1st February, 1950, all as now amended, provided such nations have applied for such benefits within the time limits prescribed therein.

(*c*)—(i) Japan acknowledges the literary and artistic property rights which existed in Japan on 6th December, 1941, in respect to the published and unpublished works of the Allied Powers and their nationals have continued in force since the date, and recognises those rights which have arisen, or but for the war would have arisen, in Japan since that date, by the operation of any conventions and agreements to which Japan was a party on that date, irrespective of whether or not such conventions or agreements were abrogated or suspended upon or since the outbreak of war by the domestic law of Japan or of the Allied Power concerned.

(ii) Without the need for application by the proprietor of the right and without the payment of any fee or compliance with any other formality, the period from 7th December, 1941, until the coming into force of the present Treaty between Japan and the Allied Power concerned shall be excluded from the running of the normal term of such rights; and such period, with an additional period of six months shall be excluded from the time within which a literary work must be translated into Japanese in order to obtain translating rights in Japan.

ARTICLE 16

As an expression of its desire to indemnify those members of the armed forces of the Allied Powers who suffered undue hardships while prisoners of war of Japan, Japan will transfer its assets and those of its nationals in countries which were neutral during the war, or which were at war with any of the Allied Powers, or, at its option, the equivalent of such assets, to the International Committee of the Red Cross which shall liquidate such assets and distribute the resultant fund to appropriate national agencies, for the benefit of former prisoners of war and their families on such basis as it may determine to be equitable. The categories of assets described in Article 14 (*a*) 2 (ii) through (v) of the present Treaty shall be excepted from transfer, as well as assets of Japanese natural persons not residents of Japan on the first coming into force of the Treaty. It is equally understood that the transfer provision of the Article has no application to the 19,770 shares in the Bank for International Settlements presently owned by Japanese financial institutions.

ARTICLE 17

(*a*) Upon the request of any of the Allied Powers, the Japanese Government shall review and revise in conformity with international law any decision or order of the Japanese Prize Courts in cases involving ownership rights of nationals of that Allied Power and shall supply copies of all documents comprising the records of these cases, including the decisions taken and orders issued. In any case in which such review or revision shows that restoration is due, the provisions of Article 15 shall apply to the property concerned.

(*b*) The Japanese Government shall take the necessary measures to enable nationals of any of the Allied Powers at any time within one year from the coming into force of the present Treaty between Japan and the Allied Power concerned to submit to the appropriate Japanese authorities for review any judgment given by a Japanese court between 7th December, 1941, and such coming into force, in any proceedings in which any such national was unable to make adequate presentation of his case either as plaintiff or defendant. The Japanese Government shall provide that, where the national has suffered injury by reason of any such judgment, he shall be restored in the position in which he was before the judgment was given or shall be afforded such relief as may be just and equitable in the circumstances.

ARTICLE 18

(*a*) It is recognised that the intervention of the state of war has not affected the obligation to pay pecuniary debts arising out of obligations and contracts (including those in respect of bonds) which existed and rights which were acquired before the existence of a state of war, and which are due by the Government or nationals of Japan to the Government or nationals of Japan to the Government or nationals of one of the Allied Powers, or are due by the Government or nationals of one of the Allied Powers to the Government or nationals of Japan. The intervention of a state of war shall equally not be regarded as affecting the obligations to consider on their merits claims for loss or damage to property or for personal injury or death which arose before the existence of a state of war, and which may be presented or re-presented by the Government of one of the Allied Powers to the Government of Japan, or by the Government of Japan to any of the Governments of the Allied Powers. The provisions of this paragraph are without prejudice to the rights conferred by Article 14.

(*b*) Japan affirms its liability for the pre-war external debt of the Japanese State and for debts of corporate bodies subsequently declared to be liabilities of the Japanese State, and expresses its intention to enter into negotiations at an early date with its creditors with respect to the resumption of payments on those debts; to encourage negotiations in respect of other pre-war claims and obligations; and to facilitate the transfer of sums accordingly.

ARTICLE 19

(a) Japan waives all claims of Japan and its nationals against the Allied Powers and their nationals arising out of war or out of actions taken because of the existence of a state of war, and waives all claims raising from the presence, operations or actions of forces or authorities of any of the Allied Powers in Japanese territory prior to the coming into force of the present Treaty.

(b) The foregoing waiver includes any claims arising out of actions taken by any of the Allied Powers with respect to Japanese ships between 1st September, 1939, and the coming into force of the present Treaty, as well as any claims and debts arising in respect to Japanese prisoners of war and civilian internees in the hands of the Allied Powers, but does not include Japanese claims specifically recognised in the laws of any Allied Power enacted since 2nd September, 1945.

(c) Subject to reciprocal renunciation, the Japanese Government also renounces all claims (including debts) against Germany and German nationals on behalf of the Japanese Government and Japanese nationals, including intergovernmental claims and claims for loss or damage sustained during the war, but excepting (a) claims in respect of contracts entered into and rights acquired before 1st September, 1939, and (b) claims arising out of trade and financial relations between Japan and Germany after 2nd September, 1945. Such renunciation shall not prejudice actions taken in accordance with Articles 16 and 20 of the present Treaty.

(d) Japan recognises the validity of all acts and omissions done during the period of occupation under or in consequence of directives of the occupation authorities or authorised by Japanese law at that time, and will take no action subjecting Allied nationals to civil or criminal liability arising out of such acts or omissions.

ARTICLE 20

Japan will take all necessary measures to ensure such disposition of German assets in Japan as has been or may be determined by those powers entitled under the Protocol of the proceedings of the Berlin Conference of 1945 to dispose of those assets, and pending the final disposition of such assets will be responsible for the conservation and administration thereof.

ARTICLE 21

Notwithstanding the provisions of Article 25 of the present Treaty, China shall be entitled to the benefits of Articles 10 and 14 (a) 2; and Korea to the benefits of Articles 2, 4, 9 and 12 of the present Treaty.

CHAPTER VI.—SETTLEMENT OF DISPUTES

ARTICLE 22

If in the opinion of any party to the present Treaty there has arisen a dispute concerning the interpretation or execution of the Treaty, which is not settled by reference to a special claims tribunal or by other agreed means, the dispute shall, at the request of any party thereto, be referred for decision to the International Court of Justice. Japan and those Allied Powers which are not already parties to the Statute of the International Court of Justice will deposit with the Registrar of the Court, at the time of their respective ratifications of the present Treaty, and in conformity with the resolution of the United Nations Security Council, dated 15th October, 1946, a general declaration accepting the jurisdiction, without special agreements, of the Court generally in respect to all disputes of the character referred to in the Article.

CHAPTER VII.—FINAL CLAUSES

ARTICLE 23

(a) The present Treaty shall be ratified by the States which sign it, including Japan, and will come into force for all the States which have then ratified it, when instruments of ratification have been deposited by Japan and by a majority, including the United States of America as the principal occupying Power, of the following States, namely Australia, Canada, Ceylon, France, Indonesia, the Kingdom of the Netherlands, New Zealand, Pakistan, the Republic of the Philippines, the United Kingdom of Great Britain and Northern Ireland and the United States of America. The present Treaty shall come into force for each State which subsequently ratifies it, on the date of the deposit of its instrument of ratification.

(b) If the Treaty has not come into force within nine months after the date of the deposit of Japan's ratification, any State which has ratified it may bring the Treaty into force between itself and Japan by a notification to that effect given to the Governments of Japan and the United States of America not later than three years after the date of deposit of Japan's ratification.

ARTICLE 24

All instruments of ratification shall be deposited with the Government of the United States of America which will notify all the signatory States of each such deposit, of the date of the coming into force of the Treaty under paragraph (a) of Article 23, and of any notifications made under paragraph (b) of Article 23.

ARTICLE 25

For the purpose of the present Treaty the Allied Powers shall be the States at war with Japan, or any State which previously formed a part of the territory of a State named in Article 23, provided that in each case the State concerned has signed and ratified the Treaty. Subject to the provisions of Article 21, the present Treaty shall not confer any rights, titles or benefits on any State which is not an Allied Power as herein defined; nor shall any right, title or interest of Japan be deemed to be diminished or prejudiced by any provision of the Treaty in favour of a State which is not an Allied Power as so defined.

ARTICLE 26

Japan will be prepared to conclude with any State which signed or adhered to the United Declaration of 1st January, 1942, and which is at war, with

Japan, or with any State which previously formed part of the territory of a State named in Article 23, which is not a signatory of the present Treaty, a bilateral Treaty of Peace on the same or substantially the same terms as are provided for in the present Treaty, but this obligation on the part of Japan will expire three years after the first coming into force of the present Treaty. Should Japan make a peace settlement or war claims settlement with any State granting that State greater advantages than those provided by the present Treaty, those same advantages shall be extended to the parties to the present Treaty.

ARTICLE 27

The present Treaty shall be deposited in the archives of the Government of the United States of America, which shall furnish each signatory State with a certified copy thereof.

Appendix 3

THE IMPERIAL FAMILY AND THE IMPERIAL HOUSEHOLD

Apart from the Emperor, the Empress, the Crown Prince and the Empress Dowager, the official members of the Imperial Family are as follows.

The second son of the Emperor and Empress is Prince Fumihito, who took the title of **Akishino-no-miya**, or Prince Akishino on his marriage. The Prince was born on 30 November 1965. He officially came of age on 30 November 1985 and graduated from Gakushūin University in March 1988. In August 1988 he began postgraduate studies of zoology at St John's College, Oxford. He returned to Japan in 1990. On 29 June 1990 he married Kawashima Kikuko, who was born in 1967, and they assumed the titles of Prince and Princess Akishino.

The Emperor and Empress's third and youngest child is their only daughter, Princess Sayako, who has the title of **Nori-no-miya**, or Princess Nori. She was born on 18 April 1969 and has been studying literature at the Gakushūin University. When she marries she will, in accordance with current Japanese law and practice, cease to be a member of the Imperial Family and to hold any title.

Prince and Princess Hitachi. Prince Hitachi is the second son of the Shōwa Emperor (Hirohito). His given name is Masahito and he was born on 28 November 1935. He graduated from the Science Faculty of Gakushūin University in 1958. In September 1958 he married Hanako, the fourth daughter of former Count Tsugaru Yoshitaka. She was born on 19 July 1940.

Princess Chichibu, whose given name is Setsuko, was born in London on 9 September 1909. She is the eldest daughter of Mr and Mrs Matsudaira Tsuneo who later became Japanese Ambassador to the United Kingdom. In 1928 she married Prince Chichibu, whose given name was Yasuhito and who was the second son of the Taishō Emperor and younger brother of the Shōwa Emperor (Hirohito). Prince Chichibu, born in June 1902, died in January 1953.

Princess Takamatsu, whose given name is Kikuko, was born in Toyko on 26 December 1911. She was the second daughter of Marquis Tokugawa Yoshihisa. In February 1930 she married Prince Takamatsu, whose given name was Nobuhito and who was the third son of the Taishō Emperor. Prince Takamatsu, born in January 1905, died in February 1987.

Prince and Princess Mikasa. Prince Mikasa, whose given name is Takahito, is the fourth and youngest son of the Taishō Emperor. He was born on 2 December 1915. He married in October 1941. Yuriko, second daughter of the late Viscount Takagi Masanari. She was born on 4 June 1923. Prince Mikasa has made specialist studies of early Middle-Eastern civilizations.

Prince and Princess Tomohito of Mikasa. Prince Tomohito, born on 5 January 1946, is the eldest son of Prince and Princess Mikasa. After graduating from Gakushūin University he studied at Magdalen College, Oxford. In November 1980 he married Nobuko, who was born on 9 April 1955 and is the third daughter of the late Mr Aso Takakichi and Mrs Aso Kazuko. They have two daughters, Princess Akiko, born on 20 December 1981, and Princess Yohko, born on 25 October 1983.

Prince Yoshihito of Mikasa, second son of Prince and Princess Mikasa, was born on 11 February 1949. After graduating from Gakushūin University he studied at the Australian National University.

Prince and Princess Takamado. Prince Takamado, whose given name is Norihito, is the third son of Prince and Princess Mikasa. He was born on 29 December 1954. He was given the title of Prince Takamado on his marrige to Hisako, only daughter of Mr and Mrs Tottori Shigejiro. After graduating from the law faculty at Gakushūin University Prince Takamado studied at Queen's University in Canada. Princess Takamado, who was born in Tokyo on 10 July 1953, graduated from Girton College, Cambridge, in 1975. Their daughter, Princess Tsuguko, was born on 8 March 1986.

Before the war the Imperial Family was much more extensive. The present Imperial Family are all direct descendants of the Emperor Meiji, whose given name was Mutsuhito. He lived from 1852–1912 and was Emperor from 1867 to 1912. The **Meiji Era** lasted from 1868 to 1912. His son by a concubine, Prince Yoshihito (who lived from 1879–1926), was Emperor from 1912 to 1926 and the era name given to his reign was **Taishō**. He is thus known as the Taishō Emperor. He suffered from an illness which made it impossible by 1919 for him to perform basic ceremonies. In 1921 the Crown Prince Hirohito was appointed regent (*Sesshō*). The era name of the present Emperor is **Heisei**. Before 1868 era names were often changed during reigns.

The Shōwa Emperor has five daughters, one of whom, Sachiko (1927–8), died in infancy. The remaining four ceased on marrige to be members of the Imperial Family. Shigeko (1926–61) married Higashikuni Morihiro (died 1961). Kazuko, born 1929, married Takatsukasa Toshimichi, who died in 1966. Atsuko, born 1931, married Ikeda Takamasa, born 1926. Takako, born 1939, married Shimazu Hisanaga, born 1934. Prince Mikasa has two daughters who have married out of the Imperial Family. Yasuko, born 1944, married Konoe Tadateru, born 1939, and Masako, born 1951, married Sen Masayuki, born 1956.

The Imperial Household Agency (*Kunaichō*) is responsible for the affairs of the Imperial Family. It is the successor to the pre-war Imperial Household Office (*Kunaishō*) which was a full government Ministry. The Agency is divided into the following divisions:

- Grand Steward's Secretariat, which is responsible for administrative matters.
- Board of the Chamberlains (*Jijū*), headed by the Grand Chamberlain assisted by Chamberlains and Ladies in Waiting (*Jokan*) who attend the Emperor and the Empress.
- Office of the Crown Prince's Household (the Crown Prince's Palace is known as the *Tōgu-gosho*).
- Board of the Ceremonies, headed by the Grand Master of the Ceremonies (*Shikibu-chōkan*), assisted by two Vice-Grand Masters, one of whom is responsible for ceremonies and the Imperial *Gagaku* (Court Music) troupe and the other for international relations.
- Archives and Mausolea Department.

- Maintenance and Works Department.
- Office of the Shōsōin Treasure House in Nara. (The Shōsōin contains treasures donated to the Tōdaiji temple in Nara by the Empress Kōmyō between 756 and 758 AD in memory of her husband, the Emperor Shōmu.)
- The Imperial Stock Farm.
- Kyoto Office (responsible for the Imperial Palace, the Katsura and Shūgakuin Villas and other Imperial properties in Kyoto.)

In 1987 the Agency had some 1130 employees.

Among the various ceremonies in which the Emperor traditionally takes part are:

- Rice-planting in June in a special rice field in the Imperial Palace.
- Harvesting in October the rice he has planted. (The rice is offered at the ancient shrine at Ise to Amaterasu-omikami-no-mikoto, the sun goddess, as part of the *Kannamesai*. The Emperor also offers rice to all the traditional deities in a shrine in the Imperial Palace on 23 November in a ceremony called the *Niinamesai*.) (The Empress, for her part, between May and July supervises the care of a collection of silkworms.)
- Poetry composition and readings in the New Year.
- Opening the annual national sport festival (each year in a different Japanese prefecture).
- Annual tree-planting ceremonies.

The Imperial Household (*Kōshitsu*) is governed by the Imperial Household Law which was enacted in January 1947. An Imperial Household Council, which consists of two members of the Imperial Family, the Speaker and Vice-Speakers of the House of Representatives and House of Councillors, the Prime Minister, the Chief Justice and one other justice of the Supreme Court, and the head of the Imperial Household Agency, is consulted on such matters as the establishment of a regency and the renunciation of imperial status. Imperial Princes, known as *Shinnō*, and Imperial Princesses (*Naishinnō*) are legally permitted (except for the Crown Prince and his eldest son) to renounce imperial status.

Despite the fact that there have been Empresses in the past, including during the Tokugawa period which ended in 1868, and despite the constitutional call for sexual equality, only males can succeed to the throne.

Appendix 4

LIST OF POST-WAR JAPANESE PRIME MINISTERS

1945	17 August	Prince Higashikuni Naruhiko
1945	9 October	Baron Shidehara Kijuro
1946	22 May	Yoshida Shigeru
1947	24 May	Katayama Tetsu
1948	10 March	Ashida Hitoshi
1948	15 October	Yoshida Shigeru
1954	10 December	Hatoyama Ichiro
1956	23 December	Ishibashi Tanzan
1957	25 February	Kishi Nobusuke
1960	19 July	Ikeda Hayato
1964	9 November	Satō Eisaku
1972	7 July	Tanaka Kakuei
1974	9 December	Miki Takeo
1976	24 December	Fukuda Takeo
1978	7 December	Ōhira Masayoshi
1980	17 July	Suzuki Zenkō
1982	27 November	Nakasone Yasuhiro
1987	6 November	Takeshita Noboru
1989	3 June	Uno Sōsuke
1989	10 August	Kaifu Toshiki
1991	5 November	Miyazawa Kiichi

Appendix 5

SOME MAJOR EVENTS IN JAPANESE POST-WAR HISTORY

1945	15 August	The Emperor (Hirohito, known now by his reign name Shōwa) broadcast to the Japanese people confirming Japan's decision to surrender.
1945	2 September	Surrender documents signed on board USS *Missouri* in Tokyo Bay.
1945	27 September	Emperor called on General Douglas MacArthur, Supreme Commander Allied Powers (SCAP) in Tokyo.
1945	4 October	Civil liberties directive issued by SCAP.
1945	15 December	Directive ordering separation of religion from the state, that is, the end of state Shintō.
1946	1 January	Emperor declared false the concept that the Emperor was divine.
1946	3 May	International Military Tribunal for the Far East (IMTFE) convened in Tokyo for trial of major war criminals.
1946	3 November	New Constitution promulgated.
1947	April	Elections held under the new Constitution.
1947	3 May	New Constitution entered into force.
1948		Joseph M. Dodge, a Detroit banker, visits Japan and recommends sweeping economic reforms, which are generally adopted.
1950	June	Outbreak of the Korean War.
1950	July	Formation of the National Police Reserve.
1951	4 September	Japanese Peace Treaty signed at San Francisco.
1952	28 April	Peace Treaty comes into force.
1952		Japan admitted to the International Monetary Fund (IMF)
1955	10 September	Japan admitted to the General Agreement on Tariffs and Trade (GATT).
1955	November	Formation of the Liberal Democratic Party (LDP).
1956	19 October	Re-establishment of diplomatic relations with the Soviet Union.
1956	18 December	Japan admitted to membership of the United Nations.
1960	19 January	Revised US/Japan Security Treaty signed.
1960	23 June	Revised US/Japan Security Treaty came into force.
1963	14 Auguast	Japan signed the partial nuclear test ban treaty.
1964	1 April	Japan accepted IMF Article 8 on currency rules.
1964	28 April	Japan joined the Organization for Economic Co-operation and Development (OECD).

1964	Autumn	Olympic Games held in Tokyo.
1964		First *Shinkansen* trains run from Tokyo to Osaka.
1965	22 June	Treaty on relations with the Republic of Korea signed.
1968	5 April	US/Japan agreement on the return to Japan of the Ogasawara Islands signed.
1970	22 June	US/Japan Security Treaty automatically renewed.
1970		World Exposition held in Osaka.
1971	17 June	US/Japan Treaty for the reversion of Okinawa to Japanese rule signed.
1971	Autumn	Emperor made a state visit to Britain and other European countries.
1972	29 September	Joint statement issued by the governments of Japan and the People's Republic of China establishing diplomatic relations.
1975	Autumn	Emperor made a state visit to the USA.
1975	November	Japanese Prime Minister Miki Takeo attended the first seven power summit in France.
1976	8 June	Japan ratified the nuclear non-proliferation treaty.
1976		Lockheed scandal exposed and former Prime Minister Tanaka Kakuei arrested.
1978	12 August	Japan/China Treaty of Peace and Friendship signed in Beijing (Peking).
1978	May	Narita International Airport (Tokyo) opened.
1979	28/29 June	Fifth summit of seven industrialised countries held in Tokyo.
1986	4/6 May	Twelfth summit held in Tokyo.
1988		'Recruit' scandal revealed, implicating leading politicians.
1989	7 January	Emperor Hirohito died.
1989	7 January	Emperor Akihito acceded to the Japanese throne. Heisei era began.
1989	24 February	State Funeral of the Emperor Shōwa
1993	9 June	Crown Prince's wedding
1993	18 June	Government of Prime Minister Miyazawa defeated in the House of Representatives on a motion of no confidence
1993	July	Nineteenth summit held in Tokyo

Appendix 6

SELECTED STATISTICS

Population   (October 1990)   123.61 million

Males		60.69	million
Females		62.92	million
Density per square km		327	
Expectation of life at birth (1990):			
Females		81.81	years
Males		75.86	years
(USA (1989) expectation of life:			
Females		78.50	years
Males		71.80	years)

Area   (1988)   378 000 square km

Percentage agriculture	14.1%	
Forests and woodland	66.5%	
Other purposes	19.4%	

GDP   Japan nominal (1990)   ¥426 trillion or US$ 2940 billion; per capita GDP US$ 23 801.

(USA nominal GDP US$ 5513 billion, per capita GDP US$ 22 062)

GDP (by type of expenditure)

Gross fixed capital formation	30.5%
Exports	10.3%
Imports	−8.0%
Agriculture	2.6%
Industrial activity	32.8%
Construction	8.4%
Wholesale and retail trade	13.2%
Transport and communications	6.0%
Other	37.0%

International reserves (end 1988)   US$ 79 707 million

Foreign trade Japan 1990   Exports (fob) US$ 314 billion
                         Imports (cif) US$ 236 billion

Degree of dependency on foreign trade (1990) Exports 9.7%
                                          Imports 7.9%

Percentage of Japan's exports going to (1990):

	USA	29.1%
	EC	18.8%
	Taiwan	5.8%
	Hong Kong	5.2%
	Singapore	3.9%
	Thailand	3.0%
	Malaysia	2.4%
	Indonesia	1.8%

Food self-sufficiency		
	Rice	100%
	Eggs	98%
	Wheat	16%
	Maize	0%
	Vegetables	91%
	Fruit	63%
	Meat (and dairy products)	72%
	Fish	83%

Calorie intake	Japan (1989)	2909 kcal
	(USA, (1985)	3644 kcal)

Employment	Japan total 1990		62.49 million
	Percentage in	primary industry	7.2%
		secondary	33.6%
		tertiary	59.2%

Production	Japan	Automobiles (1991)	9.75 mllion
		Iron and steel (1991)	109 million tonnes

Shipping	Japan (1990)	Gross tons	27.1 million
		Dead weight	40.8 million

Industrial robots Japan (end 1990)   274 210

Fortune **ranking of Japanese industrial companies (1991)**
The top ten Japanese companies in terms of sales were:
Toyota Motor
Hitachi
Matsushita Electric Industries
Nissan Motor
Toshiba
Honda Motor
NEC
Sony
Mitsubishi Electric
New Japan Steel

Trading companies
The top six trading companies in 1990 in terms of sales were:
Itōchū
Sumitomo
Marubeni
Mitsui
Mitsubishi
Nisshō Iwai

Electricity generation	Japan (1989) Total	791 168 gw
	From solid fuel	14.7%
	petroleum products	32.0%
	gas	18.7%
	nuclear	23.1%
	hydro, geothermal and solar	11.5%

Labour unions Japan (1990)

Number of unions		33 270
Number of union members		12 266 000
Number of employees		48 750 000
Rate of unionization	25.2%	
Days lost in disputes (1989)		176 000
Number unemployed (male and female, 1990)		1 360 000
Unemployed percentage	2.2%	

Tax revenue Japan (1990)

Direct taxes	72.5%
Of which income tax	39.4%
corporate tax	30.1%
inheritance tax	3.0%
Indirect taxes	27.5%

Appendix 7

PARTIES IN THE DIET

House of Representatives

The 512 seats in the House, as of February 1993, were held as follows:

Liberal democratic Party (LDP)	274
Social Democratic Party of Japan SDPJ (formerly JSP)	141
Kōmeitō	46
Japan Communist Party (JCP)	16
Democratic Socialist Party (DSP)	13
Independent	7
Vacancies	15
	512

House of Councillors

The 252 seats in the House, as of 7 August 1992, were held as follows:

Liberal Democratic Party (LDP) 106.	
Social Democratic Party of Japan SDPJ (formerly JSP)	73
Komeito	24
Japan Communist Party (JCP)	11
Democratic Socialist Party (JSP)	11
Democratic Reform Alliance (Rengō)	11
Niin Club	5
Japan New Party (*Nihon Shinto*)	4
Independent	7

Figure A7.1   Voters turn out at elections, 1946–92

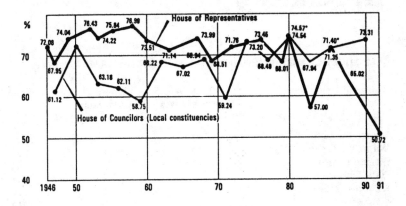

Figure A7.2   Seats won in House of Representative elections, 1960–90

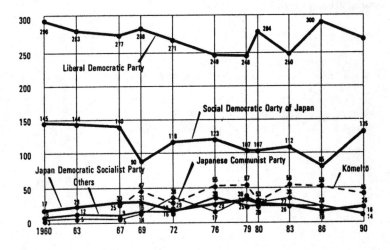

Appendix 8

LDP MEMBERS OF THE DIET BY FACTION (FEBRUARY 1993)

	House of Representatives	House of Councillors	Total
Mitsuzuka faction	57	17	74
Miyazawa faction	60	13	73
Watanabe faction	49	18	67
Obuchi faction	29	34	63
Hata faction	35	9	44
Kōmoto faction	23	6	29
Katō group	7	6	13
Non-affiliated	14	4	18
	274	107	381

Source: Kyodo Press, February 1993.

Suggestions for Further Reading

General

JAPAN ALMANAC 1993, (1992) *Asahi Shimbun*, Tokyo.
JAPAN ECONOMIC ALMANAC 1991 (1991) *Nihon Keizai Shimbun*, Tokyo.
KEIZAI KŌHŌ CENTER (1993) *Japan 1993: An International Comparison*, Tokyo.
JAPAN TRAVEL BUREAU (1991) *Japan: The New Official Guide*, Tokyo.
ECONOMIST (1990) *Japan: The Economist Guide*, London.
FOREIGN PRESS CENTER Japan (A pocket guide produced annually by the Foreign Press Center, Tokyo.)
NATIONAL DIET OF JAPAN (1986/1987) Tokyo: House of Representatives and the House of Councillors.
NIPPON: A CHARTED SURVEY OF JAPAN 1992/3 (1992) Tokyo: Kokuseisha Corporation.

Guides to Specific Areas

GOMI MUJI (1990) *Guide to Japanese Taxes 1990/91*, Zaikei Shohosha, Tokyo.
HEALTH AND WELFARE STATISTICS ASSOCIATION (1990) *Health and Welfare Statistics in Japan*, Tokyo.
SOCIAL INSURANCE AGENCY (1990) *Outline of Social Insurance in Japan*, Tokyo.
STATISTICS BUREAU, MANAGEMENT AND CO-ORDINATION AGENCY, Tokyo (1992) *Statistical Handbook of Japan*.

Reference Works

THE CAMBRIDGE ENCYCLOPEDIA OF JAPAN (1993) edited by Richard Bowring and Peter Kornicki, Cambridge University Press.
ENCYCLOPEDIA OF JAPAN (1983) (9 volumes including index) Tokyo: Kodansha.
COLCUTT, MARTIN, MARIUS JANSEN and ISAO KUMAKURA (1988) *A Cultural Atlas of Japan*, Oxford: Phaidon.
INTERNATIONAL CULTURAL ASSOCIATION OF JAPAN (1990) *Who's Who in Japanese Government 1990/91*, Tokyo.

History

BEASLEY, W. G. (1963) *The Modern Hitory of Japan*, London: Weidenfeld and Nicolson.

—— *Japanese Imperialism, 1894-1945* (1987) Oxford: Clarendon Press.
—— *The Rise of Modern Japan* (1990) Tokyo: Tuttle.
BOXER, Charles (1951) *The Christian Century in Japan*, London and Cambridge University Press, California: University of California Press.
TOSHIYA Torao and BROWN, Delmer M. (1987) *Chronology of Japan*, Tokyo: Hitoshi Haga.
CORTAZZI, Sir Hugh (1991) *The Japanese Achievement*, London: Sidgwick and Jackson.
HALL, JOHN WHITNEY (1971) *Japan from Prehistory to Modern Times*, Tokyo: Tuttle.
MASON, R.H.P. and CAIGER, J.G. (1973) *A History of Japan*, Tokyo: Tuttle.
REISCHAUER, EDWIN, O. (1987) *Japan, The Story of a Nation*, Tokyo: Tuttle.
SANSOM, GEORGE B. (1946) *A Short Cultural History*, London: Cresset Press, and subsequent reprints.
STORRY, RICHARD (1960) *A History of Modern Japan*, Harmondsworth: Penguin.
VARLEY, H. PAUL (1986) *Japanese Culture*, Tokyo: Tuttle.

Religion

AGENCY FOR CULTURAL AFFAIRS (1981) *Japanese Religion: A Survey*, Tokyo: Kodansha.
READER, IAN (1991) *Religion in Contemporary Japan*, London: Macmillan.

Literature

KEENE, DONALD (1956) *Anthology of Japanese Literature. From the Earliest Era to the Nineteenth Century*, London: George Allen & Unwin, and various reprints.
KEENE, DONALD (1956/57) *Modern Japanese Literature from 1868 to the Present Day*, New York: Grove Press (1956), Tokyo: Tuttle (1957) and various reprints.
MINER, EARL, ODAGIRI HIROKO and MORRELL, ROBERT E. (1985) *The Princeton Companion to Japanese Literature*, Princeton, NJ: Princeton University Press.
MORRIS, IVAN (1964) *The World of the Shining Prince*, London: Oxford University Press.
RIMER, J. THOMAS (1988) *A Reader's Guide to Japanese Literature: From the Eighth Century to the Present*, Tokyo: Kodansha.

Outstanding Examples of Japanese Literature in Translation

MURASAKI, SHIKIBU (1935, 1976) *The Tale of Genji*, translations by Arthur Waley, London: George Allen & Unwin, and subsequent reprints and Edward Seidensticker, New York: Alfred A. Knopf, and subsequent editions.
SEI, SHŌNAGON (1967) *The Pillow Book* (*Makura no Sōshi*), translation by Ivan Morris, London: Oxford University Press, and reprints.

WALEY, ARTHUR (1921) *The Nō Plays of Japan*, London: George Allen & Unwin, and reprints.

Art

MUNSTERBERG, HUGO (1963) *The Arts of Japan. An Illustrated History*, Tokyo: Tuttle.

NOMA, SEIROKU (1968) *The Arts of Japan*, 2 vols, Tokyo: Kodansha, 2nd edn.

PAINE, R.T. and SOPER, A. (1960) *The Art and Architecture of Japan*, Harmondsworth: Penguin.

SWANN, PETER C. (1958) *An Introduction to the Arts of Japan*, Oxford: Bruno Cassirer.

YASHIRO, YUKIO (1960) *Art Treasures of Japan*, 2 vols, Tokyo: Kokusai Bunka Shinkokai.

Modern Japan

ABBEGLEN, JAMES and STALK, GEORGE Jnr (1985) *Kaisha, The Japanese Corporation*, New York: Harper and Row.

BENEDICT, RUTH (1947) *The Chrysanthemum and the Sword: Patterns of Japanese Culture*, London: Secker and Warburg, and reprints.

BINGMAN, CHARLES F. (1989) *Japanese Government, Leadership and Management*, London: Macmillan.

CHRISTOPHER, ROBERT C. (1983) *The Japanese Mind: The Goliath Explained*, New York: Linden Press, and London: Simon and Schuster.

CLARK, RODNEY (1987) *The Japanese Company*, Tokyo: Tuttle.

CURTIS, GERALD L. (1988) *The Japanese Way of Politics*, New York: Columbia University Press.

THE JAPAN TIMES *Defence of Japan*, official White Papers translated and published annually by *The Japan Times*.

DOI, TAKEO (1981) *The Anatomy of Dependence*, Tokyo: Kodansha.

DORE, R.P. (1986) *Flexible Rigidities: Industrial Policy and Structural Adjustment in the Japanese Economy*, London: Athlone.

———— (1987) *Taking Japan Seriously: A Confucian Perspective on Leading Economic Issues*, London: Athlone.

DRIFTE, REINHARD (1990) *Japan's Foreign Policy*, London: Chatham House.

EMMOTT, BILL (1989) *THE SUN ALSO SETS*, LONDON: SIMON AND SCHUSTER.

HARRIES, MEIRION and SUSIE (1987) *Sheathing the Sword: The Demilitarisation of Japan*, London: Hamish Hamilton.

HENDRY, JOY (1987) *Understanding Japanese Society*, London: Croom Helm.

DODWELL MARKETING CONSULTANTS, *Industrial Groupings in Japan*, regular editions published by Dodwell, Tokyo, one of the Inchcape Group of companies.

JOHNSON, CHALMERS (1982) *MITI and the Japanese Miracle: The Growth of Industrial Policy*, California: Stanford University Press.

KISHIMOTO, KOICHI (1988) *Politics in Modern Japan: Development and Organization*, Tokyo: Japan Echo Inc.

LYNN, RICHARD (1988) *Educational Achievement in Japan: Lessons for the West*, London: Macmillan.

MARUYAMA, MASAO (1963) *Thought and Behaviour in Modern Japanese Politics*, London: Oxford University Press.

MORITA, AKIO (1986) *Made in Japan: Akio Morita and Sony*, New York: Dutton.

NAKANE, CHIE (1970) *Japanese Society*, Berkeley, California: University of California Press.

NEWLAND, KATHLEEN (ed.) (1990) *The International Relations of Japan*, London: Macmillan.

NODA, YOSHIYUKI (1976) *Introduction to Japanese Law*, Tokyo: University of Tokyo Press.

PARKER, L. CRAIG Jnr (1987) *The Japanese Police System Today: An American Perspective*, Tokyo: Kodansha.

PASSIN, HERBERT (1980) *Japanese and the Japanese*, Tokyo: Kinseido.

ROSENBLUTH, FRANCES McCALL (1989) *Financial Politics in Contemporary Japan*, Ithaca, NY: Cornell University Press.

SCHOPPA, JAMES (1991) *Educational Reform in Japan*, London: Routledge.

SINGER, KURT (1951, 1973) *Mirror, Jewel and Sword: The Geometry of Japanese Life*, Tokyo: Kodansha, London: Croom Helm.

STEPHENS, MICHAEL (1991) *Education and the Future of Japan*, Folkestone: Japan Library Ltd.

SUZUKI, YOSHIO (ed.) (1987) *The Japanese Financial System*, London: Oxford University Press.

TASKER, PETER (1987) *Inside Japan*, London: Sidgwick and Jackson.

TURNER, LOUIS (1987) *Industrial Collaboration with Japan*, London: Chatham House, .

VAN WOLFEREN, KAREL (1989) *The Enigma of Japanese Power*, London: Macmillan .

VOGEL, EZRA F. (1979) *Japan as No. 1: Lessons for America*, Tokyo: Tuttle.

WORONOFF, JAN (1992) *The No-Nonsense Guide to Doing Business in Japan*, London: Macmillan.

YOSHIDA KENICHI (1981) *Japan is a Circle*, Tokyo: Kodansha.

ZIMMERMAN, MARK (1985) *Dealing with the Japanese*, London: George Allen and Unwin.

Index

Matsuyama (Shikoku) 149
Matsuzakaya Co. 125
Mazda Motor Corp. 121
meat 140, 141, 164, 218
media 60, 185–7
Meiji Emperor 26, 32, 184
Meiji government 29
Meiji group of companies 130
Meiji Mutual Life Insurance
    Co. 109, 129
Meiji period 30–2
Meiji restoration 26, 182, 183
Meiji shrine (Tokyo) 184, 185
mental health 162
metal work 20, 25, 31
Meteorological Agency 147
Michiko *see* Empress
Middle East 85, 116
Midorikai 128, 130
Mikado (Emperor) 44
Mikasa, Prince and Princess 211
Miki Takeo (politician) 214, 216
Minamata disease 15
Minamoto Yoshitomo and
    Yoshitsune (medieval
    leaders) 14
mingei (crafts) 36
Mingeikan (museum) 181
Minister(s) of State 58, 61, 77, 92,
    115, App. 1
Ministry of Agriculture, Forestry and
    Fisheries (*Nōrinshō*) 62,
    140–3
Ministry of Construction
    (*Kensetsushō*) 62, 64, 143
Ministry of Education
    (*Mombushō*) 62, 171–5, 179
Ministry (Minister) of Finance
    (*Ōkurashō*) 46, 58, 61–3, 91–3,
    97–9, 106–8, 111
Ministry (Minister) of Foreign
    Affairs (*Gaimushō*) 46, 58, 61,
    65, 81, 82, 179, 180
Ministry of Health and Welfare
    (*Kōseishō*) 62, 64, 161–70
Ministry of Home Affairs
    (*Jijishō*) 62, 66, 67
Ministry (Minister) of International
    Trade and Industry (MITI)

(*Tsūsanshō*) 38, 58, 62, 63, 65,
    111–16
Ministry (Minister) of Justice
    (*Hōmushō*) 59, 61, 75, 76, 158
Ministry of Labour (*Rōdōshō*) 62,
    152–8
Ministry of Posts and
    Telecommunications
    (*Yūseishō*) 62, 100, 117
Ministry of Transport
    (*Unyūshō*) 62, 64, 69, 147, 149,
    150
Miroku Bosatsu (Buddhist) 9
Misawa (northern Honshū) 89
Misawa Homes Co. 149
Mishima Yukio (novelist) 39
Mitsubishi Bank 104, 106, 127, 129
Mitsubishi Corp. 124, 129, 219
Mitsubishi Electric Corp. 120, 122,
    129, 218
Mitsubishi group 30, 104, 127–9
Mitsubishi Heavy Industries 121,
    122, 129
Mitsubishi Motors Corp. 105, 127,
    129
Mitsubishi Trust and Banking
    Corp. 105, 127, 129
Mitsui and Co. 124, 128–30, 219
Mitsui Engineering and Shipbuilding
    Co. 122, 129
Mitsui Fire and Marine Insurance
    Co. 109, 129
Mitsui group 30, 104, 127–9
Mitsui Mutual Life Insurance 109,
    129
Mitsui Mining Co. 129
Mitsui OSK (shipping) 129, 149
Mitsui Trust and Banking Co. 105,
    127
Mitsukoshi Ltd (department
    store) 125, 127, 129
Miyajima (western Honshū) 13
MOA Foundation (new religion,
    museum) 181, 185
Mombushō see Ministry of
    Education
Momoyama period 18–20
monetary policy 98. 99
Mongols 15